797,885 Books

are available to read at

Forgotten Books

www.ForgottenBooks.com

Forgotten Books' App
Available for mobile, tablet & eReader

ISBN 978-1-331-08149-4
PIBN 10142366

This book is a reproduction of an important historical work. Forgotten Books uses state-of-the-art technology to digitally reconstruct the work, preserving the original format whilst repairing imperfections present in the aged copy. In rare cases, an imperfection in the original, such as a blemish or missing page, may be replicated in our edition. We do, however, repair the vast majority of imperfections successfully; any imperfections that remain are intentionally left to preserve the state of such historical works.

Forgotten Books is a registered trademark of FB &c Ltd.
Copyright © 2015 FB &c Ltd.
FB &c Ltd, Dalton House, 60 Windsor Avenue, London, SW19 2RR.
Company number 08720141. Registered in England and Wales.

For support please visit www.forgottenbooks.com

1 MONTH OF FREE READING

at

www.ForgottenBooks.com

By purchasing this book you are eligible for one month membership to ForgottenBooks.com, giving you unlimited access to our entire collection of over 700,000 titles via our web site and mobile apps.

To claim your free month visit:
www.forgottenbooks.com/free142366

* Offer is valid for 45 days from date of purchase. Terms and conditions apply.

Similar Books Are Available from
www.forgottenbooks.com

A Genealogical Register of the First Settlers of New England
To Which Are Added Various Genealogical and Biographical Notes, by John Farmer

The New York Genealogical and Biographical Record
by Richard Henry Greene

Pennsylvania Genealogies
Scotch-Irish and German, by William Henry Egle

A Genealogical and Heraldic Dictionary of the Landed Gentry of Great Britain and Ireland
by Bernard Burke

The Putnam Lineage
by Eben Putnam

Seldens of Virginia and Allied Families
by Mary Selden Kennedy

Peabody (Paybody, Pabody, Pabodie) Genealogy
by Selim Hobart Peabody

Old Pembroke Families in the Ancient County Palatine of Pembroke
by Henry Owen

Materials Toward a Genealogy of the Emmerton Family
by James A. Emmerton

Genealogical Gleanings in England, Vol. 1
by Henry F. Waters

Descendants of Captain Samuel Church, of Churchville
by Etta A. Emens

Countryman Genealogy, Vol. 1
by Alvin Countryman

A Genealogical History of the Rice Family
Descendants of Deacon Edmund Rice, by Andrew Henshaw Ward

The Pioneers of Massachusetts
A Descriptive List, Drawn from Records of the Colonies, Towns and Churches, and Other Contemporaneous Documents, by Charles Henry Pope

The Genealogy of the Brainerd Family in the United States
With Numerous Sketches of Individuals, by David D. Field

Genealogy of Some Descendants of Edward Fuller of the Mayflower
by William Hyslop Fuller

Ancestral Line of Clark Chamberlain Gregg
by J. Gardner Bartlett

Pettingell Genealogy
Notes Concerning Those of the Name, by John Mason Pettingell

The Larimer, McMasters and Allied Families
by Rachel H. L. Mellon

FAMOUS FAMILIES
OF
NEW YORK

Historical and Biographical
Sketches of Families
which
in successive generations
have been Identified with the
Development of the Nation

BY
MARGHERITA·ARLINA·HAMM

ILLUSTRATED

VOL. II

G. P. PUTNAM'S SONS
NEW YORK   LONDON

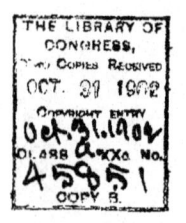

COPYRIGHT, 1901, BY *THE NEW YORK EVENING POST*

COPYRIGHT, 1902, BY G. P. PUTNAM'S SONS

The Knicker

CONTENTS

		PAGE
XXII.—LIVINGSTON	. . . .	1
XXIII.—MORRIS	. . . .	19
XXIV.—OSGOOD	. . . .	39
XXV.—POTTER	. . . .	49
XXVI.—RAPALJE	. . . .	61
XXVII.—REMSEN	. . . .	71
XXVIII.—RENWICK	. . . .	81
XXIX.—ROOSEVELT	. . . .	93
XXX.—RUTGERS	. . . .	103
XXXI.—SCHERMERHORN	. . . . . .	115
XXXII.—SCHUYLER	. . . .	125
XXXIII.—SMITH	. . . .	139
XXXIV.—STUYVESANT	. . . . . .	149
XXXV.—TAPPEN	. . . .	161
XXXVI.—VAN BUREN	. . . . . .	171
XXXVII.—VAN CORTLANDT	. . . . .	183
XXXVIII.—VAN COTT	. . . . . .	193
XXXIX.—VANDERBILT	. . . . . .	203
XL.—VAN RENSSELAER	. . . . . .	213
XLI.—VAN SICLEN	. . . . . .	225
XLII.—WENDELL	. . . .	237

THE LIBRARY
OF CONGRESS

ILLUSTRATIONS

	PAGE
Robert Livingston . . . . . *Frontispiece*	
First Lord of the Manor	
Judge Robert R. Livingston	10
From the original portrait	
Mrs. Robert R. Livingston (Margaret Beekman) . . .	10
From the original portrait	
Rev. Dr. John H. Livingston	14
Maturin Livingston	16
From a miniature	
Mrs. Maturin Livingston (Margaret Lewis)	16
From a miniature	
Lewis Morris	20
Signer of the Declaration of Independence	
Robert Hunter Morris	26
Governor of Pennsylvania, 1754	
"Old Morrisania," New York	26
Gouverneur Morris's residence	
Mrs. Lewis Morris III. (Katrintje Staats)	28
Richard Morris	30
Chief Justice under the Crown	
Frances Ludlum	32
Wife of Robert Morris	
Lewis Gouverneur Morris	34
From a steel engraving by Samuel Sartain	
Samuel Osgood	40
From the painting by J. Trumbull	
Rev. Dr. Samuel Osgood	46
From a steel engraving	

Illustrations

	PAGE
Mrs. Samuel Osgood	46
From the painting by J. Trumbull	
Bishop Alonzo Potter	50
From a painting	
Maria Nott	56
Wife of Bishop Alonzo Potter	
Clarkson N. Potter	56
From a photograph	
Jacob Rapalje	62
From a steel engraving	
The Rapalje Family Bible, in possession of Henry S. Rapalje, Esq.	66
Title-page of the Rapalje Family Bible and page showing family records	66
The Rapalje Estate, 35th Street and North River	68
Redrawn from an old print	
George Rapalje	70
From a photograph in possession of Henry S. Rapalje, Esq.	
The Remsen Farmhouse	76
From an old print	
Bedford Corners in 1776	76
From a print in Valentine's Manual, 1858	
Professor James Renwick	82
From an oil painting owned by Mrs. James Renwick	
Grace Church, Broadway	86
St. Patrick's Cathedral, Fifth Avenue	88
Mrs. William Rhinelander Renwick (Eliza S. Crosby)	90
From a miniature owned by Edmund Abdy Hurry, Esq.	
William Rhinelander Renwick	90
From a miniature owned by Edmund Abdy Hurry, Esq.	
Jean Jeffrey	92
From a picture in the possession of Edmund Abdy Hurry, Esq.	
Theodore Roosevelt	94
From a photograph by Rockwood	
Isaac Roosevelt	98
From an India ink drawing in the Emmett Collection, Lenox Library	

Illustrations

	PAGE
The Administration Building.	100
Roosevelt Hospital	
Colonel Henry Rutgers.	104
From a steel engraving	
The Old Rutgers Mansion, New York, 1768. . . .	108
From a print in Valentine's *Manual*	
The Old "Glebe House," Woodbury, Conn. . .	112
(At the time of the Revolution it was the home of the Rev. John Rutgers Marshall)	
The Rutgers House, Rutgers Place	112
Between Jefferson and Clinton Streets	
From a print in Valentine's *Manual*, 1858	
The Schermerhorn Residence, 84th Street and East River	120
From a print in Valentine's *Manual*, 1866	
General Philip Schuyler	126
From the painting by Trumbull	
Philip Jeremiah Schuyler	128
From an oil painting	
Mrs. Philip Jeremiah Schuyler (Mary Anna Sawyer)	128
From an oil painting	
Philip Schuyler	132
From a miniature	
Grace Hunter	132
Wife of Philip Schuyler	
From a miniature	
Louise Lee Schuyler	134
The Interior of the Schuyler House on 31st Street	134
Philip Schuyler	136
From a painting by R. M. Stagg	
The Schuyler Home "Nevis," at Tarrytown on the Hudson	136
William Smith	140
Justice of the Supreme Court	
William Smith	144
Chief Justice of New York and of Canada	
From a steel engraving	
Peter Stuyvesant	150
After an engraving of the picture owned by the N. Y. Historical Society	

Illustrations

	PAGE
The Residence of Nicholas W. Stuyvesant	156
Which stood in 8th Street, between First and Second Avenues From a print in Valentine's *Manual*, 1857	
Frederick D. Tappen	162
From a photograph	
Martin Van Buren	172
From a steel engraving	
Pierre Van Cortlandt	184
From the painting by J. W. Jarvis	
Cornelius Vanderbilt	204
From a steel engraving	
William H. Vanderbilt	206
From a steel engraving	
The Obelisk in Central Park	208
Brought from Egypt by Wm. H. Vanderbilt	
Residence of the late Cornelius Vanderbilt, 57th Street and Fifth Avenue	210
Kiliaen Van Rensselaer	214
First Lord of the Manor	
Margaret Schuyler	216
Wife of Stephen Van Rensselaer III.	
Philip Van Rensselaer	216
Mayor of Albany	
Maria Van Cortlandt	218
Wife of Kiliaen Van Rensselaer the Fourth Patroon	
Anna Van Wely	218
Second wife of Kiliaen Van Rensselaer, the First Patroon	
Stephen Van Rensselaer III.	220
Patroon of the Manor of Van Rensselaerwyck Major-General of the United States Army	
Cornelia Paterson	222
Second wife of Stephen Van Rensselaer III. From a miniature	
The Old Van Siclen House in Ghent, Belgium	228
Built about 1338, and still standing	

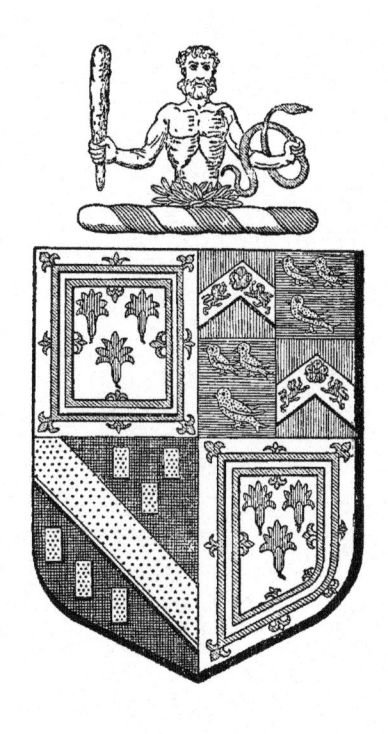

Livingston

XXII

LIVINGSTON

RELIGIOUS zeal and persecution were powerful factors in the settlement of the New Netherlands, as of New England. With the Dutch colonists went Huguenots, seeking that freedom in the New World which was denied to them in the Old, and British independents who could not adapt themselves to the conditions of life then existing in England and Scotland. Settlers of this type exert a more potent influence than do such as emigrate from motives of gain, glory, or power. The intensity of their moral and intellectual life reacts upon their social environment, causing them, it may be said, to become either martyrs or monarchs.

Running through the agricultural and commercial fabric of Dutch life in America, were strong threads of religious devotion and heroism. They modified their surroundings and imparted their force and tendencies to whatever came within the circle of their influence.

Fanaticism caused the exile of the Rev. John Livingston, a Scotch clergyman of remarkable ability. Like other non-conformists, he went to Holland, where he became a noted preacher. His family tree runs back to 1124 A.D. During the five centuries between that time and the exile, they were Lords Livingston and Earls of Linlithgow. They were among the noblest families of Scotland, and for generations were in the front rank of the courtiers at Holyrood. The distinguished divine had, therefore, the strongest social influence and position when he began his sacred calling anew in the Netherlands. There he became acquainted with the merchant princes of the time, among them Kiliaen Van Rensselaer, the First Patroon. The New Netherlands were a frequent subject of conversation in the society wherein these men moved, and those who were far-sighted perceived the future importance of the fertile territories in America. None took a livelier interest than the Scotch minister, who made no less than two unsuccessful attempts to emigrate.

What the father was unable to do, the son, Robert [1654], achieved. Provided with strong letters of introduction, and well acquainted with many of the foremost Dutchmen already in the New Netherlands, he sailed from Greenock, April 18, 1673, bound for Charlestown, in New England, and arrived in New Amsterdam about 1674. He was a well-educated man, and had a fair knowledge of surveying and certain useful arts. He worked hard from the day of landing, saved all he could, and in a few years seems to have accumulated a large amount of money. At the end of five years, he married, July 9, 1679, Alida, *née* Schuyler, the widow of Dr. Nicolaus Van Rensselaer. The union proved a happy one. The issue was four sons and two daughters. In 1686, Robert obtained from Governor Dongan a patent of Livingston Manor, which consisted of one hundred and sixty thousand acres of fertile country on the Hudson River, half way between New York and Albany, and opposite the Catskills. It seems curious that the cost of this magnificent estate amounted to not more than two hundred dollars worth of merchandise, including blankets, shirts, stockings, axes, adzes, paint, scissors, jack-knives, and pocket looking-glasses.

He led a busy life, attending to his great domain and serving in many offices of honor and trust. The records show that he was a secretary to the Albany Commissary, Town Clerk and

Town Collector, Secretary of Indian Affairs, member of the Council, member of the General Assembly (1709-1711), and Speaker of the General Assembly (1718). He bestowed great care upon the education of his children, and lived to see several of them occupy high places in the community. He loved adventure, and was noted, even among the Indians, for his skill in hunting. In 1694, he made a trip across the ocean, and was wrecked on the coast of Portugal. He displayed great fortitude during the disaster, and was instrumental in saving several lives. A thoroughly pious man, he saw in his preservation the answer to his prayers, and commemorated his escape, family tradition says, by making an appropriate change in the family escutcheon. For the ancient crest of a demi-savage, he substituted the figure of a ship in distress. This will account for the fact that both coats-of-arms are found in the family records.

During the latter part of his life, he built a church near his Manor House, now known as Linlithgow—a tomb within its portals. Here his body was laid away. The building, in the course of years, decayed and was torn down. Upon this site his descendants have erected a memorial church, and over the tomb have placed a tablet in honor of the founder of their race in the United States.

The four sons of the first "Lord" were worthy of their father. The oldest, John, embraced a military career, and rose to be a colonel in the Connecticut militia. He married twice, his first wife being the only daughter of Governor Winthrop of Connecticut, and his second, Elizabeth Knight. As he left no issue, and as he died before his father (in London, 1717), the title of "Lord" as well as the oldest son's share of the family estate went to Philip, who was born in 1686. The latter, dissatisfied with farming, turned his attention to commercial life, and, owing to his great wealth as well as to his natural ability, became, if not the greatest, at least one of the great merchants of his period. He married Katherine Van Brugh, by whom he had six sons and two daughters. In the latter half of his life he became famous for his hospitality. He kept his three houses, in

Philip the Princely

New York, Clermont, and Albany, always open to his friends and acquaintances, and gave entertainment for man and beast to whomsoever called. To him was applied the term "The Princely Livingston." He did not allow private business to engross his attention to the neglect of public duties. He served as Town Clerk, Secretary of Indian Affairs, and member of the Legislative Council.

The third son, Robert, was the most cultured and intellectual, if not the ablest, of the generation. He received a collegiate education in Scotland, and studied law at the Temple in London, where he won high praise for his legal acumen.

Robert of Clermont

Upon his return to the New World, he opened a law office at Albany, where he soon built up a lucrative practice. It was about this time that he surprised a burglar who was breaking into his father's house by climbing down the chimney. He seized the fellow by his legs, hauling him down into the ashes, and frightened him into making a full confession, which included the details of a plot to rob and murder the white people of the district. The father was so pleased with his son's courage that he presented him with a section of the manor land containing thirteen thousand acres. From this piece of land the young man received his name, Robert of Clermont, and the place was called for generations the Lower Manor. He was a member of the General Assembly from 1711 to 1727. He married Miss Howarden.

Gilbert, the fourth son, was the least conspicuous of the four; he devoted himself to his estate, to reading, and to social duties. He married Cornelia Beekman, and was the founder of the Poughkeepsie branch of the family. From 1728 to 1737, he was a member of the General Assembly.

Gilbert

Margaret, one of the daughters of the founder, made a notable marriage when she espoused Colonel Samuel Vetch, the first English Governor of Annapolis. The other daughter, Johanna, married Cornelius Van Horne, a well-to-do property-owner of that time.

Robert "the Nephew"

It would not be fair, in commenting upon this generation, to omit Robert Livingston, a nephew of the first "Lord of the Manor," who came to this country in 1684,

Livingston

ten years after his uncle. While he did not occupy so large a place in the public view, nevertheless he and his did much for the State, and added to the glory of the race.

His wife was Margaretta Schuyler, niece of Alida, his uncle's wife, by whom he had sons and daughters. Three of his sons —Peter, John, and James—became prominent in their time.

The third generation made the golden age of the Livingston family; each of the four branches (Philip, Gilbert, and Robert of Clermont, of the founder's side, and Robert, the nephew) had able and vigorous sons, who led lives of the greatest activity and, in the main, of beneficence. The Philip branch was the most notable on account of its numbers, there having been no less than six sons, each of whom rose superior to the average of his time. Nearly all had daughters of physical, mental, and social charm, who strengthened the house through marriage. Genealogically, the head of the family was Robert, the third "Lord of the Manor," son of Philip, who was born in 1708, and died at the good old age of eighty-two. He inherited his father's business ability, enterprise, and thrift, and increased the large fortune which he had inherited. He married Mary Thong, a great-granddaughter of Rip Van Dam, by whom he had six sons and two daughters. **Robert, Third Lord of the Manor** Like nearly all the men of his family, he served the State for a long time, having been a member of the General Assembly, and held minor offices. His three brothers—Philip, who signed the Declaration of Independence, Peter Van Brugh, and William, the war-Governor of New Jersey— are known as the "Revolutionary trio." Philip [1716] was a Yale graduate; in 1746, he was referred to as one of the fifteen collegians in the colony. From college he went into mercantile life, and became an importer in New York. **Philip the Signer** He was successful in business, and in 1755 had become a leader in the commercial world. He took an active part in the politics of the day; he was one of the seven New York Aldermen in 1754; and thereafter a member of the Provincial Assembly. As early as 1760, he identified himself with the opposition to the methods of the British Government. He was a prominent correspondent of

Edmund Burke, and supplied that statesman with much knowledge of colonial affairs.

While most of the men, especially the merchants of the time, were afraid to take part in the questions of the day, Philip never hesitated. In 1764, he drew up an address to Lieutenant-Governor Colden, in which he used language so bold as to warrant the charge of treason. He was a delegate to the "Stamp-Act Congress" in 1765, and was cordially hated by the Royalists, who made open war upon him and unseated him when he was elected to the Assembly. He was unanimously elected a member of the First Continental Congress, and remained a member of the House until his death. On behalf of New York, he signed the Declaration of Independence; and he has ever since been known as "Philip the Signer." He also served in the Senate of New York. His benevolence was great; he gave away seldom less than one third of his income. He founded the professorship of divinity in Yale, took part in the organization of the Society Library of New York, and was one of the founders of Columbia College. In his time, Brooklyn was a poor farming country, and not at all popular with Knickerbocker society. He foresaw its future and purchased considerable land on what is now known as Brooklyn Heights. He built a mansion at about the present corner of Hicks and Joralemon streets, and laid out a fine carriage-road from his estate to Red Hook Lane. This road is now Livingston Street. In this mansion Washington held a council of war in August, 1776. In 1770, Philip took part in organizing the Chamber of Commerce. Though his family were non-conformists, he manifested a singular catholicity in religious sentiment, establishing a chair of divinity in Yale, aiding Columbia, which was of the Church of England; contributing to the Presbyterian Church, and aiding liberally in the construction of the first Methodist church in the United States. His wife was Christina, daughter of Colonel Ten Broeck.

Peter Van Brugh [1710], was a Yale man of 1731. As did his brother, he went to New York and entered upon a mercantile career. He built a handsome mansion on the east side of what is now Hanover Square, whose beautiful gardens extended to the East River. His partner was Lord Stirling, whose sister he married in 1739. His official services to the State were long and honorable; he was member of the Provincial Council and of the Committee of One Hundred, delegate to the First and Second Provincial Congresses of New York, Treasurer of Congress (1776), trustee of the College of New Jersey (now Princeton), and a member of numerous Revolutionary and patriotic organizations. John Adams spoke of him as "an old man, extremely stanch in the cause, and very sensible," which, coming from the grim Massachusetts statesman, was high praise, indeed.

William [1723] was the most picturesque of the six sons. He was brought up by his maternal grandmother, Sarah Van Brugh, who seems to have had eccentric ideas as to a boy's education. She did not neglect his book-learning, but made physical development a point. *William the War-Governor* By the time he was thirteen, he was skilled in horsemanship, woodcraft, fishing, and agriculture. At fourteen, he was sent into the forest, where he lived a year among the Mohawks, under the care of a missionary and an Indian chief. He came back with a thorough knowledge of the Mohawk language and a master of all the Indian dances. Sent to Yale, he proved himself the best fighter and best scholar of his class, which was that of 1741. He studied law and became a leader of the bar, with the quaint sobriquet of "the Presbyterian lawyer." He served in the Provincial Legislature for three years, and then removed to Elizabethtown, N. J. Here he built a fine country seat, which in after years became celebrated as Liberty Hall. Elizabethtown was then said to be in the wilderness; from New York it was at least one day's journey. Nevertheless, so fascinating was the man, and so attractive his four daughters, that the house was always crowded with visitors. Among these were Alexander Hamilton, John Jay, and other leading men of that period. William foresaw the Revolution, and from the first was a fierce and uncompromising patriot. When it came to nominating a delegate to the Continental Congress, he was so fearful that the people would send a weak representative that, it is said, he made a personal canvass of the electors, and only stopped when he found that he was the one candidate who had been thought of by the people. He was a delegate twice, serving upon the more important committees. He gave up Congressional life to become a brigadier-general and governor, holding the latter office until his death. In this double capacity he was a thorn in the flesh to the British, by whom he was called the "Don Quixote of the Jerseys." He gave them so much trouble that they set a price upon him, and induced reckless adventurers to attempt his kidnapping, as well as to burn his mansion. Many attempts were made, but all proved failures. Before three years had gone by, many of the ignorant British troops believed that the war-Governor was in league with Satan and had supernatural powers of appearing and disappearing.

In 1777, William recommended in his message to the Assembly the abolition of slavery, and eleven years later he secured the passage of an act forbidding the importation of slaves into the State. He had inherited or had obtained many slaves himself, but these he liberated and helped on as free citizens. His versatility was notable. He wrote a digest of the laws of New York, several volumes on law and politics, a long and somewhat heavy poem entitled "Philosophical Solitude," and many bits of lighter verse, essays, theses, and pamphlets. In writing about him, President Timothy Dwight, of Yale College, said: "The talents of Governor Livingston were very various. His imagination was brilliant, his wit sprightly and pungent, his understanding powerful, his taste refined, and his conceptions bold and powerful. His views of political subjects were expansive, clear, and just. Of freedom, both civil and religious, he was a distinguished champion."

Robert of Clermont had but one son, Robert R. Livingston [1718]. Upon his father's death he became the owner of the estate, which made him one of the wealthy men of the colony. Owing partly to his wealth and partly to his ability, he became a person of much distinction, and was appointed Judge by the English Crown. He is known as "Judge Robert," to distinguish him from his famous son of the same name, the Chancellor. Like nearly all of his relatives, he

Robert R., or Robert the Judge

Judge Robert R. Livingston
From the original portrait

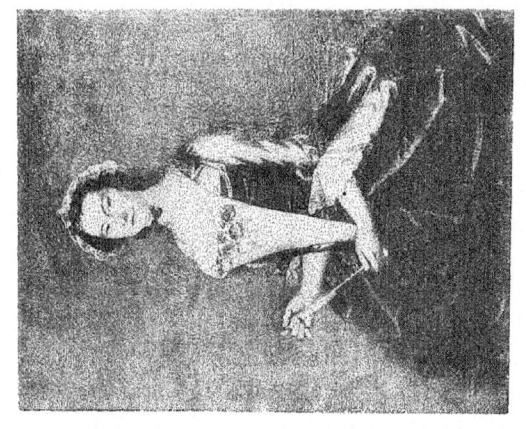

M s. Robert R. Livingston
Margaret Beekman)
From the original portrait

was an ardent patriot, and was elected a delegate to the Colonial Congress held in New York in 1765, better known as the Stamp Act Congress. He married Miss Margaret Beekman, daughter of Colonel Henry Beekman of Rhinebeck. By her he had many children, of whom at least three were to become famous in law and politics. Of Judge Robert, an interesting story is told by a friend. At a family party in Clermont one evening he was talking with his father, Robert of Clermont, his son, the future Chancellor, and his son-in-law, Captain, afterwards General, Richard Montgomery. The conversation turned upon the relations of the colonies to Great Britain, and soon became excited. The argument culminated in a bit of prophecy from the aged head of the house, who exclaimed: "It is intolerable that a continent like America should be governed by a little island three thousand miles away. America must and will be independent. My son, you will not live to see it; Montgomery, you may; Robert," turning to his grandson, "you will." The prophecy was fulfilled. Montgomery was killed at the siege of Quebec, 1775; the son died before independence was achieved, while the grandson became one of the leaders of the new republic.

James, son of Robert the nephew, left his country home to engage in commercial life at New York. He became an opulent merchant. His wife was Maria Kiersted, by whom he had issue.

<small>John</small>

John, his brother, devoted his life to the family estates. He espoused Catharine Ten Broeck, daughter of General Ten Broeck. Among their children were three of the most brilliant soldiers of the Revolution.

<small>James the Merchant</small>

The fourth generation produced many eminent men. They were so numerous that it is difficult to select a few representatives without being guilty of neglecting others as worthy. Robert, the third "Lord of the Manor," had five sons, whose names are familiar to all students: Peter R., Walter, Robert Cambridge, John, and Henry; and three daughters: Mary, who married James Decare, Alida, and Catharine. Each of three sons has left long lines of descent.

Lieut.-Gov. Peter R.
Peter R. was a wealthy landed proprietor in Dutchess County, and took a lively part in State affairs. In 1828, he was elected Lieutenant-Governor.

Judge Walter
Walter [1740], son of Robert, the third Lord, was an able lawyer and statesman. His public services were numerous and valued. Among other positions he held with success were the following: Member of the Provincial Congress (1775), Judge for Albany (1777), Member of Congress (1784-5), Commissioner of the U. S. Treasury (1785). His wife was Cornelia Schuyler, by whom he had issue.

Judge Henry W.
His son, Henry Walter [1768], was graduated from Yale (1786) and admitted to the New York bar. In 1792, he was appointed secretary to Minister Gouverneur Morris, and served two years at Versailles. 1796 saw him Judge of Common Pleas, and in 1803 and 1805 he was elected to Congress. His wife was Mary Penn Allen, by whom he had children.

From Robert Cambridge came John Swift [1785], Johnston, who married his kinswoman Sylvia Livingston, Robert Cambridge II., Robert Cambridge III., Robert Cambridge IV., John Griswold, Johnston II., Henry W., and Louis.

From John, the last Lord of the Manor, known as John of Oak Hill, come Herman and Cornelia, who married Clermont Livingston. The Oak Hill mansion is now in the possession of John Henry, a grandson of Herman of Oak Hill.

Lieut.-Governor Edward P.
From Philip come Walter and Edward Philip. The latter was a leading citizen of Columbia County, who was elected Lieutenant-Governor in 1830. His descendants included Philip Jr., Henry, and Philip VI.

Lieut.-Colonel Brockholst
William, the war-Governor, had one distinguished son, Brockholst [1757]. He entered Princeton, but left college to go into the army, where he rose to be a lieutenant-colonel. He became private secretary to John Jay, studied law, and was a member of the New York bar. In 1802, he was Judge of the New York Supreme Court, and in 1806 was made a Justice of the United States Supreme Court by President Jefferson. He was married thrice and had many children. His oldest

son was Hon. Carroll, a merchant and financier, who was graduated from Columbia (1822).

His present representative is Charles Carroll.

Of Gilbert, the most distinguished descendant was his grandson, the Rev. John Henry [1746], who was graduated from Yale in 1762, and took up the study of law. He went as far as the limited opportunities of the colonies would permit, and then crossed the sea and entered the University of Utrecht. Here a change came over his ambition, and after his law course he took up theology, and received the university degree and ordination by the Classis of Amsterdam. He returned to New York in 1770, becoming pastor of the Dutch Church at the corner of Fulton and William Streets, which office he held until 1810. During this period he was made a professor of theology by the General Synod, and in 1807 President of Queens, now Rutgers, College of New Brunswick, N. J. During the Revolution he was an enthusiastic rebel, and was ready to pray and to fight at all hours. He was one of the founders of the first missionary society in New York, Regent of the State University, and in his later years was universally known as "the father of the Dutch Reformed Church in America." *Reverend John Henry*

In the fourth generation, the Clermont branch rose to the head. They seem to have inherited and to have added to the legal and intellectual talents of their father, "Judge Robert," and their grandsire, Robert of Clermont. The two greatest were Robert R., the Chancellor, and Edward, the jurist. Chancellor Robert R. [1746] was graduated from Columbia in 1764, and studied law under William Smith, the historian, and his cousin, William Livingston, of New Jersey. After admission to the bar he became a partner of John Jay. He was a brilliant lawyer, and was made Recorder of the city of New York, relinquishing this office, in 1775, to become a delegate to Congress. He was one of the five who drafted the Declaration of Independence, and was prevented from signing by being called away to take part in the Provincial Congress of New York. In 1776, he was a member of the Provincial Convention which changed the title of the *Chancellor Robert* colony to the State of New York, and was made a member of the committee which drew up the first State constitution. He was made Chancellor, and held that honorable office from 1777 to 1801. From 1781 to 1783 he served as United States Secretary of Foreign Affairs. He administered the oath of office to George Washington at the City Hall, which then occupied the site of the present Sub-Treasury at Wall and Nassau streets. When the New York Convention adopted the Federal Constitution, he was its chief advocate.

In 1801, the Government appointed him Minister Plenipotentiary to France, where he negotiated the cession of Louisiana to the United States as well as the settlement of the French claims. It was while abroad that he made the acquaintance of Robert Fulton, with whom he formed a quasi-partnership for the development of steam navigation, in which he had already done much hard work. His capital built the *Clermont,* the first steamboat in the New World, which was named after his family home. His other public services would fill a volume: he was prominent in the construction of the canal system of New York State, in adjusting the eastern boundary which gave the State of Vermont to the Union, and in establishing the American Academy of Fine Arts, which is now the National Academy of Design. He contributed to agricultural literature and was noted as an authority upon the subject. So great was his talent as an advocate that Franklin called him "the Cicero of America." When Congress asked each State of the Union to place the statues of two of its prominent citizens in the Capitol, he and George Clinton were selected for the high honor by the Empire State.

His homestead at Clermont is still in the possession of his grandson, Clermont.

Edward, the jurist [1764], was graduated from Princeton in 1781, studied law, and was admitted to the bar upon attaining his majority. He built up a large practice, made quite a fortune in ten years, and was elected to Congress in 1794, 1796, and 1798. There was considerable opposition to the policy of Washington's Cabinet at one time, and among its leaders he, Madison, and

Rev. Dr. John H. Livingston

Gallatin were the foremost. His were the resolutions which demanded copies of the papers given to John Jay in respect to the treaty with Great Britain. Washington, backed by the unanimous vote of his Cabinet, declined, and for a few days there was talk of a conflict between the two branches of the Government. In 1801, the Government made him United States Attorney for the District of New York, and the people elected him Mayor. During his term of office the present City Hall was built, the front and sides being of white marble, while the back was of cheap brown-stone, since "it would be out of sight to all the world."

When the yellow fever broke out in 1803, and all who could afford it deserted the city, he remained at his post, fighting the epidemic, and finally contracting the disease. During his illness he was robbed and almost ruined by his confidential agent and was compelled to start life anew. He conveyed all his property to a trustee for the payment of his debts, and on the expiration of his term of office as mayor went to New Orleans, which was then an American city, where he opened a law office in order to retrieve his wealth. With great shrewdness, he accepted land instead of money for his fees, and thus established the beginnings of a new fortune.

Finding the law of the new State a confused muddle of English common law, French code, and Spanish law, he drew up a code of procedure, of which a part in 1805 was adopted by the Louisiana Legislature. This was the beginning of the first great code ever drawn up in an English-speaking community, and in its final form has been held up to the admiration of the world by the great jurists of every land. It began a new era in American jurisprudence. Edward was sent to Congress three times from Louisiana and in 1824 finished his civil code, which completed the codification of the State law. In 1826, he paid off the last of his debts, and in 1829 was elected United States Senator from Louisiana. In 1831, he was made Secretary of State, and in 1833, Minister to France. A patriot, a statesman, a scholar, and a diplomat, his claim to a high place will be his record as a jurist.

A brother of Edward, Henry Beekman [1750], raised a company of soldiers in 1775, and took part in the invasion of Canada. For his valor he received a sword of honor from Congress. He was aide to General Philip Schuyler, Colonel of the Fourth New York, aide to Lafayette in Rhode Island, and an officer at Valley Forge. He served in the War of 1812, where he rose to be a major-general. He married Ann Horne Shippen, with whom he lived happily many years in the Beekman mansion at Rhinebeck, which he inherited from his mother.

Major-Gen. Henry Beekman

Among others who have added distinction to the family name is John William, a descendant of John, the third son of the second Lord of the Manor [1804]. His father was Dr. William Turk, surgeon in the United States Navy, and his mother Eliza Livingston. In 1843, the Legislature sanctioned his assumption of his mother's name. He entered the navy in 1824, served in the war with the Mediterranean pirates, in the war of Mexico, and during the great civil conflict. In 1868, he was commissioned Rear-Admiral, and placed upon the retired list, after which he made his home in New York City.

John William the Admiral

Colonel James [1747] was a son of John and grandson of Robert the nephew. He served in the Revolution, where he proved a faithful and efficient soldier, to whom Washington expressed his gratification "that the post was in the hands of an officer so devoted as yourself to the cause of your country." The reference is to Stony Point, and the time the treason of Benedict Arnold.

Col. James

With him in the same command, during the first part of the conflict, were his fearless brothers, Lieutenant-Colonel Richard and Captain Abraham. A son of the last named was Captain John P., who served with distinction in the War of 1812.

Lieut.-Col. Richard

Colonel James married Elizabeth Simpson, a belle of Montreal, by whom he had issue. His daughter Margaret became the wife of Judge Daniel Cady of New York, and the child of this union, Elizabeth [1815], became Mrs. Elizabeth

Elizabeth Cady Stanton

Mrs. Maturin Livingston
(Margaret Lewis)
From a miniature

Maturin Livingston
From a miniature

Cady Stanton, the most eminent woman-reformer of the nineteenth century.

From Robert, the nephew of the first Lord of the Manor, comes a long and important branch, which includes James, John, Robert, James II., Maturin, Maturin II., and is represented to-day by Mrs. Cavendish-Bentinck and Mrs. Ogden Mills.

In point of numbers, the Livingstons are almost unrivalled. They have been marked by high patriotism, a warm love for humanity, and a progressive spirit, which at times amounted to radicalism. Through their blood runs the hereditary Scotch tendency towards strong feelings and forcible action. They have been characterized by great physical and mental vitality, and, unlike many successful families, have not borne fruit and then withered away. The old Scotch character has reappeared in many ways. They have been strong friends—and strong foes, and have never feared to express their convictions or to beard authority in the cause of right. The clannish spirit has expressed itself in an intense family feeling, which has caused each to help all relatives in trouble, and has gone so far as to cause many intermarriages. To this feeling may be ascribed the care with which they have preserved memorials and souvenirs of their ancestors, and the self-sacrifice displayed whenever called upon to serve the family, the State, and the nation.

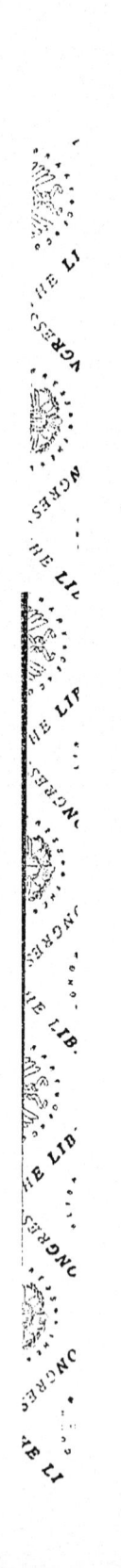

Lewis Morris
Signer of the Declaration of In

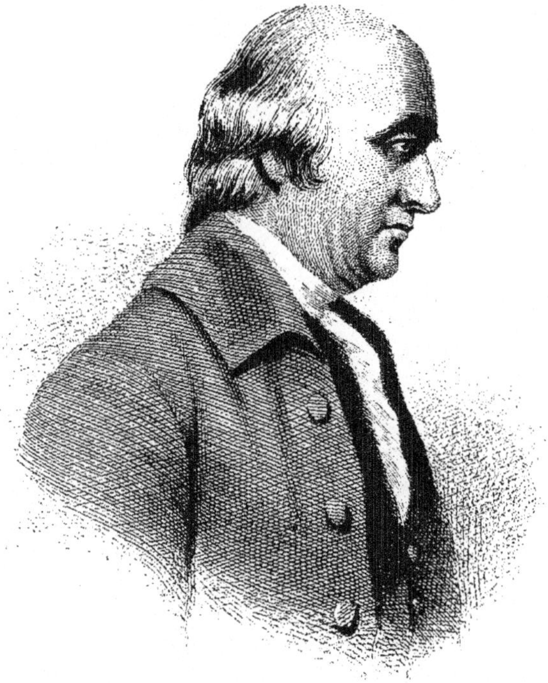

XXIII

MORRIS

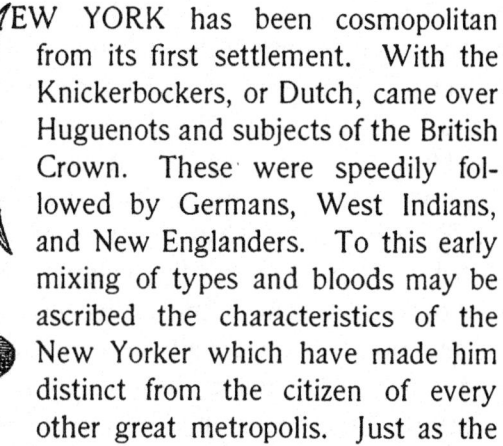

NEW YORK has been cosmopolitan from its first settlement. With the Knickerbockers, or Dutch, came over Huguenots and subjects of the British Crown. These were speedily followed by Germans, West Indians, and New Englanders. To this early mixing of types and bloods may be ascribed the characteristics of the New Yorker which have made him distinct from the citizen of every other great metropolis. Just as the Dutch were made up of people from the various provinces of Holland, so the British contingent was drawn from the different types which constitute the population of the United Kingdom.

As if to preserve a spiritual equilibrium, the solid Englishman was offset by the impetuous Scotchman and the strong and indomitable Welshman. To the little principality of Wales, Manhattan owes many of its most distinguished citizens. Of these, the head and front was the Morris family, which for more than two centuries has been in the foreground of municipal, state, and national activity. From a genealogical as well as an historical viewpoint, its career in both the Old World and the New has been of deep interest. Long before the Land of the Silures had become an appanage of the British Crown, it took a leading part in the councils of the little nation. Its very name is derived from Maur-Rhys, the Great Rhys, who was a Prince of Guintland (now embodied in Monmouthshire) in the latter part of the twelfth century. Maur is the Cymric for great, and was prefixed to the name qualified, unlike the Romance practice of suffixing, as exemplified in Charle-Magne. It was not until the seventeenth century that the present orthography was adopted.

The first Maur-Rhys was one of the conspicuous figures in British history. He was the neighbor and friend of Strong-Bow, Earl of Striguill, and, with that reckless warrior, invaded Southern Ireland, and conquered all the country around Waterford. The two adventurers might have become great Irish princes, but Henry II., their monarch, was a very thrifty and diplomatic character, who rewarded their prowess by giving them complimentary letters and titles, but added their conquests to the Crown possessions. The descendants of Maur-Rhys were proud and fierce warriors in the Plantagenet period, when they enjoyed great prosperity. Their star changed in the fifteenth century, during the wars of York and Lancaster, in which they lost much of their property, and at one time were in danger of extermination by political foes. During this period one of their princesses, a woman of rare beauty, married the Duke of Saxony, from whom was descended the Elector of Saxony.

In the reign of the Stuarts, ill-fortune again overtook them. They incurred the displeasure of King James, and their estates were confiscated by his son, Charles I. At that time the heads of the house were three brothers, Lewis, William, and Richard. William, after a vain struggle, determined to emigrate to the New World. He sold his property, and giving a moiety to his son John, set sail for the American plantations. He died upon the voyage. His son John was of a more adventurous disposition. He remained in Wales, trying to regain his ancestral lands, and when the Civil War broke out, was among the first to join the Parliamentary army, in which in 1651 he was a captain. In 1652, he went with a British expedition to Barbadoes, which was conquered and added to the British kingdom.

Captain John

He received grants of land in the new possessions and increased his fortune by marrying an heiress. This was the beginning of the West-Indian branch of the family.

William's brothers, Lewis and Richard, remained at home. They also entered the Parliamentary service, the former raising a regiment at his own expense, from which he gained the title of colonel. Richard was a captain in this regiment, and afterwards lieutenant-colonel. Notwithstanding the result of the war, they did not recover their confiscated estates, Cromwell paying them handsome indemnities instead. The two men were among the bravest of Cromwell's warriors. Their most famous exploit was the capture of Chepstow Castle, which they carried by fire and sword. From this feat they took as a crest a castle in flames on a rock, with the motto, *Tandem vincitur.* The uncles kept up a correspondence with their nephew John, and upon the latter's advice Lewis bought an estate in Barbadoes. He still yearned for the excitement of war, and urged Cromwell to attack Spain in the West Indies. He was apparently unsuccessful, because he sailed for his plantations as a settler and not a soldier. His action seems to have been a ruse of some sort, as he had scarcely arrived in his new home when Cromwell organized an expedition to attack Hispaniola (now Hayti and San Domingo), and with the announcement came a commission for Colonel Lewis Morris. For his gallantry in this little war, the Colonel received many pressing invitations to return to England, and, just before the Restoration, had begun to arrange for the voyage. The advent of Charles II. changed his plans. Instead of returning, he sent post-haste for his brother Richard, who came out by the next sailing vessel. Subsequent events showed the wisdom of the course. The two brothers had made many enemies during the wars, and proceedings had been begun against them, when Richard left home forever. There were many ex-Parliamentarians in Barbadoes, so that Richard had a hearty welcome when he arrived. Here he met, wooed, and won Sarah Pole, an heiress and belle. He remained in Barbadoes several years, attending to his brother's estate

<small>Colonel Lewis</small>

<small>Captain Richard</small>

and the one he had secured by marriage. The brothers were dissatisfied with the slow life of the West Indies, and determined upon a change. In pursuance of this, Richard in 1668 sailed for New York. He took with him a large amount of money, which he invested sagaciously in New York and New Jersey real estate shortly after his arrival.

The New York property consisted of three thousand odd acres near the Harlem, which he named Bronxland from the River Bronx lying to its north. This purchase made Richard Morris one of the largest landed proprietors in Westchester County. In 1671, Richard had a son whom he named Lewis, after the great Colonel. Captain Richard was very active in public affairs and served upon many bodies during the administrations of Lovelace, Evertse, and Colve. He died suddenly about 1675. There must have been a deep love between the two brothers, because the death disclosed a singular contract between them to the effect that if Captain Richard died Colonel Lewis would come on and become a father to the former's child or children. The Colonel was true to his word. When the news reached him of his brother's death, he disposed of most of his estates in Barbadoes and came on to New York (1676). In October of that year he invested his wealth in New Jersey property, purchasing 3540 acres in East Jersey, which he named Tinton, and another tract in the same neighborhood. He called the entire territory Monmouth, and from this name Monmouth County took its title. It seems quite odd that the English shire which had produced so many fearless opponents to the British Crown in the days of Cromwell should give its name to an American county on which again the British Crown was to meet opposition and defeat. The first opponents transported the name across the sea, and in the course of years their descendants renewed the wars of a previous century.

Lewis II. the Chief Justice and Governor

Colonel Lewis was indefatigable in all business matters. He attended to his own estate and to that of his nephew, Lewis II. He served upon the staff of Governor Andros and engaged in many private enterprises. One of these was the establishment of iron works in New Jersey, which for many years turned out an excellent grade of pig iron. He died in 1691 without issue, leaving his great estate to his nephew.

The bluff soldier had a warm heart and took pleasure in charitable and religious work. His contributions were many, and when he found that St. Peter's Church in Westchester had no bell, he presented a handsome one to it, which is still extant. Upon its lip in ancient lettering is the inscription: "Colonel Lewis Morris, 1677."

Lewis II., better known as Lewis the Chief Justice, is one of the most romantic characters in colonial history. He was a dreamer and yet sternly practical, a born soldier, and yet a good business man; an able judge, but one who never seemed to read or study precedents; ambitious, and yet scornful of the opinions of those in authority; a fountain of fun and humor, and yet so vitriolic in his bitterness as to keep his enemies in perpetual suspense; and, rarest of all, a successful politician, who despised tact and placating, and depended entirely upon truth and even brusquerie. His uncle, Colonel Lewis, became his guardian when he was five years old, and the iron-willed soldier soon found that the boy was a second edition of himself. They played a game of cross-purposes which even after two centuries sounds like a bit of delicious comedy. The uncle secured a tutor, a pious Quaker, whose ambition was to become an Indian missionary. The boy objected to the tutor and discharged him. The uncle reinstated him. The boy attempted to chastise the tutor, and was roundly flogged by the uncle.

Nothing discouraged, the youngster immediately started a new plan of campaign. He found out the Quaker's aspirations, and then studied his habits. He soon learned that the pious pedagogue was in the habit of praying every day at a stated hour beneath a certain tree. The boy went there an hour ahead of the expected time, climbed the tree, and hid himself in the thick foliage. As he expected, the teacher appeared, knelt, and, according to the custom of the times, wrestled with the Lord. Finally, when he paused for lack of breath, the boy piped out in a simulated voice: "Hugh Copperthwaite! Hugh Copperthwaite!" The simple-minded Quaker answered: "Here am I, Lord. What wouldst thou with me?" There was a pause, and then from the depth of the leaves came the command in the solemn words: "Go, preach my Gospel to the Mohawks, thou true and faithful servant!"

The tutor went back to the house, offered his resignation, and had packed his trunks for his departure, when the trick was betrayed. There was a stormy scene, and the old Colonel administered the rod in a way that would have pleased King Solomon. The next morning there was no boy around the place. The Colonel gave himself no uneasiness, believing that his nephew had stayed out over-night in the woods, or had gone to a neighbor's and would be back in a day or two. A week passed with no news of the youth. Inquiries were instituted, and it was found that he had run away to Virginia. Here he stayed some time, and then took ship and went to the West Indies. He earned a poor subsistence by serving as a scrivener. Even then he wrote a fine hand, and spelled with an accuracy that was uncommon in those years. But he tired of the work, and sighed for home. He managed to get to New York, where the Colonel received him with open arms. There was a council of war between the two, which must have been unique. The Colonel confessed that he could not govern his nephew, and then declared that, as the latter had to be governed in order to make him a man, the only thing left was to marry him off as quickly as possible. He accordingly brought about the union of his ward with Isabella, daughter of Sir James Graham, when the former was but twenty years of age.

The marriage had the desired effect. Lewis II. became a serious man and entered upon a public career immediately. He became a member of the Governor's Council and soon afterwards Judge of the Court of Common Pleas in East Jersey. In 1697, he added lands to his estate in Bronxland, and the same year erected it into a Lordship or Manor, called Morrisania. The charter was very liberal, giving him the right to deodands, wrecks, estrays,

Robert Hunter Morris
Governor of Pennsylvania, 1754

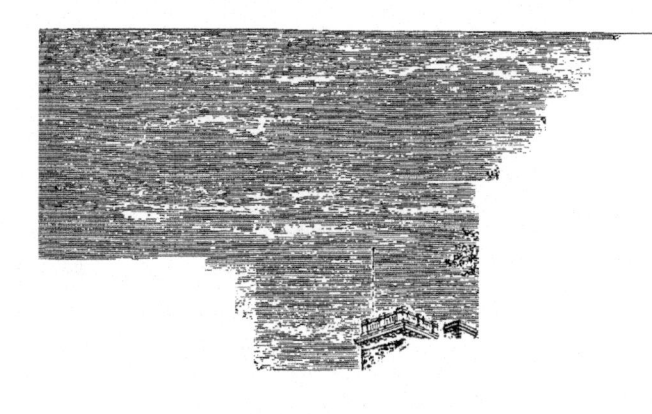

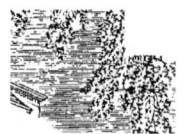

"Old Morrisania," New York
Gouverneur Morris's Residence

flotsam, and jetsam. This charter made the Morris family one of the five which possessed manorial estates in Westchester County. In 1700, he was made President of the Governor's Council, and two years afterwards, Governor of New Jersey.

He was elected a member of Cornbury's Council, and while there became champion of the people's cause against the tyranny of the Governor. In 1707, he was sent to the General Assembly, where he was soon the leader of that body. In 1718, he was made Chief Justice of the Supreme Court of New York, being the first native to hold the office. In 1734, he made a voyage to England, where he laid the grievances of New York before the Crown. On his return he advocated the separation of New York from New Jersey, which was afterwards accomplished. In 1738, New Jersey became a province or State, with Morris as Governor.

He did not care for the position, but accepted it as a matter of principle. It involved leaving his beautiful home in Morrisania and renting a farm near Trenton. His administration was very successful and was marked by a deep interest in the welfare of the agricultural and industrial conditions of the commonwealth. He was one of the creators of the Council of Colonial Governors, which devised plans of offence and defence against the French and Indians, and kept a courier service between his State, Pennsylvania, New York, and Connecticut. New Jersey was poor, compared with New York, and to prevent increasing the burden of the taxpayers, the big-hearted Governor defrayed all these extra expenses, a series of actions in full keeping with what he had done in preceding years, when he served as Chief Justice without salary. He was Governor for eight years when he died at the ripe age of seventy-five.

Almost fifty-five years of his life were passed in public affairs. The records of the time are filled with odd incidents illustrating his many-sided character. When they were building Trinity Church he donated the timber and sent the best logs which he could secure, many of them being massive enough for a building three times the size of the church. He did this, according to tradition, because the logs were not for man's service, but for the

Lord's. The trustees were so pleased with his generous gift that they voted a square pew to him and his family, which, in the social code of those days, was the highest compliment that could be paid to a citizen.

The directions he left as to his funeral were worthy of a Norse Viking. He desired to be buried at Morrisania in a plain coffin, without ostentation, and with no funeral sermon; but "nevertheless, if any clergyman, no matter the denomination, desired to make a few remarks over the grave, the privilege should be accorded as he had no objection." Neither, he declared, "did he wish that any mourning rings or mourning scarfs should be given, or that any mourning should be worn for him," saying in his will, "I die when I shall die, and no one ought to mourn because I do so."

He was an excellent husband and father, and in his wife had an invaluable partner and helpmeet. There were eight children by the marriage, two sons and six daughters. The oldest son was Lewis III., and the other Robert Hunter. The former succeeded to the great New York estate of Morrisania, and the latter to the mansion and lands at Tinton, Monmouth County, N. J. Both of these estates had been managed with admirable business ability by the Governor, so that the sons began life much richer than did their distinguished father.

The third generation continued the achievements of the second, the two sons proving talented men of affairs. Lewis III., **Judge Lewis** or Lewis, Jr. [1698], entered public life at the age of twenty-four, when he became a member of Governor Burnet's Council. In 1737, he was chosen Speaker of the New York Provincial Assembly, and was returned to the Twenty-second, Twenty-third, Twenty-fourth, and Twenty-fifth Provincial Assemblies, closing his service in 1750. A good speaker and parliamentarian, with an unusual talent for repartee and humor, he was a commanding personality in the Assembly. He was impulsive, like his father, but, unlike the latter, had rare suavity and tact. His fame, however, rests upon his judicial rather than upon his legislative career. He was Judge of the Court of Admiralty,

Mrs. Lewis Morris III.
(Katrintje Staats)

which at that time had jurisdiction over New York, New Jersey, and Connecticut. To the bench he brought great learning and remarkable dignity. His decisions were sound, and his administration of justice reflected credit upon both himself and his court. There was a grim kind of merriment in his nature, which expressed itself often in fantastic forms.

At one time he astonished people by an extraordinary head-dress. Instead of the hat and the bag-wig of the period, he wore a loon-skin with all its feathers. The bird was of goodly size, and the massive plumage covered the Judge's head in a way that aroused attention wherever he went. He wore this queer contrivance for a long time, displaying it at social functions as well as in his office and the chambers of his court. Whether it was intended as a practical satire upon the elaborate hair-dressing of the fashionables of that age, or whether it was a piece of nonsensical humor, is undetermined. The Judge was twice married, his first wife being Katrintje Staats, daughter of Dr. Samuel Staats, by whom he had three sons: Lewis IV. [1726], the signer of the Declaration of Independence, Staats Long [1728], and Richard [1730]. His second wife was Sarah Gouverneur, daughter of Nicholas Gouverneur, by whom he had one son, Gouverneur [1752].

Robert Hunter, the second son of Lewis II., the Chief Justice, enjoyed an equally brilliant career. In early manhood he was a member of the Council, thereafter Chief Justice of New Jersey, and in 1754 Governor of Pennsylvania. Thus in two generations the family had filled two gubernatorial chairs and three high places upon the bench. This is a record of which they may well be proud. To Robert Hunter, Franklin refers in friendly terms in his autobiography, throwing a pleasant side-light upon the Morris character·

Governor Robert Hunter

"In my journey to Boston this year (1754) I met at New York our new Governor, Mr. Morris, just arrived from England, with whom I had been before intimately acquainted. Mr. Morris asked me if I thought he 'must expect as uncomfortable an administration as Governor Hamilton, his predecessor, had had.' I said, 'No; you may on the contrary have a very comfortable one, if you will only take care not to enter into any dispute with the Assembly.' 'My dear friend,' said he, pleasantly, 'how can you advise my avoiding disputes? You know I love disputing. It is one of my greatest pleasures. However, to show the regard I have for your counsels, I promise you I will if possible avoid them.' He had some reason for loving to dispute, being eloquent and an acute sophist, and therefore generally successful in argumentative conversation. He had been brought up to it from a boy, his father, as I have heard, accustoming his children to dispute with one another for his diversion while talking at the table after dinner."

Later on, when Franklin returned to his seat in the Assembly, he was put on every committee for answering the Governor's speeches and messages. The communications "on both sides," he says, "were sometimes very abusive. I might imagine that, as he knew I wrote for the Assembly, should we meet, we could hardly avoid cutting throats; but he was so good-natured a man that no personal difference between us was occasioned by the contest, and we often dined together.

"One afternoon in the height of this public quarrel we met in the street. 'Franklin,' said he, 'you must go home with me and spend the evening. I am to have some company that you will like,' and taking me by the arm led me to his house. In gay conversation after supper he told us jokingly that he much admired the idea of Sancho Panza, who, when it was proposed to give him a government, requested it might be a government of blacks, as then, if he could not agree with his people, he might sell them."

Robert Hunter died in 1764 when dancing at a village party. The Governor led the dance with the wife of the village clergy man, and while bowing to his partner expired without a word or groan. He never married, and his estate went to his brother.

His code of living was quaintly expressed in a pleasant jingle which is treasured by the family.

Richard Morris
Chief Justice under the Crown

I am neither high church, nor low church, tory or whig;
No flattering young coxcomb, no formal old prig;
Not eternally talking or silently quaint;
No profligate sinner, no pragmatical saint.
I think freely, I own, yet I firmly believe,
I'm not vain of my judgment or pinned on a sleeve.
To lift truth from all rubbish, I'll do what I can,—
God knows if I err I'm a fallible man.
Any faults of my friends, I would scorn to expose
And detest private scandal, tho' cast on my foes.
When merit appears, though in rags, I'll respect it;
Will plead virtue's cause should the whole world reject it.
Cool reason I bow to, wherever 't is found,
Rejoice in sound learning with modesty crowned.
To no party I'm slave; in no squabble I'll join;
Nor damn the opinion opposing my own.
Length of days I desire, yet at my last breath
I hope to betray no mean terrors of death;
While as to the way after death to be trod
I submit to the will of a merciful God.

Lewis IV., or the Signer [1726], was graduated from Yale in 1764, and utilized his education by taking up what we would call scientific farming. In this field he did much commendable work, applying the latest ideas in European agriculture and modifying them to suit American conditions. In 1775, he was sent from New York to the Continental Congress, and, in 1776, he was one of the immortal fifty-six signers of the Declaration of Independence. It was after the great debate upon the Declaration, and just before the signing, that he received a letter from his brother, Staats Morris, who was a general in the British Army, begging him not to take so rash a step, and to think of the consequences. "Damn the consequences; give me the pen," was the reply of the impetuous Morris.

Gen. Lewis the Signer

He was one of the party when Franklin enunciated a famous *bon mot*. A delegate remarked: "Gentlemen, now that we have signed this document, we must all hang together." Franklin replied quickly: "Most certainly! if we do not, we shall all hang separately."

Lewis served in the field and afterwards was a valued and industrious member of the New York Legislature, holding office in 1777 and 1778. He was deeply interested in the National Guard, and rose to the rank of a major-general. He married Mary, daughter of Jacob Walton. Of his children, five sons served in the army, three of them making such brilliant records as to receive the thanks of Congress, and one son served commendably in the navy.

Staats [1728] was educated at Yale, entered the British Army, and through his powerful family influence attained the rank of major when he was thirty. He married the Duchess of Gordon, who accompanied him to India, where he distinguished himself at the siege of Pondicherry. When ordered to repair to America at the breaking out of the Revolution, he resigned his commission. The British Government, respecting his feelings, appointed him major-general, and detailed him to garrison duty. In 1796, he became a general, and in the following year was appointed Governor of Quebec. He died in 1800, without issue.

Staats, Maj.-General and Governor

Richard, the third son of Lewis III., was graduated from Yale in 1748 and took up the study of law. He was admitted to the bar, where he became known for his wide legal reading. In 1762, he was made a Judge of the Vice-Admiralty, which position he resigned in 1775 to take up the cause of the people against the Crown. Governor Tryon, on receiving the resignation, requested Richard to remain in office until quieter times. He answered that "he could never sacrifice his principles to his interests, and that his office was at the Governor's disposal."

Richard the Chief Justice

In 1776, he was made Judge of the High Court of Admiralty of New York, but declined the office. Two years afterwards, he was made Senator from the Southern District, and in the following year Chief Justice of the New York Supreme Court. In 1788, he was a member of the State Convention which ratified the Federal Constitution. In 1790, having reached the age of sixty, he resigned all his offices and retired to his estate at Scarsdale, Westchester County, where he passed the remaining twenty years of his life. He married Sarah Ludlow,

Frances Ludlum
Wife of Robert Morris

daughter of Henry Ludlow, by whom he had two sons and a daughter.

Gouverneur [1752], the fourth son of Lewis III., was graduated at King's College (1768), studied law, and was admitted to the bar in 1771. Here he made a brilliant success. In 1775, he was a delegate to the Provincial Congress and signed the Articles of Confederation. During the Revolution he was employed in many capacities, and in all displayed signal ability and zeal. He was an active member of the Convention which framed the Constitution, and was a Commissioner to England in 1789. Three years later, he was Minister to France, and after the expiration of his term spent several years abroad in study and travel. He became United States Senator in 1800, but served only three years of the six. In literature, he was almost as successful as in law and diplomacy. His writings were numerous and highly esteemed, if not popular. Taine, the French critic, said that of all our early statesmen he had the keenest sense of humor, and Hamilton summed him up: "He was by birth a native of this country, but by genius an exotic." Gouverneur the Statesman

Congress paid him the high compliment of assigning to him the task of delivering the funeral orations over Washington and Hamilton. The addresses produced a profound impression upon the American people, and are even to-day placed among the best examples of American eloquence. He was the second President of the New York Historical Society, and during the latter part of his life was a commanding figure in New York society. He married Annie Cary Randolph, daughter of Thomas Randolph of Virginia, a descendant of Pocahontas, by whom he had one son, Gouverneur II.

The fifth generation reached manhood about the time of the Revolution, and, as might be expected, was noted for its military record and prowess. Of its members, probably the most celebrated was General Jacob, son of Lewis the Signer. He served through the war, and distinguished himself in many battles. When peace came, in 1783, he retired to private life, but took a strong part in public affairs. The energy which he had displayed as a soldier was now turned into pacific channels. The State of New York, recognizing the losses sustained by Lewis and Richard Morris during the Revolution, in which their Morrisania property had been well-nigh destroyed, granted the brothers a tract of land, consisting of three thousand acres, in Montgomery County, as an indemnity as well as a compliment. The General was the pioneer of this patent, and established his home in the very heart of what was then a wilderness. The hardships of pioneering seemed to exert a beneficial influence upon the stout-hearted General and his wife. They changed the forest land into magnificent farms, and at the close of long lives they saw happy towns and villages where before there had been naught but the Indian and the wild beast. Their union was fruitful, his wife, Mary Cox, bearing him twelve children, nearly all of whom lived to a ripe old age. When he was over seventy he married a second time, and was blessed with one child, a son, A. P. Morris.

Next in importance to General Jacob was Commodore Richard Valentine, son of Lewis the Signer, an able, energetic, and progressive officer of the American Navy. He was the head of a cadet branch, which had many representatives in the next three generations. A third son of Lewis the Signer was Colonel Lewis, aide-de-camp to General Sullivan and General Greene. A fourth was James, who was a captain in the Revolution, and who married Helen Van Cortlandt, daughter of Augustus Van Cortlandt.

Commodore Richard Valentine

Colonel Lewis

Of the children of Richard the Chief Justice, the third son of Lewis III., the best known was Robert of Fordham. He devoted his life to the care of his estate in Westchester County, and was instrumental in effecting many reforms and improvements in that shire. Two of his children played active parts in the middle of the nineteenth century, Robert Hunter and Lewis Gouverneur.

Robert of Fordham

Gouverneur II. [1813], son of Gouverneur, Minister to France, was noted for his activity in the development of the internal resources of the United States in the first half of the nineteenth

Lewis Gouverneur Morris
From a steel engraving by Samuel Sartain

century. He was twice married: first to his cousin, Martha Jefferson Cary, of Virginia, and, second, to his cousin, Anna Morris. He left two sons, Gouverneur III. the ^{Gouverneur II.} journalist, and Randolph. Gouverneur III. is represented in the seventh generation by Gouverneur IV.

In the sixth generation, the Signer was represented by the three sons of Commodore Richard Valentine: Gerard Walton, who was graduated from Columbia in 1818, and was for ^{Gerard Walton} many years a leading lawyer in New York; Henry, who was graduated from Columbia in 1826, and was also a barrister; and Richard Valentine II.

Robert Hunter II., son of Robert of Fordham, was a member of the Constitutional Convention of 1848, Recorder and ^{Mayor Robert Hunter} Mayor of the city of New York for three terms, and Justice of the Supreme Court.

Lewis Gouverneur [1808], son of Robert of Fordham, took up his father's work, and devoted himself to the development of the southern port of Westchester County. As early as ^{Lewis Gouverneur the Patriot} 1838, he began the movement for the deepening and rectification of the Harlem River, and for the drainage of the marshes in its neighborhood. He encountered considerable opposition from the conservative elements of the district, but by sheer pluck and indomitable patience carried his plans through to a triumphant end. His greatest victory has its memorial in that noble structure, the High Bridge. When it was determined to bring the Croton water through to New York, the first proposition was to build a solid structure, which would have rendered the Harlem unnavigable. Lewis fought the project with all his strength, and urged an aqueduct along the lines of the present structure. His plans excited an outburst of protestations upon the ground of extravagance, corruption, and folly. He even went so far as to employ force.

When the contractors began driving strong piles which threatened to close the stream, he studied the laws and found some precedents whereby he could legally sail a heavily laden craft through the navigable stream even when this was impeded by trespassers. He chartered an unwieldy craft, loaded it in Philadelphia with coal, sailed it up the Harlem at flood-tide, and as he approached the piling refused to drop anchor. The tide made the vessel an enormous battering ram, which swept away the works like reeds. He anchored a quarter of a mile above, and upon the ebb raised the anchors and swept back, demolishing, it is said, the little of the structure that remained. This was too much for the contractors. They gave up their attempt, and the Harlem River was preserved in its integrity. In the fifties, he wrote a monograph in favor of a ship canal at Spuyten Duyvil. The project was regarded as visionary at the time, but was adopted by the United States Government, and made a fact in the nineties. He was active in the breeding of fine stock, and was one of the earliest importers of Devonshires, Shorthorns, and Southdowns. He prospered so well in this enterprise that, after a few years, he became an exporter, and sent valuable cargoes to Cuba, Canada, the Western States, and the Sandwich Islands. He married Emily Lorillard, daughter of Jacob Lorillard, by whom he had two sons, Fordham Morris, now living, and Commander Francis, U. S. N., who died before him.

Fordham

In the seventh generation, the main line from Lewis the Signer is well represented by Henry Lewis, son of Henry of Morrisania. He married Anna R. Russell, daughter of Archibald Russell and Helen Rutherford Watts. He is a lawyer, a member of many clubs and scientific societies, and a patron of the Metropolitan Museum of Art and of the American Museum of Natural History. Lewis the Signer is represented in the eighth generation by Lewis Spencer and Eleanor R.

Henry Lewis

The Morris family resembles the old landed gentry of England. For more than two centuries they have been identified with great estates on the one side and public affairs on the other. Few of their long roll have ever touched trade, and only a minority have cared for the professions. Where they have taken up the latter, it has almost invariably been the law, and in this they have attained the highest success. They make magnificent soldiers, and can look back upon an illustrious record in the three great wars of American history. From the first they have been marked by studious habits, broad culture, philanthropy, and patriotism. By marriage, they have become connected with most of the old families of the State, but, unlike many others, they have not been swallowed up, but have on the contrary impressed themselves upon the other bloods. Starting with a single ancestor in Captain Richard, they have increased in numbers, generation after generation, until to-day they can point to more than two hundred living representatives of their name.

Osgood

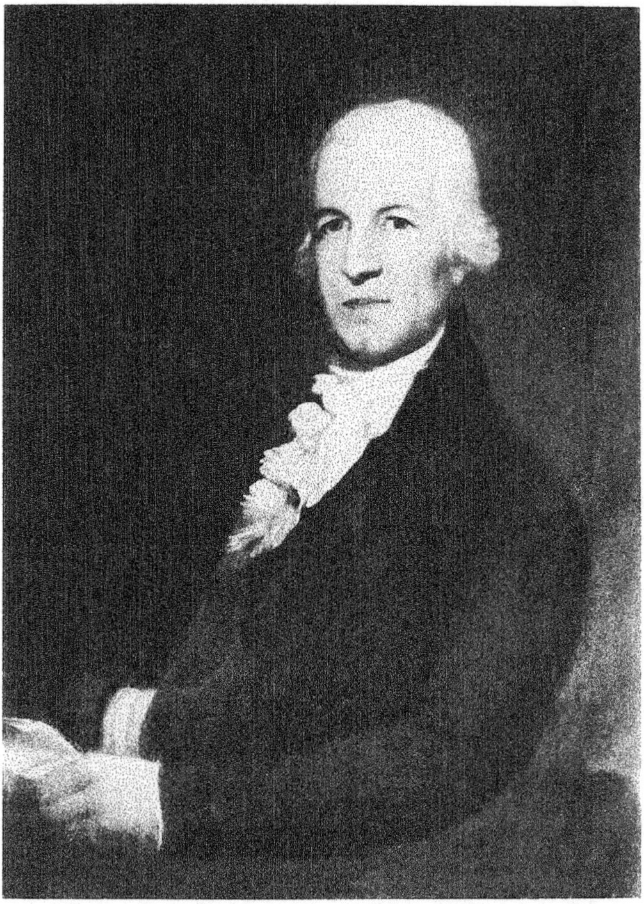

XXIV

OSGOOD

FAMILIES have characters, like individuals. Some are stationary, others move from place to place, and a third type separates and sends its fragments in various directions. Thus, the famous King family is identified with many States. Somewhat similar to it is the Osgood family, which for two centuries has been a power in both Massachusetts and New York. The founder was Captain John [1595], who came to New England about 1635, and settled in the Bay State. In 1639, he was admitted a freeman of the town of Newbury. Subsequently, he joined the pioneer party which settled in the virgin forest, cleared the land, and established the celebrated town of Andover. *Capt. John the Founder* He was a religious enthusiast, and devoted all his leisure time "to the glory of God," to use the quaint language of the Puritan days. His was the second house to be erected in the little settlement, and it had hardly been completed before it was utilized as the church or "meeting-house" of the neighborhood. The original homestead remained in the possession of the family for more than two hundred years.

According to his contemporaries, he feared neither the theological devil nor the red ones who prowled in the neighborhood.

He went to church with a musket, and whenever Indian conditions looked threatening, he and his sons went about their business armed to the teeth. No better type of the God-fearing and stout-hearted pioneer can be found in the early pages of New England.

For a century, the family remained in the neighborhood of its first home. It grew in numbers, wealth, and influence. The records show them to have been prominent in commercial, agricultural, political, and ecclesiastical affairs. They were farmers, merchants, and traders, grand-jurymen, town clerks, assessors, highway commissioners, selectmen, and chairmen and secretaries of town meetings, deacons, elders, trustees, moderators, and clergymen. They had high ideals as to public virtue, and were honest and patriotic to a fault. From the beginning, they set store upon public education, and gave their children the best instruction which could be obtained. The sons were sent to Boston, and afterwards to Cambridge, when Harvard was established; while the daughters were carefully brought up in the woman's curriculum of New England. To this period belong such characters as Colonel Isaac, Dr. Henry, Colonel John, the Rev. Thaddeus, the Rev. Daniel, Captain Isaac, the Rev. David, Dr. Kendall, Captain Samuel, and Colonel John.

When the agitation began throughout the colonies in favor of greater liberty and in opposition to the tyrannical features of the colonial government, it found the Osgoods among the strongest supporters of popular rights. They were not agitators, but zealots. They were not to be bribed nor corrupted, because their wealth rendered them independent and above temptation, and their high social position made them superior in many respects to the officials who were sent across the sea from Westminster to govern the Crown possessions.

Between 1760 and 1776, their name dots the record of the campaign for freedom. In 1765, Captain Peter and Colonel John were members of a committee which drew up resolutions against the Stamp Act and other inequitable imposts. In 1768, Captain Peter was the leading member of the committee

Capt. Peter

formed to encourage home manufactures in defiance of the policy of the Crown and to discourage the importation of all superfluities from Great Britain. When Captain Peter was asked what were superfluities, he responded with grim Yankee humor: "Everything imported from England."

In 1774, the indomitable Captain and Dr. Joseph, his cousin, were members of the Committee of Safety. Of their record in the Revolution, naught can be said but praise. They did not manifest high military talent, but made up for this by a patience, discipline, endurance, and stoical courage which are of equal value in the field of Mars. At least thirty served in the great struggle, one and all of whom made model soldiers. *Dr. Joseph*

In this group of distinguished patriots was Samuel [1748], the statesman, the founder of the branch in New York City. He was graduated from Harvard in 1770, and took up the study of theology. His health breaking down, he relinquished the pulpit for public life. In 1774, he was elected to the Provincial Congress of Massachusetts. When the British sent their expeditions to Lexington and Concord in 1775, he organized a company of minute-men, and fought the redcoats at both places. The same year he was made major, and in the fall aide-de-camp to General Ward, with the rank of colonel. His popularity was so great that a colonelcy of a regiment was offered to him, but he declined on the ground that there were many better soldiers than himself who could take the command, and that he could do more good for his fellow-countrymen as a member of the Provincial Congress. *Colonel Samuel the Statesman*

Upon entering that body, he was made a member of the Board of War, on which he served with signal success for four years. He then became a Senator and a member of the Continental Congress, where he remained until 1784. He was again elected, and in 1785 was made a Judge. A few months afterwards, the Federal Government appointed him First Commissioner of the United States Treasury, which he remained until 1789. He was then appointed Postmaster-General, which post he held until 1791, when he resigned because he preferred remaining a private citizen in New

York City to being a Cabinet officer in Philadelphia, to which city the national capital was then removed. The people of New York must have appreciated the compliment thus paid, because they elected him to the State Legislature (1800-1801-1802), and during the first two years of that period he was made the Speaker of the Assembly. From 1801 to 1803, he was State Supervisor, and from the last-named year to his death in 1813 he was the Naval Officer of the Port of New York.

During the thirty years in which he resided in the metropolis he was one of its most distinguished citizens. No man had more at heart the welfare of the community. When the present public-school system was devised, on the list of the incorporators the first two names were those of De Witt Clinton and Samuel Osgood. It may be interesting to know the names of the public-spirited men to whom the present City of New York is under so many obligations. In addition to the two mentioned, were Brockholst Livingston, John Murray, Jr., Jacob Morton, Thomas Eddy, Daniel D. Tompkins, John Pintard, Thomas Pearsall, the Rev. Dr. Samuel Miller, Joseph Constant, Robert Bowne, Matthew Clarkson, Archibald Gracie, John McVickar, Charles Wilkes, Henry Ten Broeck, Gilbert Aspinwall, Valentine Seaman, William Johnson, William Coit, Matthew Franklin, Adrian Hegeman, Leonard Bleecker, Benjamin G. Minturn, Thomas Franklin, Samuel Russell, Samuel Doughty, Alexander Robertson, Samuel Torbert, John Withington, William Edgar, George Turnbull, William Boyd, Jacob Mott, Benjamin Egbert, Thomas Farmer, and Dr. Samuel Latham Mitchell.

When the New York City Dispensary was founded, he was one of the first trustees, and in nearly all of the public movements in the last part of the eighteenth century he was a conspicuous figure. Beneath the man of affairs was the thinker and the scholar. Late at night and early in the morning he devoted his time to studying topics utterly disconnected with the routine of his life. Among the works which he published were a monograph on *Chronology,* a curious study upon *Daniel and Revelation, Theology and Metaphysics, Letters on Episcopacy,* and other philosophic,

Biblical, historical, and ecclesiastical topics. He was twice married, his first wife being Martha Brandon, who had no issue, and his second, Maria Bowne Franklin, widow of Walter Franklin, after whom Franklin Square, New York City, was named, by whom he had three daughters. Of these, Martha Brandon married the French Minister, Edmond C. Genet, from whom comes the Genet family of New York; Julia married her cousin, Samuel Osgood, and Susan Maria married Moses Field, and was the mother of Judge Maunsell B. Field.

Samuel [1812], of the sixth generation, a famous divine, was graduated from Harvard College (1832), and from the Harvard Divinity School (1835). After a brief career as an editor, he took a pulpit in Nashua, N. H., and in 1849 accepted the pastorate of the Church of the Messiah in New York City, in which place he died in 1880. His life may be divided into two epochs: twenty years in active clerical labor and eleven in hard literary work. Rev. Dr. Samuel

His contributions to American literature were numerous and valuable. Among his chief productions were *Studies in Christian Biography, God with Men, The Hearthstone, Milestones in Our Life's Journey, Student Life, American Leaves,* and an address before the New York Historical Society upon "Thomas Crawford on Art in America." He translated from the German Herman Olshausen's *History of the Passion,* and De Wette's *Human Life.* For four years he was editor of the *Christian Inquirer,* while his magazine articles, lectures, college addresses, and critical studies were more than two hundred in number.

In the seventh generation were several conspicuous members. Walter Franklin [1791] was educated at Columbia College (1809), from which he also received the degree of A.M. He inherited a handsome fortune, of which he took good care. He was prominent in church and social circles, and was connected with several moneyed institutions. The Rev. Alfred [1807] was a scholarly and enthusiastic home missionary. Ordained in 1835, he took up the onerous life of an evangelist in newly opened or sparsely peopled districts. For ten years he labored in

Ulster County and adjacent districts in the Catskills, and then, at the request of the Missionary Board, he went to La Salle, Ill., where he worked with remarkable success. Besides founding several churches, he mapped out and planned a settlement upon the open prairie which grew into the present community of Hope town. He married Paulia C. Pelt, by whom he had three children. Of these, Alfred T., the only son [1844], was prominent in financial matters. He married Clara Kenyon, by whom he had issue.

The Rev. David [1813] was notable in the Methodist Episcopal Church. His eloquence and scholarship have given him an enviable celebrity. He was twice married: first, to Harriet K. Ladd, and, second, to Maria Carle. His children were three in number: David L. [1843], Mary M. [1851], and Harriet K. [1854].

<small>Reverend David</small>

Samuel Stillman, the artist [1808], was for many years prominent in the world of painting. His specialty was portrait-making, and many of his canvases are treasured in the great public collections of the country. He married twice — first, Frances Sargent Locke of Boston, and, second, Sarah R. Howland of New York. The first wife, Frances, was the author known by the pen name of "Fanny Forrester." Her literary talent was developed at an early age, and she wrote several fine poems when a mere child. Her contributions to periodicals were many and attractive. Most of them were collected and published in book form. Among her works were *The Casket of Fate, A Wreath of Wild Flowers from New England, The Poetry of Flowers and the Flowers of Poetry, Poems, The Floral Offering,* and *Poems.* From 1840 to her death the Osgoods resided in New York, during which time their home was a literary and artistic centre.

<small>Samuel S., Artist</small>

In the eighth generation, the Rev. Howard [1831] was the most distinguished. He took sacred orders and settled finally in Rochester, where he conducted a very successful pastorate. He was a contributor to the religious press. He married Caroline Townsend Lawrence of New York, by whom he had issue.

<small>Reverend Howard</small>

Mrs. Samuel Osgood
From the painting by J. Trumbull

Rev. Dr. Samuel Osgood
From a steel engraving

In the ninth generation, a conspicuous member is Professor Herbert Levi. He was graduated from Amherst (1877), where he took the degree of A.M. in 1880. He entered the Post-Graduate School of Political Science at Columbia University, where in 1889 he received the degree of Ph.D. He is an educator by profession, and is now professor of history at Columbia.

Professor Herbert Levi

Howard Lawrence [1855], son of the Rev. Howard, was a lawyer at Rochester, and was identified with the affairs of that city. He married Catharine Rochester Montgomery, by whom he has had issue.

The characteristic of the Osgood race has been a strong religious nature. At the beginning of their career they were stern, and it may be narrow, Puritans. The pioneers of Massachusetts were tolerant only of themselves and denied to others the liberty of worship for which they themselves were ready to die. With the increase of wealth and culture, their natures broadened, and their religious conceptions grew more generous. In the eighteenth century, the leading representatives had departed from the iron creed of the seventeenth, while in the nineteenth, many of them belonged to the most liberal faiths.

No family has given a larger number of sons to the pulpit. There have been so many that the name has a distinctly religious sound. The tendencies which are involved in this field of spiritual endeavor have shaped the destinies of those who did not enter the sacred calling. Many Osgoods have been famous in charities, institutional work, the Red Cross Society, prison reform, and the management of asylums and hospitals. The wealth and culture of the race have been expressed by the contingent who have entered other learned professions. Among them are editors, poets, playwrights, historians, lawyers, physicians, archæologists, pedagogues, and artists. Few seem to have cared for commercial life, and while intensely patriotic, they have not enjoyed the perpetual clash and struggle which prevail in political life.

Their career in the Empire State has been paralleled by that in the Bay State. Those who have gone into other commonwealths have carried with them their simple modes of living, their culture and love of learning, and their intense civic and patriotic spirit. While the family has never been marked by great wealth, high military genius, or political skill, it has impressed itself upon the State and nation by its indomitable moral and religious force. It has been a power for good, from the first pioneer, who worshipped God with his loaded musket in hand, down to the score of clergymen who are trying to raise the moral standards of to-day.

Potter

Bishop
From

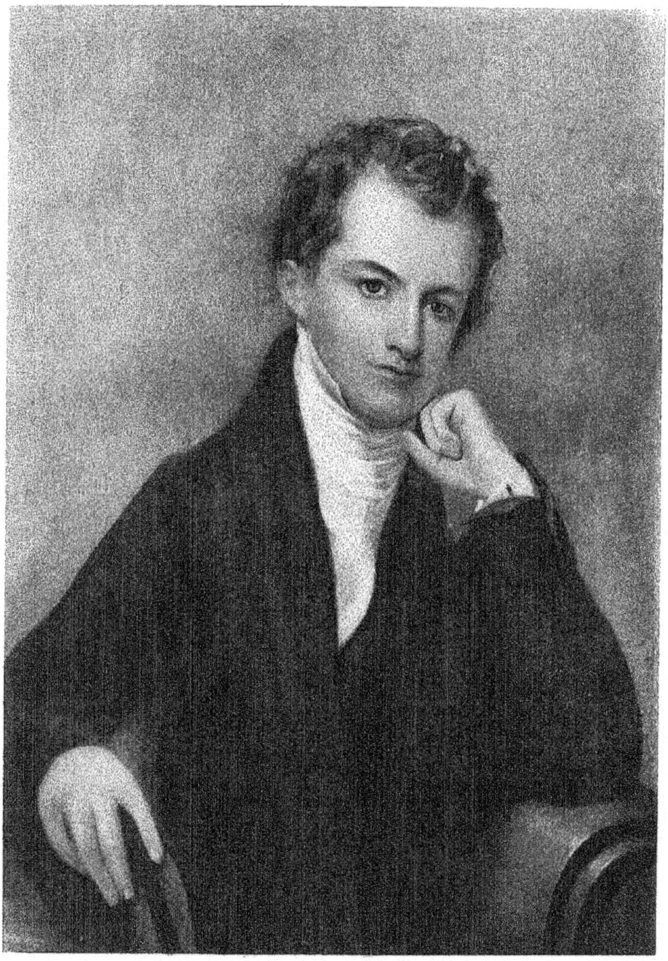

XXV

POTTER

THERE is something heroic about a **religious zealot**. The sacrifice of self upon the altar of an ideal appeals to the heart, no matter whether the sacrifice consists of an anchoritic life of abnegation and suffering, of an evangelist's career in the dark communities of the world, or of the turbulent existence of the reformer, trying to arouse his generation to a loftier manhood. In the early settlement of New England, these types of men were numerous and noticeable. What could be more picturesque than Miles Standish praying with extreme unction for God's blessing upon the heathen redskins, and then sallying forth with the sword and gun to send as many as he possibly could into the presence of their Creator? What dramatic possibilities are bound up in the experience of Lion Gardiner at Fort Saybrook, where his day was divided into fragments which were applied to study, engineering, manual labor, prayer, praise, and taking arms against "the hellish Indians." No less memorable was the fierce enthusiasm of Robert Potter, of Warwick, R. I., who founded a race which added lustre to American annals. **Robert the Founder**

He came from Coventry, England, which seems to have been a hotbed of religious zeal, and in his early manhood had evolved a stern and heroic belief which made him a thorn in the flesh to his neighbors. It is hard for us who enjoy the liberal spirit of the twentieth century to understand the exact position of the man's mind concerning affairs spiritual. He has been called a Quaker, but he certainly had little in common with that meek and long-suffering sect. Other critics have called him an Antinomian, both of the Lutheran and Calvinistic varieties, and yet his opinions cannot be interpreted according to either of those schools of religious thought. As a matter of fact, he probably was a law unto himself. Intensely devout, full of enthusiasm and energy, he tried to live according to his own canons and resented all attempts to circumscribe his liberty by well-meaning but officious third parties.

He came to the Massachusetts Plantations in 1634, and the same year was made a freeman under the ancient law. This indicates that he was a man of education, high intelligence, and some means. He settled first at Lynn, and thence removed to Roxbury. Here he had a violent altercation with the church, in which he was haled before the courts and compelled to give bonds for his appearance unless "hee bee with his family removed out of the plantation before." This decorous way of exiling a citizen resulted in his migrating to Rhode Island, where, with a group of associates, he bought the tract of land called the Shawomet purchase, which was christened Warwick, in honor of the Earl of that name who had espoused their cause during their quarrels with Massachusetts. Although Rhode Island was exceedingly liberal compared with Massachusetts, it was not long before the fearless agitator found himself in hot water with his new neighbors, and was imprisoned and otherwise punished for his "blasphemies." In 1643, he had the honor of being excommunicated by his bigoted neighbors.

During the next four generations the family prospered and waxed numerous. Its stern fanaticism changed to intellectual and civic activity, and its members rose to become prominent actors in the drama of colonial life. The records of Rhode Island show them to have held many offices, and to have been marked by probity, intellectuality, and sound sense. One branch settled in Massachusetts, and gave many distinguished sons to the service of the colony, and afterwards to the State; a second became prominent in the development of New Hampshire, while a third settled in New York, and in the course of time came to rival the main branch in the distinction and public service of its members.

The line of descent of the New York branch is clear and simple. Robert's son, John [1639], married Ruth Fisher; their son John [1669] married Jane Burlingame; their son John [1695] married Mrs. Phœbe Arnold Greene, widow, a daughter of Stephen and Mary (Sheldon) Arnold; and their son Thomas [1735] married Esther Sheldon. Of their offspring, Joseph [1757], who married Anna Knight, was the founder of the New York family. John [1695], Thomas [1735], and Joseph [1757] were Quakers.

Joseph the New York Head

Joseph, of New York, was a well-educated and industrious character, who on arrival in New York State settled in Beekman, now La Grange, Dutchess County. He became prominent in his new home, and enjoyed the affection of his fellow-citizens. They elected him to many positions of honor, of which the most important was the Assemblymanship, he being sent to Albany as a representative in 1798 and 1814. Here he proved an intelligent legislator and an incorruptible politician.

The great characters of the seventh generation were his two sons, Bishops Alonzo and Horatio. Alonzo [1800] was graduated from Union College (1818), where he was the honor man of his class. Shortly after his graduation, he took up theological studies with a view of entering the pulpit. In the meantime, he served as a tutor at his Alma Mater, and on coming of age was made professor of mathematics and physics at that institution.

Bishop Alonzo

In 1824, he took orders and married, his wife being Sarah Maria Nott, daughter of the Rev. Dr. Eliphalet Nott, President of Union College. In 1832, he was appointed to fill the chair of moral and intellectual philosophy and political economy. Six years later, he became Vice-President of Union, which position he administered with great ability up to the time of his election as

Protestant Episcopal Bishop of Pennsylvania. This new honor was the opportunity of his lifetime. Too often the position is viewed as a reward for past services and as a vacation after years of earnest effort. In the case of Bishop Alonzo, it was the opening of a field for greater energy and efficiency.

He had no more than taken the cathedral chair, when he began a campaign of work which attracted the attention of the country and made him immortal in the annals of the Protestant Episcopal Church. He advocated human liberty, and though he incurred the displeasure of many rabid pro-slavery enthusiasts, he won the respect and affection of the great masses of the North. He lectured with marked success, proving himself one of the brilliant orators of his time. He contributed largely to American literature, his writings displaying an almost phenomenal versatility. These writings include a treatise on logarithms and a course of lectures on the evidences of Christianity, a treatise on descriptive geometry, a noble volume on "Religious Philosophy," a sound text-book on "Political Economy," and a critical edition of a volume of poems. His most notable achievement was the organization of the forces of his Church into instrumentalities for practical work. His eloquence and goodness, coupled with extraordinary executive ability, made easy for him what to others would have been insuperable, and resulted in an advance of his Church in every direction.

Among other things that were accomplished during this time were the building and endowment of the Protestant Episcopal hospital of his diocese, the establishment of the Protestant Episcopal Academy, the foundation of the Protestant Episcopal Divinity School of Philadelphia, and the erection of no less than thirty-five new churches in the city of Philadelphia. So great was the amount of labor involved that his health broke down under the strain and he was compelled to seek the relief of an assistant. The consequences of his work were a growth of his diocese in wealth, numbers, and activity, which necessitated its division into two separate organizations. He married three times. By his first wife, Sarah Maria Nott, he had the Hon. Clarkson N. [1825], who married Virginia Mitchell; Howard [1826], who married Mary L. Brown; General Robert B. [1829], who married, first, Francis Tileston, and second, Abigail Stevens; Edward Tuckerman [1831], who married Julia Blatchford; the Right Rev. Henry Codman [1835], who married Eliza Rogers; Eliphalet N. [1837], who married Helen Fuller; and Maria [1839], who married Launt Thompson. By his second wife, Sarah Porter, he had James Neilson [1841], who married Harriet Duer Jones; William A. [1842]; and Frank Hunter [1851], who married Alice Key. His third wife was Frances Seton.

Bishop Horatio [1802] was graduated from Union in 1826, and admitted to the priesthood two years later. The same year he was made professor of mathematics and physics in Washington, now Trinity, College. Five years later, he became rector of St. Peter's Church, Albany, where he labored with great power and success twenty-one years. In 1845, he was made Provisional Bishop of the Diocese of New York, and in 1861, Bishop.

Bishop Horatio

His work in New York may be compared with that of his brother in Philadelphia, being marked by the same great administrative talent, contagious enthusiasm, and deep belief in the efficacy of organized effort. The Church grew rapidly, and in 1868 the diocese had become so unwieldy that it was divided into three parts, Albany and Long Island being erected into separate jurisdictions. Marked by ripe scholarship and literary skill, his addresses, sermons, and occasional contributions to Church literature exerted a strong and wholesome influence wherever read. During the war his patriotism was marked, and at all times his labors for the ignorant, poor, and sick were continuous and efficient. He married, first, Mary Jane Tomlinson, and, second, Margaret Pollock. Among his children were Charles Henry [1828], Mary Jane [1830], Anna [1831], David T. [1836], Phœbe [1838], Horatio [1840], Robert Minturn [1843], Professor William Bleecker [1846], and Mary J. [1848].

The eighth generation was marked by many men of eminence. The Hon. Clarkson Nott [1825] was graduated from

Union (1842), studied civil engineering at the Rensselaer Polytechnic, and thereafter law, and was admitted to the bar. This thorough education made him a valued member of the community, and in 1868 he was elected to Congress, where he served three terms until 1875, and thereafter served two terms, from 1877 to 1881. From the first he was a prominent character in the House of Representatives. His greatest achievement was his exposure of the frauds in the Presidential election of 1876, being chairman of the committee which investigated the matter, and doing the lion's share of the work. For many years he was one of the great leaders of the New York Democracy, and was at one time President of the American Bar Association.

Clarkson Nott, Statesman

Howard, the banker [1826], was born at Union College, and graduated therefrom in 1846. He came into great prominence during the Civil War, when he organized many relief associations and other patriotic societies, and may be justly called one of the fathers of the famous United States Sanitary Commission. He was an incorporator of the American Museum of Natural History and of the Metropolitan Museum of Art, and an organizer of the New York State Charities Aid Association. In 1873, he was elected President of the New York Association for Improving the Condition of the Poor. He has played an important part in the various societies which have been established for the preservation of scenery and historical monuments, the establishment of state and local parks, and the reservation of Niagara Falls as a public pleasure-ground.

Howard the Banker

The soldier of this generation was General Robert B. [1829]. He studied at Union College, and afterwards took up law, and was admitted to the bar. At the breaking out of the Civil War he gave up a lucrative practice to aid in the defence of the Union. He fought like a hero, and rose rapidly, becoming a brigadier-general in 1863. The following year he was brevetted major-general, and on his wedding day Secretary-of-War Stanton presented the wife with his commission as full major-general. At the close of the war he gave up army life and

Major-General Robert B.

Maria Nott
Wife of Bishop Alonzo Potter

Hon. Clarkson N. Potter
From a photograph

became interested in railway corporations. According to General Hancock, General Potter was one of the twelve best officers in the American Army.

Edward Tuckerman [1831], architect and musician, was graduated from Union (1853), and devoted his life to study, architecture, and music. He was as well known in Europe, where he resided for a long time, as in his native country. *Edward Tuckerman, Architect*

For forty years he made a special study of the problem of housing the masses, during which time he personally investigated every type of model tenement in the great cities of the world and compiled an immense mass of valuable facts bearing upon every phase of the subject. He embodied these studies in a model tenement, which was exhibited at the Columbian Exposition in Chicago in 1893, for which he received a medal from the Exposition authorities, and which has been widely approved by students of the tenement-house question. In 1897, he was made an honorary member of the New York Chapter of the American Institute of Architects. The position of Supervising Architect of the Treasury Department was offered to him by President Grant, and, on his declining it, was given to his brother, William Appleton.

The Right Rev. Henry Codman [1835], Bishop of the Protestant Episcopal Church of New York, was a worthy successor of both his distinguished father and uncle. He was educated at the Episcopal Academy, Philadelphia, and the Virginia Theological Seminary, where he was graduated in 1857. He served with marked success at Greensburg, Pa., St. John's, Troy, and Trinity, Boston. In 1868, he became rector of Grace Church, New York, where he remained sixteen years. During this time, he declined the Presidency of Kenyon College (1863), and the Bishopric of Iowa (1875). In 1883, he was elected Assistant Bishop to his uncle, the Right Rev. Horatio. Four years later, on the death of the latter, he became his successor. *Bishop Henry C.*

His policy has been that which has marked the great divines of his race—that of a patriot upon all national matters, a civic leader upon municipal questions, a tireless advocate of educational reform and progress, and a resolute worker in philanthropic enterprises. During a life of the hardest kind of work, he has found time to publish several books of literary excellence and general value. His most notable work of recent years has been his statesmanlike effort to harmonize the interests of labor and capital, and to Christianize the "Submerged Tenth," in both of which cases his endeavors have met with gratifying success.

The Rev. Eliphalet Nott [1837] was a graduate of Union College (1861), and of Berkeley Divinity School (1862). In 1866, he **President Eliphalet N.** was made professor of ethics at Lehigh University, and in 1871 President of Union College, and afterwards President when the college was made into a university. In 1884, he declined the Bishopric of Nebraska to accept the Presidency of Hobart College. He died on February 16, 1901.

Professor William Bleecker [1846] was one of the great educators of the country. He was graduated from Columbia **Professor William B.** with high honors in 1866, and thereupon entered the celebrated School of Mines of that university, where he took the degree of E.M. in 1869. For two years he was assistant professor of geology, and at the same time served as a geologist upon the State Geological Survey of Ohio. In 1871, he became professor of mining engineering and metallurgy at Washington University, St. Louis, Mo. No one stands higher among the scientific experts of the land, nor enjoys a greater esteem among the learned societies of this country and Europe. In 1888, he was made President of the American Institute of Mining Engineers.

It would be difficult to surpass the record of the Potter family so far as intellectuality and mental achievements are concerned. It is difficult, indeed, to equal it. The record of the main branch is longer and marked by a greater number of distinguished men, but it may be questioned whether, in general, they have attained the high levels of their New York kinsmen. They have achieved fame in the pulpit as orators, and in the cathedral chair as executives and organizers. In science, pedagogy, architecture, music, literature, and at the bar, they have won enviable reputations for that high ability which borders upon genius.

In national and civic affairs they have been marked by patriotism, humanity, and philanthropy, and in private life they have been characterized by a culture, refinement, and grace which have made them leaders of society for a hundred years.

Rapalje

Jacob Rapalje
From a steel engraving

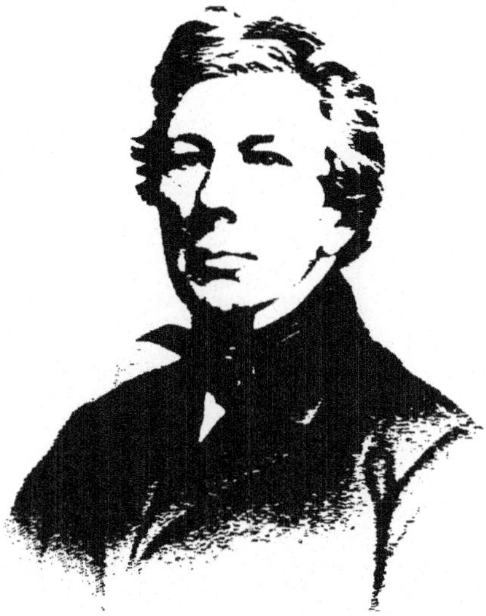

XXVI

RAPALJE

RELIGIOUS forces are potent factors in the breaking up of old and in the establishment of new communities. The wars between the Romanists and Huguenots of France are an interesting exemplification of this fact, especially to an American student. The revocation of the Edict of Nantes drove tens of thousands of the Reformed faith into more liberal countries, and of these a considerable portion crossed the Atlantic and settled in the Dutch colonies of America, where they soon became a large and influential element in the community.

Among the first settlers in the New Netherlands, was Joris Janes de Rapalie, a noble Huguenot of La Rochelle, France, better known under the Dutch form of his name, Jan Joris Rapaelje. His family had been distinguished in the history of Brittany from the middle of the eleventh century. In this romantic province they owned large estates, and were famous for their valor and patriotism. Many of them took part in the Crusades, while others achieved distinction in the French wars at home and abroad. They were among the first converts to the Reformed faith, and paid the usual penalty for their non-conformity. Some were killed, while the majority were forced to flee to Switzerland, Belgium, and Holland.

Jan Joris, Founder

Joris was among those who escaped to Holland. Here he remained a short time, and then, with a company of venturous men and women, he took passage in the ship *Unity* of the Dutch West India Company, and arrived in New Amsterdam in 1623, being one of the earliest settlers. He stayed a short while at New Amsterdam, and then went to Fort Orange, now Albany. Here he remained three years, and returned to New Amsterdam, where he lived until 1637. In June of that year he bought a large tract of land from the Indians on the Long Island side of the East River, and there made his permanent home. The tract was of 335 acres, and included a large part of what was called the Wallabout. He was a man of high integrity, and a few years after his arrival in Brooklyn he was made a magistrate. He married Catalina Trico, daughter of Joris Trico of Paris, by whom he had eleven children: Sarah [1625], Marritje [1627], Jannetje [1629], Judith [1635], Jan [1637], Jacob [1639,] Catalyntje [1641], Jeronimus [1643], Annetje [1646], Elizabeth [1648], and Daniel [1650].

Of these Sarah, the eldest, was the first female child born in the New Netherlands. In honor of this fact, the authorities presented her with a tract of land on the Wallabout adjacent to her father's farm. Sarah was a woman of great talent and physical vigor, and during her long life was the acknowledged social head of Brooklyn. She was twice married, her husbands being Hans Hansen Bergen and Tunis Gysbert Bogaert. By these unions she had fourteen children, becoming thereby the maternal ancestress of the Bergen and Bogart families of Long Island.

Sarah, the First Girl

Jeronimus, in the second generation, was a man of prominence in both New York and Brooklyn. He was a farmer and merchant, Justice of the Peace, and a deacon of the Brooklyn Church. He owned several small craft, with which he supplied the market of New York with produce, and turned an honest penny by carrying freight for his neighbors. He accumulated considerable property, and left his children well provided for. His wife was Anna, daughter of Tunis Denys, by whom he had six sons and three daughters.

Jeronimus

Daniel, the youngest child of Joris, was a man of high character and of a strong religious nature. He took comparatively little interest in public affairs, but devoted his time and wealth to church work. He was an elder of the Brooklyn Church the larger part of his life, and made it a point of duty to visit regularly all the places of worship belonging to his denomination. The church records of that period speak of him in very high terms, and ascribe the prosperity of his denomination largely to his generous aid. He married Sarah Klock, daughter of Abraham Klock, by whom he had six children. Daniel the Devout

In the third generation were several male members of ability and influence. Tunis [1671], son of Jeronimus, was active and versatile, having been a farmer, stock-raiser, merchant, and sheep-owner. He was an enthusiastic churchman, and served as deacon of the Brooklyn Church for many years. He married Sarah Van Vechten, by whom he had seven children. Tunis the Deacon

Jacob [1679], son of Jeronimus, married Sarah Brinckerhoff, daughter of Abraham Brinckerhoff, by whom he had a large family. He settled in Raritan, N. J., where he founded the New Jersey branch of his race.

Cornelius [1690] married Joanna Antonides, daughter of the Rev. Vincentius Antonides, by whom he had many daughters, nearly all of whom grew up and married advantageously. He resided in New York, and from his branch came the Rapaljes who married into the New York families of that period.

Jeronimus [1682] was a prosperous land-owner, shipper, and merchant, who was active in religious and philanthropic affairs, and who served twenty-five years as a trustee of the town of Brooklyn. He took delight in good roads and bridges, and was marked by great fidelity to his trusteeship. He married Hilletie Van Vechten, daughter of Hendrick Van Vechten, by whom he had five children. Jeronimus, Town-trustee

Daniel, son of Daniel [1691], settled in Newtown, where he established the Queens County branch of the family. He married Aletie Cornell, daughter of Johannes Cornell, by whom he had ten children. He was a prosperous farmer, and founded an estate which grew to large proportions, under the management of his descendants.

In the fourth generation, the male descendants began to change from agricultural to mercantile pursuits. In the meantime, the growth of Brooklyn and New York had enhanced the value of farm property and of garden produce, so that nearly all the sons were quite well to do. George, son of Tunis, bought property in Bedford, which was then developing into a very prosperous village. He improved it, so that its value almost doubled during his lifetime. He married Elizabeth Remsen, daughter of Joris Remsen, by whom he had five children—Sarah [1722], George [1724], Tunis [1726], Rem [1728], and Phœbe [1731].

Jeronimus and his brother Derrick (sons of Jeronimus) followed their uncle Jacob and migrated to New Jersey, settling first at Raritan and afterwards at Brunswick. Each married, the former having two sons, Cornelius and Tunis, and the latter, George and Jeronimus.

Daniel, son of Daniel, was the thriftiest member of the family. He was very successful in business, and eight years after his father died bought the paternal estate at Newtown. He managed it with prudence and amassed great wealth. He was a magistrate of the town, and held many positions of honor and trust in the ecclesiastical, commercial, legal, and social world.

Judge Daniel

About this time the conflict of English and Dutch spelling brought about a curious change of the name. Heretofore it had been spelled Rapalie; now, on account of slurs cast upon the Dutch Knickerbockers, the family adopted the Holland spelling. They could not agree, however, upon the form, and no less than three versions appeared. The largest number accepted Rapalje, while two other groups employed Rapaelje and Rapelje respectively. The French particle of place, "de," was now omitted altogether.

Folkert [1719], son of Tunis, resided at Cripplebush, and devoted himself to horticulture. He married Matilda Polhemus,

the management of his

descendants began to
sults. In the meantime
had enhanced the value
t, so that nearly all th
son of Tunis, bought
developing into a very
so that its value almos
ried Elizabeth Remsen,
he had five children—
7:0], Rem [1728], and

(sons of Jeronimus) fol
to New Jersey, settling
wi.k. Each married, th
⁴ Tunis, and the latter

st member of the family.
ght years after his father
: at Newtown. He man
assed great wealth. He
many positions of honor
ercial, legal, and socia

ish and Dutch spe ling
name. Heretofore it had
s of slurs cast upon the
ed the Holland spel ing
re form, and no less than
.mber accepted Rapalje
le and Rapelje respecti
de." was now omitted

ted at Cripplebush, and
..ried Matilda Po hemus

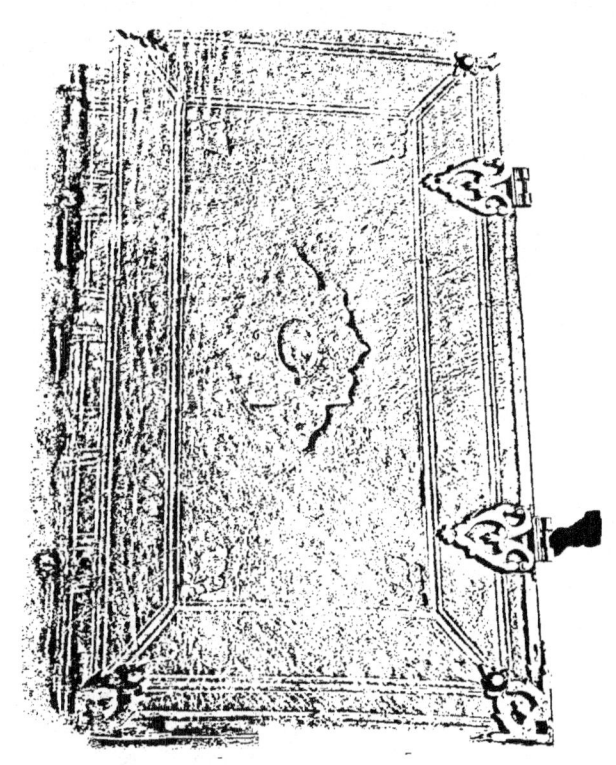

The Rapalje Family Bible, in Possession of Henr S. Rapalje, Esq.

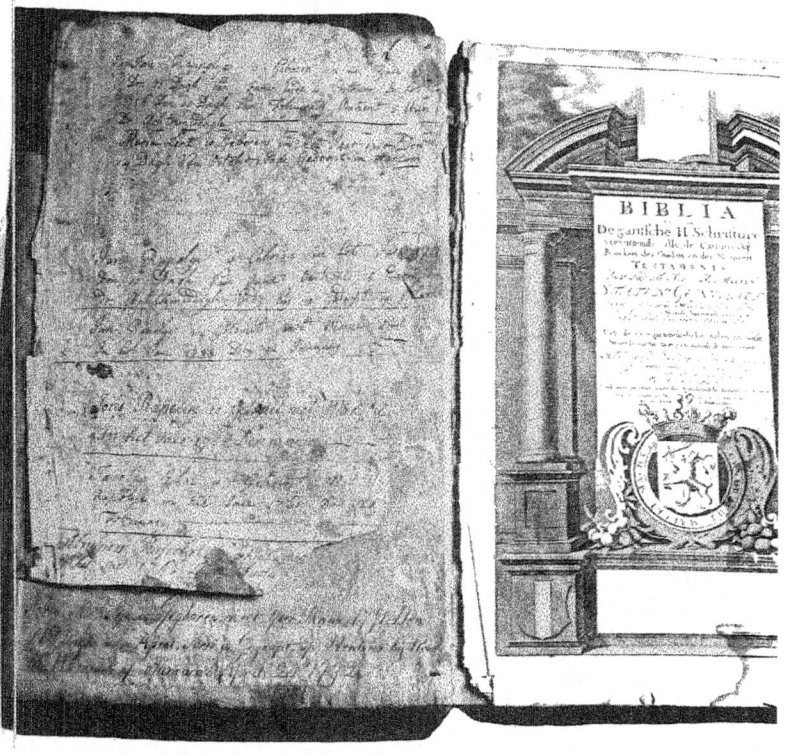

daughter of Cornelius Polhemus, by whom he had one son and three daughters.

In the fifth generation, Major Daniel [1748], son of Johannes and grandson of Daniel, was a brave Revolutionary soldier. Upon the breaking out of the war he took up arms, served as lieutenant during the conflict, and reached the rank of major at its close. The British holding the western end of Long Island, he was compelled to fly the country, and did not see his home until after the British troops had evacuated New York. He married Agnes Bergen, daughter of Johannes Bergen, and had a large farm at New Lots. His children were John, Daniel, Samuel, and Michael.

Major Daniel

From this branch are descended several men of distinction. His grandson, Williamson, was a skilful portrait painter and a prosperous man of affairs. His great-grandson, Daniel [1836], was educated at Rutgers, and after graduation entered the theological department and took orders. As soon as he was ordained he offered his services to the Foreign Missionary Society, which sent him to the Amoy Mission, in China, of the Reformed Church in America. Here he labored for over thirty years, building up a large and faithful congregation of Chinese converts. The work accomplished by Dr. Rapalje and his heroic assistants borders on the marvellous. When he went there in the early sixties, the place was the most notoriously evil on the China coast. Superstition was rife, and the Tong-An district, just back of the city of Amoy, had supplied pirates to the China Sea from time immemorial.

Williamson, Artist

Daniel the Evangelist

The good doctor determined upon invading the latter field. He organized all the missionaries of the district into a compact whole and assigned to each a specific duty. He established preaching centres throughout the large territory and placed several at the more important points among the rough populace of Tong-An. For many years the task seemed fruitless, and then it began to bring forth a harvest. Chapels, schools, and, finally, churches, were founded. In 1890, the turbulent district had become quiet and orderly, and the evangelists found themselves supported by fifty native exhorters of ability and courage. Then began the foundations of a college on the Island of Kulang-Su, and, in 1895, several hundred children attended the schools of Dr. Daniel and his associates.

Rem [1728], the son of George, took up mercantile life in New York, which he made his residence. Here he amassed a handsome fortune, and finally retired from business and settled in Pelham. He married Ellen Hardenbrook, by whom he had issue.

George the Scholar His son George [1771] was graduated from Columbia in 1791, and admitted to the bar in 1794. He had a large practice, but finally confined his work to the management of his estate, especially after 1805, when his father died, leaving him a fortune. He was a man of strong literary tastes, and devoted his leisure to travel and study. He published many monographs upon special topics, and, in 1834, a volume upon his travels. He married Susan Eliza Provost, daughter of Bishop Provost.

George B., grandson of George, who was a grandson of Joris, was a famous character in his time, and was noted for his strange ill-luck. His grandfather, George, was drowned in New York Bay in 1781, his cousin George in 1795, and his uncle George, in 1799, met a similar fate. This singular coincidence of a man, his son, and grandson, each bearing the same name and meeting the same doom, attracted great attention. George B. was a talented business man and prospered from the first. In his youth he fell in love with a very beautiful girl named Miss Sherred, and became affianced to her. A month before the wedding-day she fell sick, and died on the very night she was to have been married. From that time on the young merchant was a changed man. He gave up all society, especially that of women, and found his solace in the excitement of trade. He lived amid the humblest surroundings in order to accumulate wealth, and invested his gains with great shrewdness. Before his death he owned numerous houses and lands between Thirtieth and Fortieth Streets, Eighth and Eleventh Avenues. His cousin, George Bernard [1784], was a merchant of high standing and wealth in the first half of the nineteenth century.

The Rapalje Estate, 35th Street and North River
Redrawn from an old prin

In the sixth generation, George, the son of Daniel, grandson of John, was distinguished as a merchant and philanthropist. He was a moving spirit in the charities and church organ-   George the izations of the early part of the nineteenth century.   Philanthropist He married Sarah Elizabeth Staples, by whom he had: Ellen Maria, George Augustus—who was educated for the Protestant Episcopal Church, but died before he was ordained,—Sarah Eliza beth, and Henry Staples, architect, who is the head of the present branch of the family in New York.

In the seventh generation, Jacob [1788] commands attention. He began his business life as a clerk in New York, where his energy and courtesy soon made him liked by his em-   Lieutenant ployers. At the outbreak of the War of 1812, he enlisted   Jacob and became a lieutenant of artillery. He made a good record as a soldier, and the regimental order-books which he wrote are still in existence and bear testimony to his administrative ability. At the close of the war he started business in Charleston, S. C., where, in 1816, he was appointed Deputy Secretary of State. In 1825, he returned to Brooklyn, where he soon became a leader in the City Council.

He labored for the widening and improving of Atlantic Avenue, and advocated the present South Ferry. In 1837, he invented a machine with which he proposed to clean the streets of New York. His invention was far ahead of the age. It did the work well, but it aroused the fierce enmity of the street sweepers of the time, who formed a mob, chased the inventor a mile, and destroyed the machine. It was fully twenty years before his idea was taken up and made a part of the street-cleaning equipment. In the forties, with Cornelius J. Bergen and Alexander Bergen, he started a movement which resulted in the laying out of Carroll Park and the reclamation of the marsh lands in South Brooklyn.

This measure changed what before had been an unhealthful territory into a fashionable neighborhood and paved the way for the Erie Basin and the great manufacturing establishments which now are so striking a characteristic of that part of the borough. He developed the district of Newtown known as Laurel

Hill, and gave it its poetic name. With J. S. T. Stranahan he was one of the first to advocate the establishment of Prospect Park, and lived to see the first steps taken towards the realization of that project. He married Elizabeth Van Mater, by whom he had seven children. Of his sons, the eldest, Gilbert Van Mater, became a prominent citizen of Staatsburgh, Dutchess County, and the youngest, Augustus, remained in New York and Brooklyn.

More than thirty of the family have been prominent merchants in the metropolis, and during the Civil War over eighty, espoused the cause of the Union. The Rapaljes are notable for the vigor of their members, the large size of their families, and the preponderance of male over female issue. In this respect they tower over the other old families of the State with but one exception, the Schencks. The strength and health of the race is accompanied or manifested by lightheartedness and geniality. This is modified by a strong religious nature, which expresses itself in enthusiastic church work. More than one hundred and fifty Rapaljes have been deacons, vestrymen, and trustees in the churches of the Greater New York. In the beginning, they were stalwart pioneers, and assisted in the settlement of at least fifty towns in New York and New Jersey. In their next stage, they were skilful farmers, graziers, and carriers. In the third, they were able merchants, owners of real estate, clergymen, and professional men. In peace, they have always striven for local improvements and municipal reform, and in war, they have been active supporters of the nation. They have cared little for office or title, finding their chief joy in the performance of their duty — domestic, social, and civil.

George Rapalje
From a photograph in possession of Henry S. Rapalje, Esq.

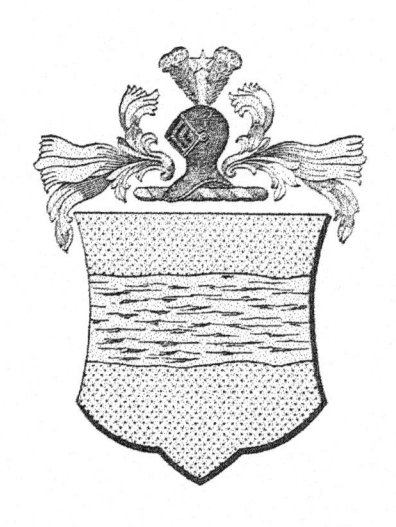

Remsen

XXVII

REMSEN

THE history of the old New York families, and especially those of Holland blood, is full of quaint features, resulting from the projection of Dutch customs into the New World. Nowhere can a better illustration be found than in the family names of the seventeenth century. To the present generation the patronymic is all-important. We reproduce it exactly as it is transmitted from the past, no matter how incorrectly our forebears may have spelled it. The good Knickerbockers had no such feeling. In them the filial qualities seem to have been much stronger than they are with the people of to-day. The son and daughter took the father's first name and added to it "s," "se," or "sen," to express filial relationship, and gave little thought to the final name of their sire. In some cases they seemed to tire of a family name and adopted a second, with the seeming approbation of the members of their race. Thus the Lents and Suydams are really Rikers.

A similar illustration is afforded by the distinguished Remsen family, which for more than two centuries and a half has been prominent in Manhattan, Brooklyn, Queens, and other districts of the Empire State. Their family name is Vanderbeek or

Vanderbeeck, meaning "of the Brook." The family belonged to the nobility of Germany and of the Netherlands at a very early period. The first reference to them in the ancient chronicles was in 1162 A.D., when the Emperor Frederick Barbarossa presented a valorous knight of their race with a handsome coat-of-arms. From that time up to the present century their name has been frequent in the annals of both Germany and Holland, where they earned honor by courage in war and public services in peace.

The founder of the race in America was Rem Jansen Vanderbeeck, who came to the New Netherlands in 1642. He was a farmer, and in addition a skilful blacksmith. At that time the young men of Holland were obliged by law and custom to learn a regular trade in addition to their ordinary calling. This was done for the protection of the community in the event of inundation by the sea or of beleaguerment by a foreign army. Soon after Rem's arrival he espoused Jannetje, the handsome daughter of Joris Jansen de Rapalje, and settled in Albany, then Fort Orange. He took up a farm, opened a forge, and prospered in both callings. He was a man of powerful physique and sweet disposition, a good-natured, laughing giant, who won the affections of young and old. A kind husband and a loving father, he soon had ample opportunity for the use of both virtues, having a family of which fifteen grew up and married.

Rem Jansen Vanderbeeck the Founder

He accumulated property and would doubtless have remained in his first home but for the rumors of an Indian uprising. He had no fear for himself, but much solicitude for his little ones. At the same time, his father-in-law, Joris, bought a large estate at the Wallabout, and added his persuasion to the other incentives for removal. Rem complied and took up a fine tract of meadow and marshland at the Wallabout, which was held by the family more than two hundred years. In Brooklyn he was as popular as at Fort Orange. Shortly after his arrival, he was made an official, and during the second Dutch administration he became a magistrate. Of his fair wife a family tradition says that in her babyhood she with her Indian nurse sailed across Buttermilk

Channel in a Dutch washtub. That body of water between Governor's Island and Brooklyn, which now floats an ocean steamer, was then a shallow estuary, which at very low tide could be waded across by a grown man.

Rem died in 1681, and at his funeral his fifteen children with their wives, husbands, and children were present. It was a seven-days' talk in New York, and made so deep an impression upon the public mind that it is probable both his offspring and the public considered the dead man as a greater personality than the race of which he was a member, and so induced the adoption of Remsen as a family name from that time on. The sons were Jan, Joris, Rem, Jacob, Jeromus, Daniel, Abraham, Isaac, and Jeremias. Of the daughters, Anna married Jan G. Dorlandt, Hildegond married Aris J. Vanderbilt, Femmetie, Joseph Hegeman, Jannetje, Garret H. Van Nostrand, Catalina, Elbert Adriense, and Sarah, Martin Adriense.

The members of the second generation left the paternal homestead and established themselves at various points. Jan [1648] became a resident at Flatbush, as did his brother Daniel. Joris settled in Brooklyn, near the ferry. Isaac [1673] became a Brooklynite. Rem, Jr., went to Flatbush. Jeremias retained the homestead, and Abraham settled in Newtown. *Jan of Flatbush* *Abraham of Newtown* No less than six of the sons left families which became the nuclei in the next generation of large and influential branches.

In this third generation, Rem, the son of Jan, removed to Staten Island, where he became a wealthy farmer and justice of the peace. John and Isaac, the sons of Isaac, settled at Oyster Bay, where they were the founders of a *Rem the Justice* powerful clan. Rem, the son of Rem, was a distinguished churchman in Brooklyn, whose chief interest in life was the education of his children. Besides the ordinary tuition of the schools, supplemented by instruction at home, he had each apprenticed to a trade. When the youths came of age he gave them each a portion of his estate so as to start them in life. The sons settled in New York, where they founded an important branch of the family.

They were seven in number, and seemed to act always upon the rule of "all for one and one for all."

Captain Jeromus [1705], the son of Abraham, was probably the most distinguished member of this generation. He was a thrifty farmer, who saved enough money from his own farm to purchase the parental homestead from the other heirs and add it to his own estate. He was active in church and state, and held many offices of honor and dignity. He had a warlike vein in his composition, and from early manhood to old age was connected with the militia, in which he rose from private to captain. Rem, the son of Jeremias, was another forceful individuality. He removed from the old homestead at the Wallabout to Bedford, where he took up a large farm. He soon became a leader in that settlement, and was chosen a trustee of Brooklyn, in which office he served from 1727 to 1776. His brother Christopher was a farmer and land-owner, who invested wisely in real estate at Fulton Ferry, the Wallabout, and Newtown. He left a large fortune, which went to his two daughters, Heyltie, who married Johannes Schenck, and Phœbe, who married William Howard.

Captain Jeromus

Rem the Trustee

In the fourth generation the sons of Rem were commanding figures. They were Abraham [1730], Garrett [1736], Aert [1737], and Luke [1749]. The four were fine specimens of Knickerbocker manhood. Their education had been excellent, and had included a thorough course in technical training. In the decade prior to the Revolution they were so outspoken in favor of colonial independence that they were frequently threatened with prosecution for treason. Even before the outbreak of hostilities they had supplied themselves with a full military equipment, and Aert and Luke, who were machinists and wheelwrights by trade, started the repair of firearms for patriotic neighbors and friends.

Major Abraham

Lieutenant Garrett

The beginning of the war found them ready and eager for action. Abraham and Garrett went to the front, where they proved superb soldiers, the former rising to be a major, and the latter to be a lieutenant. Luke and Aert, on ac-

Luke the Ordnance-Master

o act always upon the

.braham, was probably
generation. He was a
h money from his own
omestead from the other
as active in church and
nd dignity. He had a
early manhood to old
ich he rose from private
Jeremias, was another
oved from the old home-
re he took up a large
t settlement, and was
e he served from 1727
farmer and land-owner,
lton Ferry, the Walla-
ortune, which went to
Johannes Schenck, and

The Remsen Farm House
From a print in *Valentine's Manual*, 1858

Rem were commanding
rrett [1736], Aert [1737],
were fine specimens of
eir education had been
rse in technical train-
e Revolution they were
onial independence that
prosecution for treason.
hey had supplied them-
nd Aert and Luke, who
ade, started the repair of
ls
em ready and eager for
went to the front, where
the former rising to be
Luke and Aert, on ac-

Bedford Corners in 1776
From an old print

count of their technical knowledge, were made masters of ordnance, their skill proving invaluable to the colonists. With the British victories on Long Island, the four brothers retreated, first destroying everything in their homes, likely to be of value to the foe, which they could not carry away. During the remainder of the war the two soldiers were at the front, while the two machinists were high in command in the Continental workshops at Peekskill. Of Aert and his wonderful strength many stories are told. On one occasion, when a speculator tried to palm off an inferior rifle upon the Government, the big Long Islander, remarking, "We don't want this kind of steel," took the weapon and bent it to a right angle with his hands and knee. At the conclusion of peace, the valiant quartet returned to their home on the paternal farm, and there passed the remainder of their days. *Aert the Strong*

No less than ten members of this generation were eminent merchants in New York. All accumulated goodly estates, and one, Hendrick [1708], became a man of great wealth. Through their opulence, education, numbers, and high character, they were prominent in New York society, where they contracted many admirable matrimonial alliances. In the main, they married into the old Knickerbocker families, more especially those of Dutch and Huguenot descent. *Hendrick the Merchant*

In the fifth generation the most noticeable figure was Hendrick, or Henry, the merchant [1736]. He inherited his father's business, as well as a handsome fortune, and from the time he reached manhood's estate he played an active rôle in commercial, religious, political, and social affairs. His strong love of liberty and his intense enthusiasm gained for him the sobriquet of "Henry the Whig" before the Revolution, and "Henry the Patriot" afterwards. He was a member of the famous Committee of One Hundred, and was chairman of the importers of New York, especially those whose trade was with Great Britain. They met, October 13, 1774, and at his suggestion formed the first boycott known in American history. This was aimed at speculators, more especially unscrupulous adventurers *Henry the Patriot* from Great Britain, who were taking advantage of the troublous times to make corners in the necessaries of life.

The chief personality of the sixth generation was Henry [1762], son of Henry the Whig. He was finely educated and began active life as a clerk in his father's counting-house. He left the desk to become private secretary to the Hon. John Jay, when the latter was Secretary for Foreign Affairs. In 1790, he returned to business life, and became his father's partner. Five years later he gave up private business to become first teller of the United States Branch Bank. From this time on his life was devoted to financial institutions, for which he displayed an aptitude bordering upon genius. The only interruption to this career was when, at the earnest solicitation of the President, he became private secretary to Thomas Jefferson. He married Elizabeth, daughter of Captain Abraham R. de Peyster, by whom he had nine children.

Henry the Banker

This generation was marked by wealth and culture. More than fifty members possessed great estates; some twenty were college graduates who attained distinction in law, medicine, and the political arena. The largest number belonged to New York City; next in importance were those of Brooklyn, while smaller groups were scattered in Staten Island, Pennsylvania, and other places.

In the seventh generation were eminent scholars and capitalists. William [1815], son of Henry, was graduated from Princeton 1836, and admitted to the New York bar in 1839. He relinquished practice to attend to the large estates left by his father and grandfather. He was deeply interested in banks and financial corporations, and left a large estate. He married Jane Suydam, by whom he had eight children. Among the organizations to which he belonged were the St. Nicholas Society and the American Geographical Society, of both of which he was a founder. Robert G., brother of William, was an active man in the financial world during the middle of the nineteenth century. He married Mary Delprat, by whom he had Georgiana **Delprat**, who married Charles Betts Hillhouse.

William the Financier

In the eighth generation have been many professional men of high repute. Dr. Charles, the son of William, was a physician, and an executor of his father's estate. He was graduated from Princeton (1877). He married Lilian Livingston Jones, by whom he had issue. He is represented in the ninth generation by his son William. He has an estate at Remsensburg.

<small>Dr. Charles</small>

Dr. Robert George was graduated from the New York University (1873), and from the College of Physicians and Surgeons, Columbia (1876). Henry [1852] was graduated from Columbia (1871). Phœnix was graduated from Columbia (1867), and resided on the family estate at West Islip, N. Y. Jacob D. [1855] was educated at Erasmus Hall and the Brooklyn Polytechnic. He early displayed talent for political life, and began his career as a justice of the peace. On the annexation of Flatlands to Brooklyn, he became a city assessor, and remained such until the consolidation of the boroughs into the greater city. In 1899, he was elected to the State Assembly, and re-elected in 1900 and 1901.

<small>Doctor Robert G.</small>

<small>Jacob D. the Assemblyman</small>

An eminent living representative of the race is Dr. Ira [1846], now President of Johns Hopkins University. He was born in New York City, studied at the City College, and was graduated from the College of Physicians and Surgeons (1867). He went abroad to continue his scientific studies, spent a year in Munich, and then took a course in Goettingen, where he took the degree of Ph.D. (1870). For the next two years he served as assistant professor in the University of Tuebingen, Germany, and at the expiration of that time accepted the professorship of chemistry and physics at Williams College. Here he achieved fame by his brilliant researches in higher inorganic and synthetic chemistry. In 1876, his rising fame attracted the attention of the founders of Johns Hopkins University, who invited him to take the chair of chemistry in that institution. He accepted the offer, and from that time until to-day has devoted himself to researches in chemical and electrical fields, in which he has become one of the greatest experts of the world. In 1879, he founded the *American Chemical Journal,* of which he has

<small>President Ira</small>

been the editor, and to which he has largely contributed ever since. He has written and translated many standard works upon chemistry, while numerous monographs have become classics in the literature of that science. Upon the resignation of Dr. Gilman from the Presidency of Johns Hopkins University, he was elected to that post. In 1893, Columbia University conferred upon him the honorary degree of LL.D., and Yale chose him for similar distinction at her bicentennial. He is a member of numerous chemical and scientific societies at home and abroad, and may be justly regarded as one of the finest scientific intellects this country has yet produced.

The history of the Remsens has followed a different line of development from that of any other Knickerbocker family. Like most of the early immigrants from the Netherlands, they were dowered with great intelligence, religiousness, and probity, and were distinguished for physical health and vigor. They took to husbandry and the manual trades, succeeding in both and displaying industrial and mechanical aptitude of a high character. Not until the closing of the eighteenth century was there any break from this mode of life. Then, as if they were no longer satisfied with their ancestral occupations, and the wealth which these had produced, they turned from the plough to the counting-house, the college, and the political forum. During the nineteenth century these tendencies developed, until to-day the family name is more or less identified with scientific, collegiate, and political affairs.

Renwick

Professor James Renwick
From an oil painting owned by Mrs. Renwick

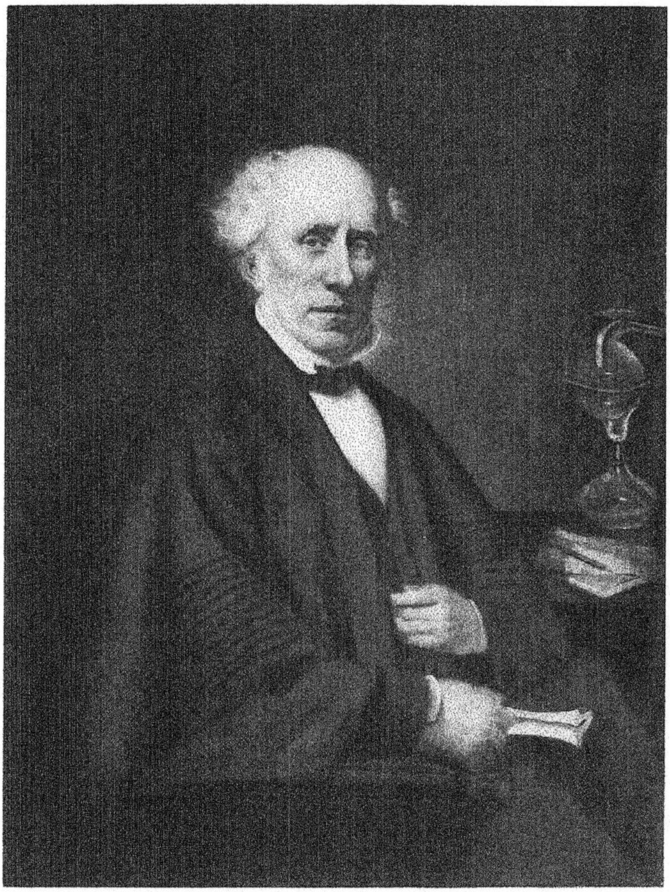

XXVIII

RENWICK

TO Scotland the Empire State owes some of its best blood. The thrift and intellectuality which so mark the Scotch character found full field for their development in the New World, and achieved triumphs which would have been impossible in the home country, for lack of opportunity. Beyond the substantial virtues of the Caledonian nature are moral and spiritual traits of even greater value. From time immemorial the people of the Land-o'-Cakes, to use Burns's pet phrase, have been noted for their affection, loyalty, fidelity to duty, and strong religious convictions. These qualities were developed by the stern and rigorous life demanded by the necessities of the country. In an inclement and sterile land Nature compels the citizens to lead simple, laborious, and upright lives. There is no other alternative. Any other course of living implies pauperism and extinction.

The qualities enumerated mark the history of the Renwick family, which has attained distinction in the land of its birth and that of its adoption. In the former they were soldiers, lawyers, merchants, and divines. One of them, James Renwick, the martyr, a famous soldier and clergyman of the

James the Martyr

seventeenth century, was put to death for his religious and political opinions. He met his fate with a serenity which impressed deeply the spectators of his execution.

The founder of the family in the United States was James [1744], who came to New York from Manchester, England, in 1783, shortly after the American Revolution. He was an enterprising and long-headed merchant, who was well known in the mercantile world of the eighteenth century. A good father and a kind husband, he was also a public-spirited and philanthropic citizen. In 1789, we find him, with a group of friends, organizing The Mercantile Society for Employing the Industrious Poor and Promoting Manufacturing. His generosity was noted, especially to church and charitable work.

<small>James the Founder</small>

Of his two children, William [1769] was an able merchant, who established a direct traffic between Liverpool and New York. At that time Liverpool was a place of but little importance, and the venture was regarded as a wild speculation. It proved a success and gave renown to its author. So far as history is concerned, he is not so commanding a figure as his beautiful wife. She was Jean Jeffrey, daughter of the Rev. Andrew Jeffrey, of the Manse, Lochmaben. Her beauty and talents made her a belle when a mere child, and attracted the admiration of the poet, Burns, who immortalized her in three of his finest poems. The union of James and Jean was very happy, and was blessed with six children, three sons and three daughters, of whom five were to become important members of New York life.

<small>William the Merchant</small>

In the third generation, Professor James [1792] was born in Liverpool, while his parents were on a visit to the old country. He was of studious habits, and entered Columbia College at the early age of eleven, being then on a par with most boys of fifteen. He was graduated in 1807, being the first in his class, which contained such brilliant men as Judge Bronk, Dr. Burrell, the Rev. John H. Hill, and James Van Cortlandt. The following year he received the degree of A.M., and in 1813, at the age of twenty-one, was appointed instructor in natural and experimental philosophy. In 1820, he was made professor of

<small>Professor James</small>

natural and experimental philosophy and chemistry. He held this double chair with rare ability for thirty-three years, when he was made professor emeritus. He served as trustee of the college from 1817 to 1820. During the topographical survey of the United States, there was a large demand for scientists, and, at the request of the authorities at Washington, he entered the service as an engineer, with the rank of major, and devoted his summers to the prosecution of Government work. This occupied him for many years.

In 1838, he was appointed a Commissioner for the exploration and delimitation of the northeast boundary between the United States and New Brunswick. In 1829, Columbia conferred upon him the degree of LL.D. For an ordinary man these labors would have been ample, but to the Professor they were stimulants to further endeavor. He seemed to begrudge all time that was not applied to intellectual work. He conducted chemical and physical experiments, translated works from the French, edited English text-books on science, compiled reports, composed biographies, text-books, and compendia; contributed to the press of the period, and frequently acted as editor. In the list of his literary labors appear two volumes of his translations, four of his editing, and fourteen of his own authorship, not to mention reports, commentaries, and fugitive articles. His was the first text book on natural philosophy or physics ever published in the United States, and also the first hand-book on geology.

He was among the first to perceive the great historical importance of the founders of the Republic, and urged upon the writers of his time the duty of recording the events and the individuals of the latter part of the eighteenth century, and not leaving them for time to cover with myth, exaggeration, and distortion. It was in pursuance of this theory that he wrote the lives of David Rittenhouse, Robert Fulton, Count Rumford, De Witt Clinton, and (with Henry B. Renwick, his oldest son) of John Jay and Alexander Hamilton. Outside of his fame as a pedagogue, a scholar, and scientist, he would have enjoyed celebrity from his contributions to American literature. He loved the great college with which he was connected, and left nothing undone to increase its influence and power. He entered there his three sons, all of whom were to make admirable records for themselves in after life; assisted poor students; secured donations from private citizens; endeavored to create closer ties between the institution and scientific branches of the national government, and advocated an enlarged curriculum in the sciences and modern languages. Looked at after the lapse of more than a half-century, he stands in the front rank of the wisest and most distinguished men of his age. He married Margaret Ann Brevoort, by whom he had three sons and one daughter.

Robert Jeffrey, brother of the Professor, was graduated from Columbia (1809), and took up a mercantile career. He prospered and increased his prosperity by marrying Mary Hobart Rhinelander, a belle and heiress. He was a leading participant in the social world and prominent in philanthropic activities. He had five children, three sons and two daughters.

Robert J

The three sisters of Professor James were society leaders, who married advantageously, as follows: Jane, Admiral Charles Wilkes; Isabella, Charles Smedburg; and Agnes, the Rev. James Henry.

In the fourth generation four sons kept up the high records of their ancestry. Henry Brevoort [1817], son of Professor James, was graduated from Columbia in 1833, and took up the profession of civil engineering. He became an assistant engineer in the United States service, where he continued six years, and was then promoted to be first assistant astronomer of the United States Boundary Commission in 1839–1842. In 1848, he was made Examiner in the Patent Office, with special reference to mechanical, chemical, and physical inventions. The life was too sedentary, and in 1853 he resigned to become Inspector of Steamboat Engines for the District of New York. He held this office some years, relinquishing it to become a consuiting mechanical engineer, in which capacity he achieved great fame. In his spare hours he wrote extensively, more particularly upon scientific topics, and in his early manhood he was joint

Henry Brevoort, Engineer

Grace Church, Broadway, N. Y.

author with his father, as before mentioned. He married Margaret Janney, daughter of Jonathan Janney, by whom he had one daughter and one son.

James, the architect [1818], second son of Professor James, was graduated from Columbia (1836). This was a famous class in college history, having among its number John Graham, the great lawyer, the Rev. John H. Hobart, Hon. John Jay II., the Rev. Henry McVicar, the Rev. D. M. Quackenbush, and the Rev. Charles Seymour. *James, the Architect* He inherited a love of architecture, of calculation, drawing, and engineering from his father. His career began as a surveyor and civil engineer on the Erie Railway. He went thence to the Croton Aqueduct, where he served as superintendent of construction of the distributing reservoir on Fifth Avenue and Forty-second Street, which was lately demolished to make room for the New York Public Library. His next work was the making of the model for a fountain in Union Square. Shortly after this came his *entrée* in the world of architecture.

The vestry of Grace Church had purchased the land on Broadway, opposite Eleventh Street, and had called for plans from the architects of the time for a church, to be erected upon the site. James submitted designs which, when exhibited, received the highest praise from the press and the public, and were finally accepted by the vestry. The building, which is one of the finest Gothic structures in the country, was completed in 1845. This is one of the few famous churches in which all the work is to be credited to one man. His were the original and final plans, the working drawings, nearly all of the delicate tracery and ornamentation of the exterior, and the furniture and ornamentation of the interior. It is one of the best specimens of the French fourteenth-century school of Gothic art upon the Western Continent. When it was finished it made its designer famous on both sides of the ocean. From this time James was a recognized authority upon church architecture in America, and was called upon to prepare plans for buildings, public and private. He was the architect of Calvary Church, on Fourth Avenue, New York, the Church of the Puritans, formerly on Union Square, New York, and of the Smithsonian Institution and the Corcoran Art Gallery at the national capital. The Smithsonian is a noble pile of brownstone in modified Elizabethan style, which suggests the ancient halls of Oxford University.

In 1853, he was commissioned by the Archbishop of New York to draw plans for St. Patrick's Cathedral, on Fifth Avenue, between Fiftieth and Fifty-first streets. The commission was the most important one in church construction which has ever been given in the history of the metropolis. James perceived the responsibility of the opportunity, and devoted himself to his task so tirelessly that he nearly broke down from overwork. The plans were finished, submitted, and accepted. When published, they elicited the highest praise from critics the world over. In 1858, the corner-stone was laid, and in 1879 the building was dedicated by Cardinal McCloskey. The structure is built of white marble, with a basement course of Quincy granite. It has magnificent twin towers on the west façade, and a main door which is of remarkable beauty. The style is the decorated or geometric of the thirteenth century, of which the cathedral at Rheims is the best foreign example. In 1887, work was begun upon the spires which terminate the two towers, and these were finished a few years ago. To-day, St. Patrick's is undoubtedly the handsomest and most impressive Gothic church in the New World.

Other buildings which illustrate the broad taste and versatility of James are St. Bartholomew's Church, Vassar College, the Church of the Covenant, in New York; St. Ann's in Brooklyn; the Young Men's Christian Association building, on Fourth Avenue and Twenty-third Street, New York; and a hundred other buildings of lesser importance. He may certainly be styled the first of the great American architects. He married Anna L. Aspinwall, daughter of William H. Aspinwall, the merchant, for whom is named the City of Aspinwall upon the Isthmus of Panama. There was no issue to the marriage.

Edward Sabine [1823], third son of Professor James, was

St. Patrick's Cathedral, Fifth Avenue

graduated from Columbia (1839), which also conferred upon him the degree of A.M. Even before he went to college he displayed a rare talent for machinery, so that upon graduation he but followed his bent in becoming the superintendent of iron works in Wilkesbarre, Pa. In a few years he was recognized as an expert in civil, mechanical, and steam engineering and the many industries upon which these professions are based. He invented a number of railway appliances of value, including a chair for holding together ends of rails, an improved frog, and an improved switch. In the world of steam navigation the credit may be ascribed to him for an efficient cut-off for steam engines, an improvement in the connection between the moving parts and the valve system, and an ingenious method of side propulsion for steamers and bulky craft.

Edward Sabine, Engineer

He shares with Cyrus Hall McCormick the honor of having created the self-binding reaper. Between 1870 and 1890, he gave careful study to the artificial hatching of poultry, and was the first to determine the condition under which this process could be applied. These studies were expressed in concrete form by many incubators, and afterwards by artificial brooders. Before he undertook the work artificial hatching had never been a profitable enterprise, but long before he finished his system it had become a source of handsome revenue to tens of thousands of farmers in this country and Canada. His careful analysis of the matter was an invaluable addition to practical poultry-raising. His researches enabled every farmer to form a clear conception of the matter and to incubate and brood with home-made mechanisms. The system was applied to the eggs of chickens, ducks, geese, turkeys, pigeons, and other birds employed for food purposes.

His greatest scientific feat was accomplished in 1862. The giant steamer *Great Eastern* had injured its bilge, a portion eighty-two feet long and ten feet wide having been broken. There was no dry dock large enough for the leviathan, and the size of the vessel made it impossible to beach or careen it sufficiently to reach the injured surface. With his brother, Henry Brevoort, he improvised an appliance upon the coffer-dam principle, which enabled the workmen to remove the damaged plates and backing and replace them with new materials. The task had been pronounced impossible by many of the chief authorities of the time, so that the exploit became a nine days' wonder to navigators, ship-builders, and naval men.

He wrote a number of monographs upon various technical subjects connected with the industries in which he was interested. His erudition and technical skill so impressed the community that from the early fifties on he was in constant employment as an expert in patent suits and scientific inquiries by public and private bodies. He married Elizabeth Alice Brevoort, daughter of Henry Brevoort, by whom he had two sons and one daughter.

Laura, only daughter of Professor James, married John A. Munroe.

Of the children of Robert Jeffrey, William Rhinelander [1816], the oldest son, was graduated from Columbia (1833), and took up a mercantile career. He was prominent in social, religious, and literary circles. He married Eliza S. Crosby, daughter of William Bedlow Crosby, by whom he had two sons and three daughters. Robert Jeffrey [1822] died unmarried at the age of thirty-two.

William R.

Frederick William, the third son, was twice married — first to Julia Kortright, by whom he had two sons, and, second, to Annie Cooke

Jane Jeffrey [1819], the oldest daughter of Robert Jeffrey, married S. Stanhope Callender, by whom she had one child, Mary Renwick Callender. Mary Rhinelander [1825] married Benjamin L. Swan II.

The head of the fifth generation is James Armstrong, oldest son of Henry Brevoort. He was graduated from Columbia (1876), where he also obtained the degrees of A.M., and of LL.B., from the Columbia Law School in 1879. He is an active member of the New York bar. He married Viola Blodget, daughter of Charles F. Blodget, by whom he had one son, Henry.

James Armstrong, Lawyer

William Rhinelander Renwick
From a miniature owned by Edmund Ely Henry, Esq

Mrs. William Rhinelander Renwick
(Eliza S. Cox by)
From a miniature owned by Edmund Ely Henry, Esq

Meta Brevoort, only daughter of Henry Brevoort, married Robert Sedgwick, by whom she had two sons, Robert J. and Henry Renwick.

Of the children of Edward Sabine, Edward Brevoort [1863], the oldest son, is an accomplished mechanical engineer. He married Emily Dilworth Hicks. *Edward B., Engineer*

William Whetten [1864], second son of Edward Sabine, is an architect and a member of the firm of Renwick, Aspinwall & Owen, which was established by his uncle James III., architect of St. Patrick's Cathedral. Elizabeth, only daughter and youngest child of Edward Sabine, married Watson Condit Wittingham. *William W., Architect*

Of the children of William Rhinelander, Philip Brevoort, the oldest son, married Ellen J. Wise, by whom he had one child, Eliza Crosby. She married A. Leland Brown, by whom she had issue.

William Crosby, second son of William Rhinelander, was twice married: first, to Harriet McDonell, by whom he had three children; and, second, to Gertrude Sears. Of the three daughters of William Rhinelander, Emily Ashton married Edmund Abdy Hurry (November 17, 1868); Mary Crosby married, first, Henry Turnstall Strong, and, second, Dr. Frederick Tilden Brown. Helen Schuyler married Anselm Schaff. *William C.*

The children of Frederick William are Frederick William II. and S. Stanhope. The latter married Evelyn Smith, by whom he had Harold Stanhope and Claire Rhinelander.

The name of Renwick has for a century been associated with creative intellectuality. It has been borne by philanthropists, merchants, professors, inventors, architects, engineers, and lawyers. It is identified with valuable inventions, standard literary works, magnificent buildings, and the proceedings of learned societies. If the value of achievement is to be measured by the creation of wealth through inventive energy and constructive skill, the family will rank high in the annals of the State. That man is said to be a public benefactor who makes two blades of grass grow where but one grew before. From this point of view the inventor is the most valuable member of society. The flower of his brain creates wealth, sometimes for himself, but always for the community at large; and it may be that he who makes wealth for others is higher in the scale of public utility than he who accumulates it for himself. A nation of inventors towers over a nation of plutocrats. The secret of American success has been its creative genius. This in turn has produced wealth and power, and from the smallest beginnings has raised the nation to a commanding place in the society of nations. In this class of forces are to be placed the mental activity and prowess of the Renwick race.

Jean Jeffrey
From a picture in the possession of Edmund Abdy Hurry, Esq.

Roosevelt

Theodore Roosevelt
From a photograph by Rockwood

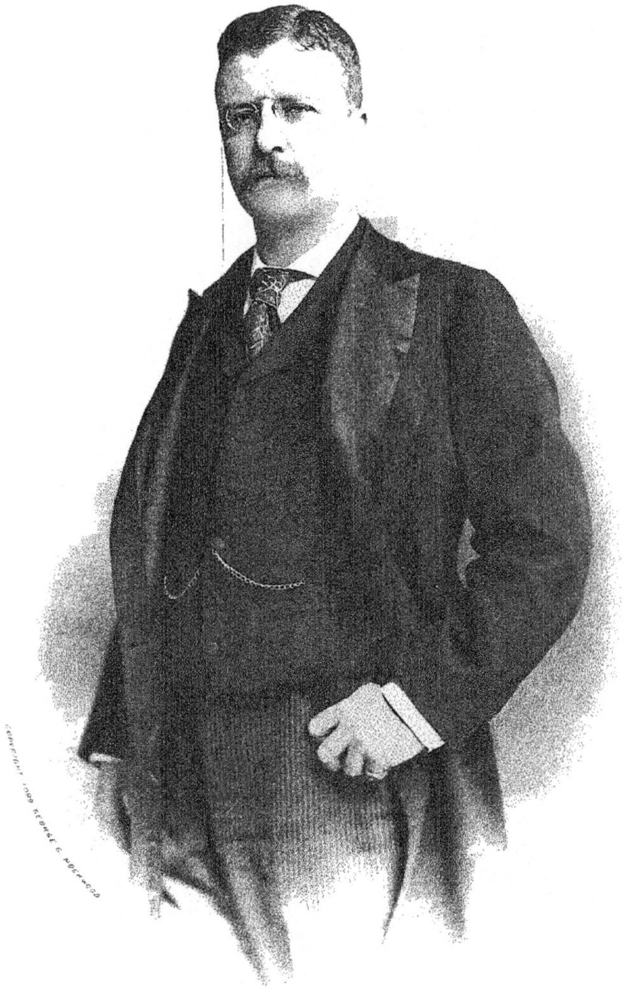

XXIX

ROOSEVELT

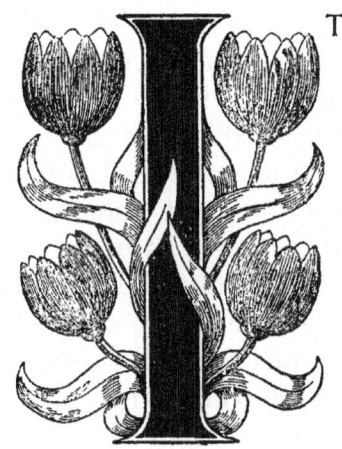

It is hard to lay down any definite standard as to what constitutes a famous family. Sometimes the laurels are won by the achievements of a single individual, which is illustrated in the case of the Washingtons and Franklins. At the very opposite extreme are those families in which, generation after generation, men of eminent ability appear, and play a large part in the national life. This is exemplified by the Adams family of Massachusetts, the Lee family of Virginia, and the Roosevelt family of New York.

In 1649, Claas Martenszen Van Roosevelt came to this country. He was a shrewd, strong, and sterling Hollander, who transferred to the New World the habits of thrift which had been developed by his race in the Old. He was successful in his undertakings, especially in that of matrimony, his wife being Jannetje Thomas, a young belle of the New Netherlands, whose personal charms were rivalled by her skill in spinning, weaving, cooking, and housekeeping. The union was a happy one, and resulted in many children, all of whom seemed to inherit their parents' virtues—moral, mental, and physical. Small families, indeed, have been the rare exception with the Roosevelts.

Claas

Owing to this fact it has extended in every direction, and by marriage has become connected with nearly every other old family both in New York City and in New York State.

The most prominent member of the second generation was Nicholas of Esopus, who married Hillotje Jans, sister of Anneke Jans of Trinity Church fame. In this generation the family began to add intellectual to agricultural talents.

Nicholas

Nicholas was a student, and by all odds the most learned and most popular man in his district. He is referred to by the old records as a citizen of great influence and authority, and one who frequently served as an arbitrator between his stiff-necked and litigious neighbors. He was one of the first settlers to perceive the business aspect of the Indian question, and during his life was on the most friendly terms with the red men. He invited them regularly to his house, and invariably made them presents when they called. For many years to his neighbors this seemed extravagance, but their eyes were opened when they learned that in Indian etiquette whoso receives a present from a friend must give back one of greater value. The gala-colored ancient weapons which Nicholas presented to the warriors came back to him in furs, which brought ten times the value of his gifts in the markets of New Amsterdam. That he was very prosperous is shown by formal charges that were brought by gossipers against his wife Hillotje and her sister Anneke for wearing and showing luxurious petticoats. Nicholas took the part of the women, and after the proceedings were dismissed he authorized his dress-loving wife to purchase another large roll of beautiful cloth to increase still further her stock of brilliant skirts.

Of the third generation, Johannes appears to have been the ablest. Early in the eighteenth century he married Hyltje Syverts, a belle and heiress. He was successful in farming and business ventures, and took what seemed to his friends a strange and extravagant delight in works of art. He is said to have been one of the first to import paintings, fine furniture, and artistic metal ware from the Netherlands. He did it on so generous a scale that his home was viewed as a wonderland by his less

Johannes

enterprising fellow-citizens. In this generation the family became allied with the Schuylers through the marriage of Sarah Van Roosevelt, a niece of Johannes, to Philip Schuyler. In the fourth generation were several sons, of whom Jacobus [1724] was the most notable. He married Annetje Bogaert, and had a large family. In Jacobus, the Dutch characteristics had changed so far that he may be regarded as an American in the modern sense of the word. He began to drop the Van from his name, and in other ways showed his Anglicization. He was a stout believer in freedom and home rule, and was looked upon as a Dutch malcontent by many of the British colonial officers. He was diplomatic and never permitted himself to do anything which could be construed into a violation of law. He attended to his commercial interests with great care and largely increased the fortune which he had inherited. Jacobus

The fifth generation seems to have been the crucial point in the family history. Up to that time the various generations had confined themselves to agriculture, trading, and the management of real estate. The race was now represented in its own names by at least fifty families, which, as a whole, were more than prosperous, capable, and prominent. The simple farmers of the first and second generations had become educated and cultured men so far as the opportunities of the time permitted. The Revolution seemed to stir up their blood and to bring into being the higher qualities which are represented by patriotism, executive power, and statesmanship. In this period the first to be noticed is Jacobus II., afterwards known as James I., his brother Nicholas, who invented the steamboat at about the same time as Fulton; Captain John J., a brilliant and wildly reckless soldier; and Isaac, who afterwards became State Senator. There were others, who were brave soldiers and faithful representatives of the people, but the four enumerated stand head and shoulders above the rest. Jacobus or James I. is often mistaken for his son James I. (II.), who was a member of Congress, a judge, and one of the great jurists of New York State. The elder

James
Nicholas
John J.
Isaac

was a good soldier, a capable commissary, and an admirable organizer.

Nicholas was America's first great inventor. He had extraordinary versatility and an almost tireless energy. He was a skilful mining engineer and metallurgist, as well as machinist, and was the first to work copper on a large scale in the United States. As contractor and ship-builder, he was engaged by Congress to superintend the building of a new navy in the eighteenth century. He was a civil engineer, and carried through contracts for supplying the city of Philadelphia with water. In this busy period he found time to prosecute studies in the then unknown field of steam engineering, and reached the same conclusions that Fulton did a few years afterwards. He submitted his researches in 1797 to Chancellor Livingston and to Colonel Stevens, who formed a partnership with him to build a boat on joint account. This was done, and in October, 1798, the new venture was tried. The engines worked perfectly, but the propelling gear, which had been designed by Livingston, proved a failure. Roosevelt was not, however, discouraged, but kept on until he had devised an efficient vertical paddle-wheel in place of the cumbrous contrivance of the Chancellor. The new design was tried upon the Ohio River, where it worked satisfactorily. In 1811, he built the first steamer to ply upon the Mississippi, so that he may be justly called the father of Mississippi navigation. Nicholas married Miss Lydia M. Latrobe. Of his descendants, Samuel Montgomery is a member of the Chamber of Commerce, and the late Nicholas III. was a lieutenant in the United States Navy.

<small>Nicholas the Inventor</small>

Jacobus or James I. married Mary Van Schaick. Among their children, two were highly distinguished in the beginning of the nineteenth century, Cornelius Van Schaick and James II. The former, who married Margaret Barnhill of Pennsylvania, was a merchant, banker, and capitalist. He was one of the five richest men in New York, and took a deep interest in the welfare of the city. He founded the famous Chemical Bank, the only bank in the country which has always paid its obligations in gold. He had five sons, all of whom were important figures in the mid-

<small>Cornelius Van Schaick</small>

Isaac Roosevelt
From an India ink drawing in the Emmett Collection
Lenox Library

dle part of the last century. These were Silas W., lawyer, wit, and School Commissioner; James Alfred, banker and capitalist; Cornelius Van Schaick II., merchant; Robert B., lawyer, author, editor, Commissioner of the first Brooklyn Bridge, Congressman, and United States Minister; and Theodore, merchant, War Commissioner, and philanthropist. The history of these five sons covers the most important years from 1850 to the present time. Each contributed in his own way to the metropolis, and stamped his name upon its history. Silas W. was a New York School Commissioner in deed as well as in name. He took an interest in educational work before he received his appointment, and may be classed as a member of the school of thought started by Horace Mann. When he accepted office he brought all his energy to bear upon the problem of books and methods, and infused a new spirit into the proceedings of the Board. The present admirable condition of the public schools and the high standards which mark all tuition in the city are under obligations to his faithful and efficient services. James Alfred, the banker, had a natural genius for finance. He was admitted to his father's firm when only twenty years of age, and while still in the prime of life had become an officer or director in a score of great financial institutions. He was Park Commissioner during the administration of Mayor Strong.

Robert B., born in 1829, is still a hale and hearty member of the community. He received a fine liberal education, studied law, and practised in New York for twenty years. He was successful in that profession and was one of the most popular members of the bar thirty years ago. He was versatile and made his mark in many fields. A fluent writer, he served as an editor of the New York *Citizen* and wrote a number of books upon fish, birds, and other similar topics. He took an active part in politics, served in Congress, and was one of the leaders of the National Democracy. The life-work by which he will be longest known was that devoted to the game interests of the State and nation. He took up the task, an almost novel field, and struggled in the beginning against many odds. By degrees he created and organized sentiment on behalf of the game birds and the fisheries of the State and secured much of the legislation which has preserved the fin and feather interests of the community. He served acceptably as Commissioner of Fisheries of New York, did much toward the restocking of the rivers, lakes, and streams of the commonwealth, the establishment and development of fish culture, the interchange of valuable fish fry, and the protection of waters from the refuse of cities and factories. To the angler and the sportsman he will be always regarded as the Izaak Walton of America. He was one of the famous Committee of Seventy which started the movement that resulted in the downfall of Tammany and Tweed, and has always been identified with the best interests of the municipality.

Theodore, the fifth of the brothers, was a brilliant Unionist during the war and one of the Allotment Commissioners. Upon the restoration of peace, he took up practical philanthropy and devoted himself to the cause of the poor and ignorant. He was one of the founders of the Newsboys' Home and the other homes which grew out of the first one, the Young Men's Christian Association, the Orthopædic Hospital, and the Children's Aid Society. He married Miss Martha Bulloch of Georgia. Their son was Theodore II.

Theodore [1858] was educated at Harvard (1880), where he displayed marked literary, scholarly, and athletic talents. The following year he entered political life and was elected to the Assembly from the 21st District, New York City. He served until 1884. In 1886, he was nominated for Mayor, but was defeated by Abram S. Hewitt. Three years afterwards he was appointed Civil Service Commissioner by President Harrison and served until May, 1895. He was chosen Assistant Secretary of the Navy in President McKinley's Cabinet in 1897. At the breaking out of the war with Spain, he resigned his position and entered the United States Army. He raised a regiment of Rough Riders, but instead of taking the command, as is the custom in such cases, he requested the President to appoint his personal friend, Dr. Leonard Wood, Colonel, and himself Lieutenant-Colonel.

The Administration Building
Roosevelt Hospital

Roosevelt

He and his men were in the army of invasion which landed at the eastern end of Cuba and took part in the first engagement between the American and Spanish forces. Both he and his Rough Riders made a famous record for gallantry during the brief campaign. The same year he was elected Governor of the State of New York. In 1900, he was chosen Vice-President of the United States and took office on March 4, 1901. On the death of Mr. McKinley, September, 1901, he became President.

He is a man of indefatigable industry, and in the last twenty years has contributed largely to the press and added twelve valuable works to American literature. He married Alice Lee of Boston, and, after her death, Edith Carow of New York. By the first he had one child, and by the second, five.

James Henry of the sixth generation has left a monument in the Roosevelt Hospital. It was the realization of his life ambition. Born in 1800, he was graduated from Columbia College, and took up the practice of law with the ambition of founding the charity described. To this he subordinated all other interests. He never married, and allowed nothing to swerve him from his path. He died in 1863, leaving a million dollars for a foundation. This, through the wise management of his trustees, was so administered that, in 1888, the hospital and its endowment represented over two millions of dollars. His epitaph is written upon the tablet which records the gift: "To the memory of James Henry Roosevelt, a true son of New York, the generous founder of this hospital, a man upright in his aims, simple in his life, sublime in his benefactions."

James Henry

Considerable impression upon New York City has been made by the so-called Pelham branch, established by Elbert [1767] of the sixth generation. He had six sons and two daughters. Of the former, Clinton, the inventor and scientist, was the chief of his generation. Peter T. and Albert J. were men who led long and eventful lives; the former died at the age of ninety-six, and the latter at eighty-eight. Washington [1802] was a scholarly Presbyterian divine, who was graduated from Middlebury, Conn., in 1829. He married Jane Maria Young, by

Elbert

whom he had four sons and one daughter. The oldest of the sons was Charles Henry [1832], who married Annie J. Jackson, by whom he had two sons, Henry Everitt and Albert Curtenius. Charles Henry has long been one of the leading citizens of Westchester County.

Here and there, in the family history, have been indications of mechanical and inventive talent. In addition to Nicholas, who was the greatest in this respect in his generation, and Clinton, who was President of the Society of Inventors, was Hilborne Lewis, who was born in 1849, and died when but thirty-seven years of age. He displayed mechanical genius in his boyhood, and entered an organ-factory in early youth. He mastered all that could be learned in this country, and then went to Europe to gain an insight into the artistic, scientific, and historic features of the craft. He was one of the first to take up electric apparatus for organ-manufacture. In a few years he developed it to an extent never before known. On his return to America he established organ-factories in New York, Philadelphia, and Baltimore, and within five years had become one of the authorities on the subject. Many of his constructions enjoy a world-wide fame among musicians. His chief ones are those in the Protestant Episcopal Cathedral at Garden City, L. I., and in Grace Church, New York, each of which contains twenty miles of electric wires. He built the famous organ for the Philadelphia Centennial Exposition. He received letters patent for improvements in organ-building, electrical apparatus, and telephony. His chief electrical invention was a telephone switch, which was adopted by telephone companies the world over.

Rutgers

Colonel Henry Rutgers.
From a steel engraving

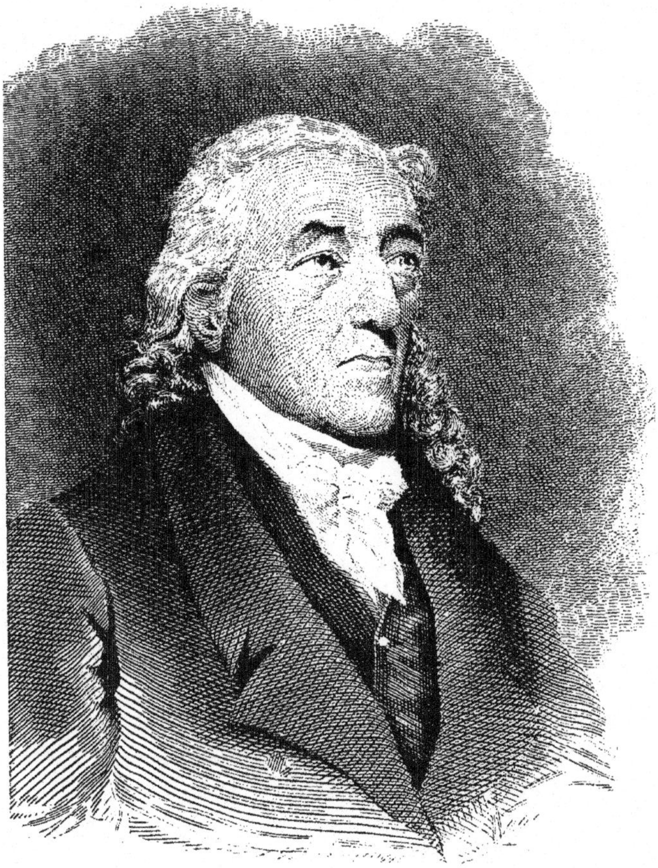

XXX

RUTGERS

To the student of New York history, each family name is identified with a set of virtues or a group of achievements. That of Rutgers suggests a warm-hearted public spirit and a deep love for humanity. It is one of the first of Knickerbocker names. On October 1, 1636, Rutgers Jacobsen Van Schoenderwoerdt set sail at Texel, Holland, on board the good craft *Rensselaerswyck,* commanded by Captain Jan Tiebkins, for the New Netherlands. The quaint name is eloquent. Schoenderwoerdt is a pretty village not far from Leerdam, and Jacobsen, or Jacobse, means that Rutgers was the son of Jacob. The family belonged to the great middle class of Holland, which had fought both man and the sea for generations and had developed a stalwart manhood, which is even to-day the admiration of the civilized world. The virtues, private and public, are developed not in ease and idleness, but under the pressure of danger and of death. Great men never come from Sybaris.

<small>Rutgers Jacobsen, Founder</small>

The voyage was uneventful, and early in the following year Rutgers landed at Fort Orange, where he immediately set to work to change the wilderness into a fertile domain. He labored long and late, and enjoyed a proportionate reward. His fields brought rich harvests and his trading ventures proved profitable. Not until he was a wealthy man did he look about him for a helpmeet. This occurred in 1646, when he married Tryntje Jansse Van Breesteede. In 1649, he formed a partnership with Goosen Gerritse Van Schaick and founded a brewing business. According to the old records, he turned out an admirable quality of beer, so excellent that it was used by the churches of the time at the feasts or repasts which were given in connection with funerals and weddings.

Even in this prosaic business he displayed a kindly heart. Whenever a poor family was unable to purchase the beer without which the funeral ceremonies were incomplete, he would send a cask of his best brew to the house of mourning. By 1660, he had become very rich. About this time he was appointed a magistrate and conducted the office up to his death with dignity and ability. His last public office was the laying of the corner-stone of the new church in Albany in 1656.

Two of his children were prominent in Knickerbocker life. His daughter Margaret married Jan Jansen Bleecker (1667), and became the maternal ancestor of the Bleecker family. Her husband Jan was Mayor of Albany in 1700. Harman, the only son, took after his father. He was an active man of affairs, and conducted successfully the brewery, the real-estate business, an Indian trade in furs and skins, and the farms which he inherited. When clouds appeared upon the political horizon, and an Indian uprising was threatened, he promptly volunteered and became a private in the Burgher Corps, bringing with him, it is said, a number of the muscular workmen in his brewery. He continued his father's practice of supplying beer to the church funerals, and, like his father, he contributed a friendly cask to poor neighbors who were in mourning. So far as can be inferred from the records of the time, the custom known as "church beer" seems to have been analogous to the modern wake, and both are undoubtedly survivals of a custom very prevalent among the early Christians. In 1693, the Indians became so threatening near Albany, that Harman removed with his family to New York. He

Harman the Trader

married Catarina de Hooges, daughter of Anthony de Hooges, Provincial Secretary of Rensselaerswyck, by whom he had issue.

In the third generation, Elsie, daughter of Harman, married David Davidse Schuyler, at one time Mayor of Albany. Anthony, the oldest son, was a wealthy brewer, who took an active part in public affairs. In 1710, 1711, 1712, he was an Assistant Alderman, and from 1727 to 1734 an Alderman. From 1726 to 1737 he was a member of the Colonial Assembly. The last was a representative body, and included such men of prominence as Henry Beekman, Jeremiah Van Rensselaer, Robert Livingston, Jr., Stephen de Lancey, Frederick Philipse, Peter Van Brugh, Benjamin Hicks, Nicholas Schuyler, and Lewis Morris. Anthony's intellectual grasp was well shown by an undertaking which in the light of to-day was an enterprise of the highest merit.

<small>Anthony the Assemblyman</small>

In the neighborhood of what is now Chambers Street and West Broadway there was a swamp, which occasioned much fever and ague. The title lay in the Crown, but under the law of the time it could not be sold in fee simple, but only leased for life or a period of years. Besides injuring public health, it was a blemish to the neighborhood, and interfered with the growth of the young city. Anthony petitioned the local authorities to obtain authority from the Crown to grant him the swamp in fee simple, so that he might drain and reclaim it, and so end the sickness which always prevailed in this neighborhood. In return, he promised to make it into habitable land at his own expense, no matter what that might be. It took no less than three years to secure the authority, and to sign the proper deeds. When this was done, the good burgher put his men to work, and within a year had changed a noisome, festering morass into one of the best meadows on Manhattan. Anthony was twice married: first, to Hendrickje Vandewater, by whom he had issue, and, second, to Mistress Cornelia Benson.

Harman II. went into business with his father upon coming of age, and thereafter purchased a farm lying east of what is now

Chatham Square. Of this farm, Rutgers Street is the relic, and undoubtedly represents the early road or path which led down to Rutgers Wharf. Harman married Catharina Meyer, and had two sons and three daughters.

Harman II. the Land-Owner

In the fourth generation, Anthony II., son of Anthony I., died a young man, leaving one son, Anthony III., and five daughters. This son is of importance, because he transmitted to his daughter Elsie or Alice one third of his great estate. She married Leonard Lispenard, who thereafter purchased from his wife's two sisters the other two thirds, thus bringing together again the old Anthony Rutgers estate, which then became known as the Lispenard estate.

Peter [1701], son of Anthony, was a wealthy brewer and merchant, and was Assistant Alderman from 1730 to 1736. He was Captain of the Independent Company of Cadets, and married Helena Hoogland, by whom he had issue. Of the children of Harman II., Harman III., a son, died before his father. The three daughters made brilliant marriages. Elsie espoused John Marshall, Catharine married Abraham Van Horne, and Eva, John Provoost. Harman III. left three sons and three daughters.

Captain Peter

Hendrick [1712], his brother, was a thrifty merchant and real-estate owner, who married Catharine de Peyster, by whom he had four sons and a daughter. None of the former left issue.

In the fifth generation the family reached its meridian. Anthony III., son of Anthony II., was the head of the family and filled a large place in social circles. He married Gertrude Gouverneur, a famous belle. In 1775, he was a captain of artillery. When he was ordered out by the British Government, he resigned, and moved to Newark, N. J., which he made his permanent home. He had three sons and four daughters, and was the founder of the Rutgers family of New Jersey.

Anthony III., Captain

Anthony the lawyer, son of Peter, was a prominent member of the New York bar in the middle of the eighteenth century. He married Elizabeth Williams.

Anthony the Lawyer

The Old Rutgers Mansion, New York, 1768
From a print in *Valentine's Manual*

Of the three sons of Harman III., the oldest, Robert, was a man of great wealth, who married Elizabeth, daughter of Dr. William Beekman. Harman IV. was a wealthy merchant, who never married. Captain Anthony, the youngest brother, took to the sea in his youth, and rose to be a captain. In 1754, he received his first command, and in 1758 was the captain of a privateer. In 1760, he received letters of marque from the Crown and sailed the good brig *King George*, with which he captured many ships and realized an independent fortune. Five years afterwards or thereabouts he retired and settled upon the land. The same year he was made an Assistant Alderman. *Anthony the Sea Captain*

Shortly afterwards he opened a rope-walk with Jacob Le Roy, and was the father of that business in the colonies. His two sisters, Catharine and Cornelia, successively married his partner, Jacob Le Roy, from whom comes the Le Roy family of New York.

Of the children of Hendrick, three command notice. His daughter Catharine married William Bedloe, grandson of Isaac, of Bedloe's Island.

Lieutenant Harman was a heroic soldier, who enlisted in the Colonial army upon the breaking out of the Revolution, and was one of the first to give up his life for the cause of liberty. He was killed by a cannon-ball at the bombardment of Red Hook, on August 28, 1776, by the British ships in the Long Island campaign. *Lieutenant Harman*

In Colonel Henry [1745], the son of Hendrick, the race produced its finest representative. He was marked by unusual attractiveness—physical, mental, and moral. In his youth he was studious and was graduated in 1776 with very high honor from King's College, now Columbia University. On leaving college, he took up a mercantile life and assisted in the management of his father's estate. The times were exciting, the troubles between the colonies and the mother country coming to a crisis. In the general controversy which prevailed he took strong sides with the Colonials. His fine appearance, culture, and ability soon made him prominent, *Colonel Henry the Statesman* and before the Revolution broke out he was looked upon as a Revolutionary leader. He was lieutenant in 1775 and a captain in 1776, serving in Malcolm's Regiment and taking part at the battle of White Plains, where he was wounded. He fought through the war and was cheered (?) from time to time by escaped or returned soldiers, who informed him that his family homestead had been converted into a British barracks and afterwards a military hospital.

At the close of the war he returned to New York City, where the following year he was elected a member of the Assembly. This honor was frequently repeated, his last term being 1807–1808. In 1802, he was made a regent of the New York State University, and held it for twenty-four years. From 1804 to 1817, he was a trustee of Princeton.

His most important work in political life was in 1800, when he was one of the Republican leaders in the movement to defeat the Federalist party. The campaign was all-important as regarded the future policy of the United States, and in it the two New York champions of popular rights were Colonel Henry and General George Clinton. Their efforts were successful, and their party carried the day and elected Thomas Jefferson President of the Republic.

In 1812, Colonel Henry was chairman of the mass-meeting held in New York, which was called to take defensive measures against a threatened attack on land and sea by the British, subscribing liberally to the campaign fund and overseeing the construction of the fortifications that were built to defend both New York and Brooklyn against a naval expedition from the harbor and a land attack from Long Island. In 1829, he was made President of the New York Public School Society, succeeding Governor De Witt Clinton in that office. He gave the money which assisted in founding Rutgers Female College, New York, and which took Queens College, New Jersey, out of bankruptcy. It was in honor of his munificence that the name of that institution was changed in 1825 to Rutgers College, by which it has been known ever since.

His benefactions to churches were large and numerous. He showed no sectarianism and treated all with equal kindness. Among the beneficiaries were the Dutch Reformed, the Scotch, the Baptist, and the Presbyterian. He made many gifts to schools, charitable societies, and to the deserving poor. The rule of his life was to spend one quarter of his income in charity. This, however, did not include what he called his "special gifts." These were numberless and extraordinary. Thus, for example, for many years he had all the boys of the ward in which he lived call upon him early New Year's morning. When the crowd was small, they were invited into the house; when large, they would stand in the yard and on the sidewalk. Punctually at the hour, the Colonel appeared in full dress, delivered a little speech appropriate to the occasion, and then presented each urchin with a large cake and an entertaining volume. The cakes were always made to order, and were "nutritious and wholesome, but not too rich nor cloying," and the books were "edifying as well as amusing." Even the Colonel's speeches were not impromptu affairs, but were the results of weeks of careful thought and preparation. A few have been, it is believed, preserved, and are models of kindliness of heart, manliness, and patriotism.

On any occasion when the city's finances were at an ebb and the schools were about to suffer, the Colonel paid repair bills, teachers' wages, and on several occasions built schoolhouses, out of his own pocket. During the last twenty years of his life he was known as the "well-beloved citizen."

His home, a large and superbly furnished mansion, stood at Rutgers' Place—what is now the corner of Jefferson and Cherry streets—and for many years was a capital of the world of fashion. Here Lafayette was entertained, "*en prince*," to use the great Frenchman's own words, and here was given the most notable reception of the time to General Washington and Colonel Willet, after the latter's return from his mission to the Creek sachems and sagamores. In the Rutgers drawing-rooms met all the Republican leaders of the period, and, despite the bitter asperities of politics, most of the great Federalists.

The names of the streets bear testimony to the man. Henry and Rutgers are his name; while Clinton and Jefferson represent General George Clinton, with whom he led the campaign which gave New York's electoral vote to their friend, Thomas Jefferson, and made him President of the nation.

Colonel Henry never married. His estate was divided by his will among his many relatives, the largest individual share going <small>William B. Crosby</small> to his great-nephew, William B. Crosby, grandson of his sister, Catharine Bedloe, who, left an orphan in his childhood, had been adopted by his generous kinsman.

In the sixth generation, the main line was represented by Gerard, who married Margaret Bayard; Robert II., and Elsie.

Elsie Rutgers married John Marshall and from this marriage came the Rutgers-Marshall family of the metropolis.

Of their issue the Rev. John Rutgers was the foremost. Graduated from King's College in 1770, he took orders, and was <small>Rev. John Rutgers-Marshall</small> ordained a minister of the Church of England at Lambeth Palace, London. He began his clerical career as a missionary at Woodbury, Connecticut, where he remained until his death, in 1789.

He took an active part in bringing about the first convention of the Protestant Episcopal Church in the United States, which was held at Woodbury in 1783. The old "glebe house," one of the earliest landmarks of that denomination in this country, is now used by the diocese as a home for aged and infirm clergymen.

The head of the present generation is Henry Rutgers-Marshall, the psychologist and architect.

No family has ever given more of itself and its belongings to the Commonwealth. From Rutgers Jacobse to the ninth generation, the members have been marked by commercial and intellectual ability and have reaped the reward which comes from these traits, when put to practical use. Instead of applying this wealth solely to the upbuilding of a great family, they have devoted it to relatives and friends, neighbors, and strangers. Colonel Henry, the greatest son, must have given away two

The Old " Glebe House," Woodbury, Conn.
(At the time of the Revolution it was the home of Rev. John Rutgers Marshall)

The Rutgers House, Rutgers Place
Between Jefferson and Clinton Streets.   From a print in *Valentine's Manual*, 1858

thirds of his vast fortune during his life; and at the close, distributed the remaining third with the same kindly thoughtfulness. The other members have been marked by this altruistic character. They have left their imprint upon the city in the names of a dozen streets, and upon the country in Rutgers College, New Jersey; but more lasting than these are the noble actions which for two hundred years have made them notable among their fellow-men.

Schermerhorn

XXXI

SCHERMERHORN

A CHARACTERISTIC Knickerbocker family is that of Schermerhorn. It embodies the so-called Dutch virtues—thrift, courtesy, probity, patience, and zealous patriotism. It was among the very first settlers, and antedates most of its Knickerbocker compeers. It has cared little for military glory or political power, but has devoted its energies to religious, philanthropic, and educational institutions. Its history is to be found in church archives, college records, and the annual reports of benevolent organizations. Such qualities exert a profound influence upon a community and give a prestige to a family name like that which clings to such characters as Wesley, Fox, and Asbury.

The founder of the Schermerhorn family in the New Netherlands was Jacob Jansen, who was born in Holland in 1622. He crossed the ocean with some relatives in 1636, and shortly afterwards settled in Beverwyck, now Albany. *Jacob Jansen the Founder* Here he married and had many children. His farm was not far from the river, and was so fertile as to make him independent. In spite of his prosperity and of the large and happy family which he saw growing up around him, he was not altogether contented with his residence. Many features of the feudal system which were applied by the West India Company and the Patroons contravened his ideas of liberty and government, so that when Arendt Van Curler proposed to his friends to migrate westward and there form a new settlement, based upon freedom and equal rights, Jacob was one of the first farmers who volunteered to take part in the expedition.

They made the journey in 1662, and established the village which is now the city of Schenectady. Here Jacob cleared the virgin soil and made a farm whose fertility was greater than that of the one he had relinquished. He resided on this estate until his death in 1688, seeing the country develop, the population increase, his wealth accumulate, and his family of nine children grow up, marry, and become esteemed citizens of the community. His wife was Jannetje Segers, daughter of Cornelius Segers Van Voohoudt. His sons were Beyer [1652], Symon [1658], Jacob, and Lucas, and his daughters, Helena, Nachtilt, Cornelia, Jannetje, and Neeltje.

Among these the chief in the second generation was Symon. He began life as a farmer and Indian trader, and was one of the **Symon the Fearless** survivors of the massacre at Schenectady in 1690 by the French and Indians. In this tragic affair he displayed rare gallantry, saving several people at the risk of his life. Even as it was, his horse was wounded under him and he himself shot through the thigh. The following year he removed to New York and became interested in the navigation of the Hudson. He seems to have been commander and part owner and, finally, owner of a large trading-sloop, which, owing to his great strength and business sense, soon became very profitable. This change in his calling affected not only his own career, but also the careers of his descendants. For the next five generations, nearly all of these showed a love for the sea and for commercial and maritime enterprises. He married Willempie Viele, by whom he had four children. The marriages of his brothers and sisters disclosed the names of several families that were to become eminent in after years. Among them were Bogart, Van Buren, Beekman, Ten Eyck, and Dame.

Schermerhorn

Arnout [1686], the second son of Symon, was the master mind of his generation. In his early boyhood he escaped the massacre at Schenectady, where his elder brother, John, was killed. After receiving such education as the period afforded, he took eagerly to his father's calling and soon became a skilful navigator and shipping-master. He led a very long and busy life. He invested his earnings with sound judgment in New York real estate, many of his transactions being on record in the New York Register's office. One of these was the purchase of three parcels of land, which cover nearly all the present site of Fulton Market. The bay at that time ran up nearly to Pearl Street, then known as Queen Street. Here Arnout built a handsome wharf, after the old Holland pattern, which lasted into the nineteenth century. This is the Schermerhorn wharf, so often referred to in the old books and records. It proved a wise investment, as it was soon called into constant use by the increasing commerce of the port, so that the wharf dues and demurrages amounted to a handsome sum every year. He displayed rare enterprise and energy. Before January, 1733, he had established a line of sailing vessels between New York and Charleston, S. C., and, in connection with this, a warehouse and ship-chandlery in the latter city. At the height of his career he was conducting this line, managing large mercantile establishments at each end, and also caring for many interests in real estate and water rights. He married Marytje Beekman, by whom he had six children, Catharina [1711], Willementje [1713], Johannes [1715], Aeltje [1717], Jannetje [1719], and Symon [1721].

Arnout the Ship-Owner

Of the two sons, Johannes proved another edition of his brilliant father. He was both a "merchant and mariner," and enlarged the lucrative business which his father had established. During the long war between England and France he secured letters of marque and reprisal from the British Government, and under this authority fitted out a number of privateers, which played havoc with French commerce and put corresponding profits in the pockets of the shrewd builder. He married Sarah Cannon. daughter of John Cannon,

Johannes, "Merchant and Mariner"

who was a descendant of a Huguenot refugee from Rochelle, France. The union was very happy and was blessed with twelve children — Arnout [1742], Mary [1743], John [1746], Symon [1748], Peter [1749], Sarah [1751], Catharine [1753], Abraham [1755], Cornelius [1756], Catharine [1759], Esther [1761], and Hester [1762].

Of the six sons of this generation, Peter, commonly known as Peter the Elder, was the greatest. He started life with a moderate fortune, on account of the great wealth of his father, and increased it largely and rapidly. At the beginning of his business-life, he took up his father's calling and conducted it until the outbreak of the Revolution in 1776. Here his forethought was displayed to rare advantage. After the frigate *Asia* fired upon the town and before the people had taken alarm, he disposed of all the property he could and then with his family and belongings removed up the Hudson to the neighborhood of Hyde Park. In this district were many coves, where his vessels would be safe from the men-of-war upon the river. What increased their security was the strong colonial spirit of the people on the land. Nearly all of his kindred withdrew from New York at the same time, so that the family lost almost nothing in the weary seven years of the Revolution. Both Peter and his relatives were strong Revolutionists and helped the colonial cause wherever it was possible. The sterling seamanship of the family enabled them to be of great usefulness to the Continental armies. They supplied transportation to the soldiers, forwarded arms and provisions, carried despatches, and even made reconnaissances, when information was needed by the American generals.

When peace was restored, Peter returned to New York and re-established himself as a ship-chandler. The business was developed with such skill that it soon became one of the first commercial concerns in the metropolis, and its owner one of the richest merchants. In the beginning of the nineteenth century the firm was changed to "P. Schermerhorn & Son," and afterwards to "P. Schermerhorn & Sons." It sustained its reputation under the new management and earned fine fortunes for the two junior

The Schermerhorn Residence, 84th Street and East River

From a print in *Valentine's Manual*, 1866

members. In 1796, Peter was elected a director of the Bank of New York, and in 1800 was prominent in all financial matters. He was one of the first to invest in Brooklyn real estate, and as early as 1795 purchased a great tract in Gowanus, which included what is now a goodly part of Greenwood Cemetery. From his interest in Brooklyn matters, the authorities of that town named one of its chief thoroughfares after him, a name which it still retains. He took an active part in church and charitable work, and was justly regarded as one of the best citizens of New York in his time. He married Elizabeth Bussing, daughter of Abraham Bussing, by whom he had six children: John [1775], Peter [1781], Abraham [1783], George [1785], Elizabeth [1787], and James [1792].

In the sixth generation, the most conspicuous member was Peter the Younger, son of Peter the Elder. When he came of age he was admitted to his father's firm as a junior partner, and, in 1810, he and his brother, ambitious to surpass their father, started a separate firm called "Schermerhorn & Co.," which they managed with success, while still retaining their connection with the other house. This duality was continued even after the father's death, the old houses being reorganized under the names of "Schermerhorn, Banker & Co." and "Schermerhorn, Willis & Co." He invested wisely in real estate, purchasing among other tracts a large piece of land between Third Avenue and the East River, from Sixty-fourth to Seventy-fifth Street.

Peter the Younger

In 1814, he was made a director of the Bank of New York, which office he held until his death in 1852. He was a pillar of Grace Church, which in the early part of the nineteenth century was a small affair, but which, owing to the hard work and munificence of the Schermerhorns, reached its present prominence in the ecclesiastical world. Peter the Younger became a vestryman in 1820 and a warden in 1845. He was an active member of the Building Committee which superintended the new church and rectory on Broadway, near Tenth Street. The two buildings with their exquisite façades are a fitting tribute to the memory of the great merchant prince. He married Sarah Jones, daughter of John Jones, by whom he had six children: Peter Henry [1805], John Jones [1806], Peter Augustus [1811], Edmond Henry [1815], James Jones [1818], and William Colford [1821].

In the seventh generation, William Colford has probably been the most eminent member of the family. He was graduated from Columbia in 1840, and admitted shortly afterwards to the bar. He received the degree of A.M. from his Alma Mater in 1860, and the same year was elected one of the trustees. In 1893, he was chosen chairman of the Board of Trustees. His life has been eventful for its many acts of philanthropy and munificence, the most notable being the presentation to Columbia University of Schermerhorn Hall, one of the noblest buildings devoted to natural science. He married Ann Elliott Huger Laight.

William Colford

His brother, Peter Augustus, gave promise of the highest scholarship. He was an honor-man at Columbia, where he was graduated in 1829, and where he took the degree of A.M. in 1833. His erudition, literary talent, and vigorous mentality were unusual. He had just begun his career as a scholar when he was overtaken by death at the age of thirty-four. He married Adeline E. Coster, by whom he had three children: Ellen, Henry Augustus, and Frederick Augustus. The first has played an active part in city philanthropy. She married the late Colonel R. T. Auchmuty, who founded the New York Trade School in 1881.

Peter Augustus the Scholar

Frederick Augustus [1844] is the head of the eighth generation. He was educated at Columbia. During his college term he enlisted in the Union army, and served in the Civil War as second lieutenant in the One Hundred and Eighty-fifth New York Infantry. He rose to be first lieutenant, and at the end of the war was brevetted captain for gallant conduct at the battle of Five Forks. At the close of the war he returned to Columbia, but instead of continuing the classical course he took up the study of science, and was graduated from the School of Mines (1868) with the degree of Engineer of Mines. In 1877, he

Frederick Augustus

was elected a trustee of the university, which office he has held ever since. He is President of the New York Institution for the Blind, a member of the Metropolitan Museum of Art, the Loyal Legion of America, the American Geographical Society, and other learned bodies.

Other distinguished members of the family were Henry Augustus [1840], a brilliant scholar, who was graduated from Columbia (1861), and took the degrees of A.M. (1863) and LL.B. (1867); Dr. Burr, who was graduated from the College of Physicians and Surgeons in 1863; William Barnewell, who was graduated from Columbia in 1863; Bruce, who was graduated from Columbia in 1833; Daniel C., who was graduated from Columbia in 1824; and Judge Cornelius, who was graduated from the same institution in 1806, and practised law for many years in this State.

The women of this race have been noted for their social graces. Nearly all married well and enjoyed long and happy wedded lives. In every generation they have been at the very head of New York society, and in the present decade they still wield that sovereignty in the person of Mrs. William Astor. They have been women of deep religious sentiments, and have been identified with church work in all of its forms. They have written their names indelibly upon the pages of philanthropy in the history of the metropolis.

The family typifies the growth of the Empire State. Its early members were active in the opening of the primeval forest-lands and thereafter in the development of travel and traffic. They were among the first to establish the higher education in New York, and have ever since been closely connected with its college and university life. In the present century they have aided generously in the formation and support of learned bodies and semi-educational institutions. They have never sought office, and of all the old families of the State, they have been the most reserved. This reserve has not been that of selfish isolation, but has, on the contrary, been accompanied by an ideally democratic conduct. They have looked after the welfare of their neighbors and fellow-citizens, and have in every generation increased the prosperity of the community.

From the earliest time they perceived the maritime importance of New York. They realized that the possession of the Hudson, the Sound, the Kills, and Newark Bay involved a mine of inexhaustible wealth to Manhattan Island. They were advocates of the Erie and Champlain Canal, the Morris and Essex, the Delaware and Raritan, and of the harbor improvements which have been going on for more than a century. They took part in the development of coastwise and river navigation, and laid the foundation for many mercantile enterprises between New York and the coast cities of the Atlantic. It was this clear statesmanlike view which enabled them to take advantage of opportunities unperceived by others, and to accumulate that wealth which is usually the reward of intelligence and determined effort. The name Schermerhorn bears the same relation to the coastwise shipping of New York that the names of Astor, Low, and Grinnell do to its huge ocean traffic.

Schuyler

General Philip Schuyler.
From the painting by Trumbull

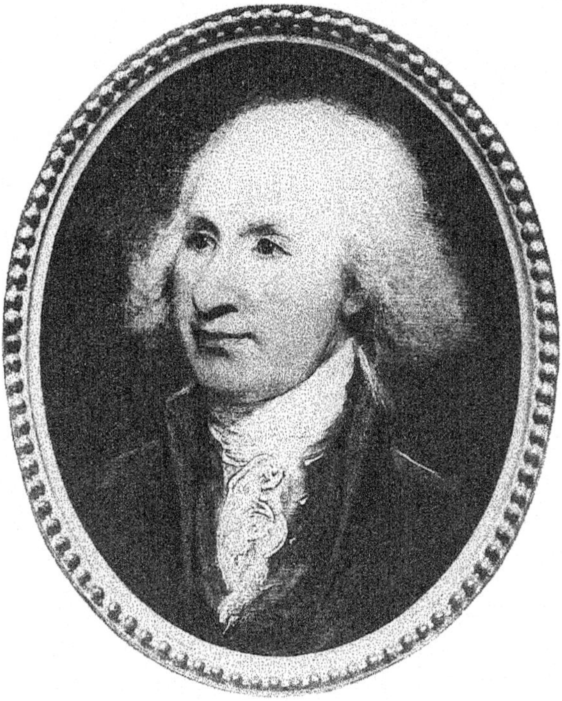

XXXII

SCHUYLER

TWO hundred and fifty years ago (1651) a handsome young Dutchman, Philip Pietersen Van Schuyler, came across the seas from Holland and settled in the town of Rensselaerswyck, known to-day as Albany. He represented the finest type of Dutch manhood, being brave, intelligent, energetic, and religious. He was a pioneer in the best sense of the word, and in addition was a commander of men and an organizer of industry. He was a successful farmer, acquiring an estate which enriched his descendants for many generations. He was eminent as a public leader, preserving friendly relations with the Indians, directing the conquest of the wilderness, and aiding newly arrived immigrants to obtain a foothold in the valleys of the Hudson and the Mohawk. He married Margherita Van Schlichtenhorst soon after his arrival, and had a numerous family, all of whom inherited his health and physical and mental strength.

Philip Pietersen

Of his children, Pieter, the oldest son, was the most conspicuous. With Dutch thrift, he circulated a petition, presented it in person, and obtained a royal charter in 1688 for the city, under the new name of Albany. Incidentally with the incorporation, came his appointment as Mayor. The mayoralty

Pieter

was more important in colonial days than at the present time. It had military and legal as well as executive obligations, and in general jurisdiction was almost the equal of the governorship. On account of the exigencies of the time, the Mayor was the Indian Commissioner or Agent. He was popular among the red men, who named him "Quedor," a sobriquet by which he was well-known in northern New York.

In 1689, the war broke out between England and France, affording the doughty Mayor the opportunity of proving himself as brilliant a soldier as he was a statesman. From this period up to his death, in 1724, his life was one of the chief glories of New York. He was indefatigable; he kept his own property well in hand, organized the people of northern New York into military companies, established forts at strategic points, led several expeditions into Canada, then an appendage to the French Crown, made treaties with the Puritan colonies in New England, and alliances with the Indian tribes in the Empire State. When affairs were looking dark for the colony, he took a delegation of Indian chiefs across the sea and presented them to Queen Anne. It is hard to say which produced the greatest sensation at the English capital — the handsome Dutch Mayor or the stalwart sagamores. They were entertained in the most lavish style of old-fashioned hospitality, which, according to old historians, nearly ruined the Honorable Pieter's digestion and half demoralized his redskin colleagues. But it had the effect desired. When the chiefs returned laden with clothing, jewels, arms, toys, watches, and baubles they created such a furor among the Iroquois that from that time on the Mayor had no difficulty in gathering an Indian army whenever needful. The historians of the time are singularly unanimous — the English, Canadians, and Americans pronouncing Pieter the best soldier and statesman of his period, while the French chroniclers refer to him as the most ferocious and bloodthirsty enemy of the King of France. The fame of Pieter has obscured his brothers, Brandt, Arent, and John, who were gallant officers and public-spirited citizens, the latter also having been Mayor of Albany. Pieter might have had a title had he so desired,

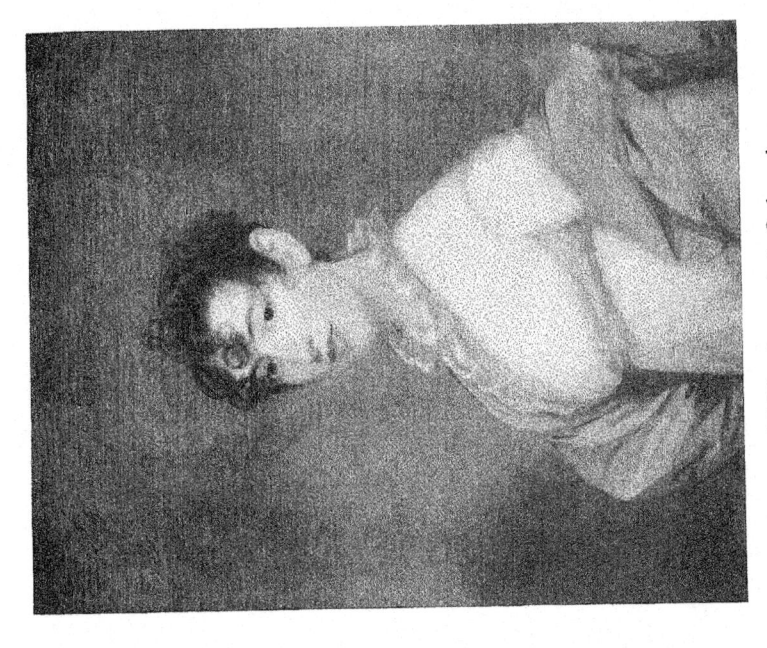

Mrs. Philip Jeremiah Schuyler
(Mary Anna Sawyer)
From an oil painting

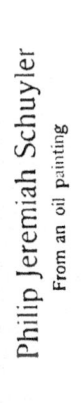

Philip Jeremiah Schuyler
From an oil painting

but when knighthood was offered him by Queen Anne he refused the honor. He explained his declination on two grounds: first, that it might humble his brothers, who were just as good men as he; and, second, that it might make the women of his family vain. Pieter's bravery came as much from his mother as his father. The former, Margherita Van Schlichtenhorst, was living in the fort at Albany when a párty of soldiers came to seize the place. The Colonel, her son, was away at the time, and the men attached to the house were at their wit's ends; but the woman was equal to the emergency. She summoned the men, called them to arms, and drove out the assailants.

In the third generation, the most conspicuous figure was that of Colonel Philip, Jr., Pieter's oldest son. According to his tombstone, he was "a gentleman improved in several public employments." He was a capable soldier, a shrewd statesman, and a good business man. He married his cousin, Margaret Schuyler (1701-1782), whose many graces have been recorded in Mrs. Grant of Laggan's interesting book, *Memoirs of an American Lady*.

From Arent, Philip Pietersen's third son, are descended the Schuylers of northern New Jersey, where many still own large estates along the Passaic River. To this branch belongs Colonel Pieter, son of Arent, the gallant commander of the "Jersey Blues" during the "Old French War," who will be remembered for his humanity and generosity while in Canada toward the captives of the French and Indians whom he rescued or ransomed, as well as toward the prisoners he himself made.

The fourth generation brings upon the boards the greatest of the family, Major-General Philip Schuyler, who was born in 1733, and died in 1804. He was a man who could have succeeded in any calling, so well rounded was his mental and moral equipment. Webster pronounced him second only to Washington among the great Revolutionary heroes. At the breaking out of the Revolution, he was practically the head of the Schuyler family. He had wealth, power, and culture; he held a commission under the British Crown, and could, had he so desired, received knighthood. His interests were bound up in the

Major-Gen. Philip

English cause, and to espouse the cause of the colonies seemed to mean ruin. He was an aristocrat by birth, breeding, and association. Nevertheless, when the conflict came he threw up his commission and gave himself to the Revolutionary cause. His career during the seven years' war is known to every one, and it is generally conceded that it was his genius which won the battle of Saratoga. After the Revolution, he took an active part in public affairs, serving as a delegate to the Continental Congress, and as a United States Senator.

General Schuyler was not covetous of public office. From boyhood he was marked by an equanimity seldom found among the children of the wealthy. He was generous to a fault. Under the law of primogeniture, which then prevailed, he was entitled to the major part of the paternal estate. He refused to accept it, however, and shared the patrimony with his brothers and sisters. The first half of the eighteenth century was not an age when education flourished. Conviviality and social pleasures engrossed the attention of the higher classes, but young Schuyler made himself conspicuous even then by his studious habits. In this determination he was greatly aided by his mother, Cornelia Van Cortlandt. He was a fluent French scholar, had a good knowledge of Dutch, German, and Latin, excelled in mathematics, and was more than proficient in civil and military engineering.

The first recognition of his ability came when he was a young man. The Commissary Department of the British Army was in a muddled condition, and Lord Viscount Howe, the commander, selected young Schuyler to take charge of an important branch of the work. There was a protest from many officers, who resented the placing over them of what they called a boy. Lord Howe is said to have replied that he did not like to appoint a boy, but when a boy was the only one who could do the work properly, he had to appoint him. It was just before this time, September 17, 1755, that Philip Schuyler married Catherine Van Rensselaer, a noted beauty of the period, daughter of Colonel John Van Rensselaer. The choice was a happy one, as the wife possessed the determination and heroism of the husband. Her daughter wrote concerning her: "Perhaps I may relate of my mother, as a judicious act of her kindness, that she not infrequently sent a milch cow to persons in poverty. When the Continental Army was retreating before Burgoyne, she drove in her chariot with four horses to Saratoga to remove her household articles. While there, she received directions from General Schuyler to set fire to his extensive fields of wheat—which she did with her own hands—and to induce his tenants and others to do the same, rather than suffer them to be reaped by the enemy. She also sent her horses on for the use of the army, and returned to Albany on a sled drawn by oxen."

Of Philip's chivalry, the best witness was his adversary, General Burgoyne. This British commander in the House of Commons delivered a speech in which he held General Schuyler up to the admiration of Parliament. He said: "By orders a very good dwelling-house, exceeding large storehouses, great sawmills, and other outbuildings, to the value altogether of perhaps ten thousand pounds, belonging to Gen. Schuyler at Saratoga, were destroyed by fire a few days before the surrender. One of the first persons I saw after the convention was signed was General Schuyler, and when I expressed to him my regret at the event which had happened to his property, he desired me to think no more of it, and said that the occasion justified it according to the rules and principles of war. He did more: he sent an aide-de-camp to conduct me to Albany, in order, as he expressed it, to procure better quarters than a stranger might be able to find. That gentleman conducted me to a very elegant house, and to my great surprise presented me to Mrs. Schuyler and her family. In that house I remained during my whole stay in Albany, with a table with more than twenty covers for me and my friends, and every other possible demonstration of hospitality."

This home in Albany saw all the great men and women of the land. The library contained the best collection of books in the colony. This room, or den, as the owner called it, was a favorite resort of Aaron Burr, who went there, when a member of the Legislature at Albany, to prepare his cases and write his orations.

There he met the daughter of General Schuyler, whom he was to make a widow by shooting her husband, Alexander Hamilton. General Schuyler displayed great political wisdom and statesmanship during his term in the Senate.

Of General Schuyler's children, eight reached maturity and married. Only one took part in public affairs—Philip J. Schuyler, who was a Representative in Congress from Dutchess County and a valued citizen. The other seven exercised great social influence in the latter part of the eighteenth century and the early part of the nineteenth. Angelica married John Barker Church; Elizabeth, Alexander Hamilton; Margarita, Stephen Van Rensselaer, the Patroon; John B., Elizabeth Van Rensselaer, the daughter of the Patroon; Rensselaer, Elizabeth Ten Broeck; Cornelia, Washington Morton; and Catherine, who will be long remembered as the godchild of Washington, married Samuel Bayard Malcolm, and, upon the latter's death, James Cochran. Six of the eight marriages proved fruitful, though in nearly every instance there was a preponderance of female over male descendants. This is seen in the small number of those who bear the General's name, and the very large number of those who carry his blood in their veins. Among the names which now represent this branch of the house are Ogden, Harison, Baxter, Bolton, Chambers, De Luze, Seabury, Peck, Morton, Van Rensselaer, Nolan, Douw, Thayer, Robb, Andrews, Berry, Townsend, Barber, Crosby, Hamilton, Church, Cruger, Pell, and Glover.

The oldest son of General Philip was John Bradstreet [1763], who was a distinguished engineer, and who died (1795) from a fever contracted while engaged in the construction of a waterway from Schenectady to Lake Ontario. He inherited the Saratoga estate. His wife was Elizabeth, daughter of Stephen Van Rensselaer.

Philip of Saratoga [1788], son of John Bradstreet, was graduated from Columbia in 1806 and immediately afterward began a brilliant career. He was a canal advocate and secured the construction of the great canal-basin at Schuylerville. He established at the latter place the second cotton-mill in New York State. He

uyler, whom he was to
Alexander Hamilton
wisdom and statesman

reached maturity and
urs—Philip J. Schuyler,
ongress from Dutchess
The other seven exer-
part of the eighteenth
nth. Angelica married
Hamilton; Margarita
hn B., Elizabeth Van
Rensselaer, Elizabeth
n. and Catherine, who
i Washington, married
latter's death, James
ed fruitful, though in
erance of female over
number of those who
number of those who
mes which now repre-
son, Baxter, Bolton,
ton. Van Rensselaer
n Townsend, Barber
nd Glover.

hn Bradstreet [1763],
ho died (1795) from a
nstruction of a water-
He inherited the Sara
ghter of Stephen Van

Bradstreet, was gradu-
ly afterward began a
and secured the con-
ville. He established
New York State. He

Philip Schuyler
From a miniature

Schuyler

served in the New York Assembly (1822) and made an excellent United States Consul at Liverpool. He married Grace, sister of Hon. John Hunter. His life was noted for its generosity and hospitality. At his first home in Schuylerville, and his second and last, at Pelham-on-the-Sound, he entertained with princely liberality He was enthusiastic in his love of humanity, giving all the time he could to church work and charity.

John [1825], son of Philip of Saratoga, was educated at the New York University and became a civil engineer. In this profession he rose to the highest rank, and became an authority on railway construction and bridge-building. He was a member of the Order of the Cincinnati, where he was elected progressively secretary, general treasurer, and vice-president. His chief relaxation was the study of astronomy and Egyptology, in both of which sciences he was a distinguished expert. He died unmarried in 1895.

Philip Jeremiah [1768], second son of General Philip, settled in Rhinebeck, where he attained great prominence. He served in the Assembly and held many responsible offices. He married Sarah Rutzen, and, after her death, Mary Anna Sawyer.

George Lee [1811], son of Philip Jeremiah, was born in Rhinebeck and came to New York early in his career, where he became a civil engineer of high repute. He was one of the organizers of the modern system of transportation upon the Hudson River and Long Island Sound, and shares with Stevens, Astor, and Stockholm the credit of having developed, if not created, that system which has been so potent in increasing the wealth of the Metropolis.

He was a stanch supporter of the Union during the Civil War, and served as an aide-de-camp with rank of Colonel on the staff of General Wool, as agent for the Union Defence Committee and as agent for the Federal Government. He enjoyed considerable reputation as a writer and historical student. He was married twice, both wives being grand-daughters of Alexander Hamilton. He was active in club life, having been a member of the Union, Knickerbocker, and New York Yacht Clubs. He was probably best known to the public as one of the original owners, with J.

C. Stevens, E. A. Stevens, Hamilton Wilkes, and J. Beekman Finley, of the *America's* Cup. In 1882, he was the sole survivor of that famous group of yachtsmen.

In 1887, he was the referee in the international race between the *Volunteer* and the *Thistle*. He had one son, Philip, and two daughters, Louisa Lee and Georgina. The present head of this branch is Philip [1836]. He was educated at Harvard (1853) and the University of Berlin (1857). He read law with the late Benjamin D. Silliman. He joined the Seventh Regiment N. Y. N. G. in 1859, and at the outbreak of the Rebellion left New York for the defence of Washington. In May, he entered the regular army as lieutenant and became major for gallant and meritorious services. He has been identified with the management of several large local institutions, including the New York Hospital and its Asylum for the Insane at White Plains and the New York Blind Asylum. He is a trustee of the New York Public Library, Astor, Lenox, and Tilden Foundation, and of the Zoölogical Gardens. He inherits his father's yachting tastes and has been fleet-captain of the New York Yacht Club.

Louisa Lee [1837], daughter of George Lee and Eliza Hamilton holds a high rank in philanthropy and patriotism. At the breaking out of the Civil War she joined the U. S. Sanitary Commission and was one of the chief volunteer workers of the New York Branch during the four years of that great struggle. So closely did she attend to her duties that her health was impaired and she was obliged to pass some time in Europe. In 1872, as a result of her visits among the poor and to institutions for their benefit, she organized the "State Charities Aid Association," which has been so potent a factor in the reforms of institutional work in the Empire State. To this Aid Association she has given her time and labor up to the present date. Her achievements include reports, recommendations, studies upon pauperism, hospitals, asylums, and the care and treatment of the pauper insane. She is especially distinguished for her ability in initiating and furthering reform measures and for her power of enlisting the sympathy of the community in such undertakings.

Louisa Lee Schuyler

She accepted the honorary position of representative of New York State on the Woman's Board of the Columbian Exposition at Chicago 1892–93, and in 1900 was chosen an honorary member of the Woman's Board of the Pan-American Exposition at Buffalo.

Arent Schuyler, a brother of Pieter, the founder, is the head of a junior branch which has been well represented in official and professional life. In the family itself it has been known as the clerical division, on account of the large number of ministers and writers it contained. To this line belongs the Rev. Dr. Montgomery Schuyler, who was born in New York City in 1814, and who studied at Geneva, now Hobart, and at Union Colleges. After graduating from the latter in 1834, he practised law, went into mercantile life, and finally entered the Protestant Episcopal Church.

Arent

Rev. Montgomery

He was a rector in Marshall, Mich., Lyons, N. Y., and Buffalo, N. Y. He then went to Christ Church, St. Louis, Mo., where he labored up to his death, in 1896, serving over forty years. When his church was made the cathedral of the diocese, he was chosen dean. He made many valuable contributions to Church literature and ecclesiastical publications.

About his son, the Rev. Louis Sanford Schuyler, is the halo of heroism. He was born at Buffalo in 1852, graduated from Hobart in 1871, entered the ministry in 1874, and, when the yellow fever broke out in 1878, was the first to volunteer upon the relief committee, and obtained an assignment at his own request for Memphis, Tenn., where the epidemic was the worst. Here he fought well, but paid the penalty of his philanthropy with his life. Memorial services for him were held in all the Protestant Episcopal churches of the country, as well as in those of other denominations.

Rev. Louis Sanford

The Rev. Dr. Anthony Schuyler, cousin of the Rev. Dr. Montgomery Schuyler, was another distinguished Episcopal divine. After graduation from Hobart College, he studied and practised law for ten years. He then took sacred orders, and was admitted to the Protestant Episcopal Church in 1850, at the age of thirty-four. For thirty-two years

Reverend Anthony

he was rector of Grace Church, Orange, N. J. A ripe scholar and author, he was rewarded by the degrees of D.D. and S.T.D. He died November, 1900.

Montgomery Schuyler [1843], son of the Rev. Dr. Anthony Schuyler, is the well-known editor, writer, and author of New York City. He received his education at Hobart College, travelled extensively at home and abroad, and has made a special study of American architecture.

<small>Montgomery</small>

Montgomery Schuyler, Jr., son of Montgomery and grandson of Anthony of the Arent line, is a fellow of Columbia University and the author of monographs upon early Persian and Sanscrit religions and dramatic literature.

<small>Montgomery II.</small>

An important branch begins with Captain Philip, fourth son of the founder. He was a stalwart farmer and brave soldier, and was the leading spirit in Old Saratoga and its vicinity. To his energy was due much of the development of that early settlement. During King George's War (1744–48) the authorities at Albany gave notice that they could not protect the outlying towns in the event of an invasion by the French and Indians, and advised the settlers to rendezvous at the northern metropolis. Captain Philip refused to leave and fortified his house. Here he remained, and when the French made their attack in 1745 he was one of the many heroes who fought and died at Saratoga in defence of their homes.

Among the descendants of Captain Philip was George Washington Schuyler, his great-grandson, who was born in 1810, and died at Ithaca, N. Y., in 1888. He was a graduate of the University of New York. He studied theology, but turned from the pulpit to commerce. In 1863, he was State Treasurer and in 1866 was appointed Superintendent of the Banking Department of New York. He served in the Assembly in 1875 and from 1876 to 1880 was auditor of the Canal Department. He was undoubtedly the first to advocate the abolition of tolls upon the canal and, after many years' agitation, saw his project become the law of the State by the passage of a Constitutional Amendment.

<small>George Washington</small>

Philip Schuyler
From a painting by R. M. Stagg

The Schuyler Home "Nevis," at Tarrytown on the Hudson

Schuyler

The high talents of George Washington were transmitted to his son, Eugene Schuyler, author and diplomat. He inherited the intense energy of the founders of his race. He was born in 1840, at Ithaca, N. Y., and died in Egypt, at fifty years of age. He held consular and diplomatic posts no less than ten times, and in all acquitted himself creditably. He was a popular contributor to the magazines of both his own country and England, and made two translations from the Russian of Turgenef and Tolstoy, and one from the Finnish. He wrote a biography of Peter the Great, and was an esteemed member of a dozen learned societies.

Eugene

Viewed as a unit, the Schuyler family has had a great influence upon the Empire State. In the colonial days it was in the front rank of the progressive patroons, and aided the conversion of the northern and eastern districts of the commonwealth from savagery to civilization. It was always liberal, generous, and tolerant. These virtues it brought from the Netherlands, and with them the love of learning, of comfort, and refinement. The Schuyler homes for two hundred years were noted for hospitality, and were crowded by the leading men and women of the time. Of the great Revolutionary characters, more than one half were guests at some time of the Schuyler mansion in Albany. They devoted their activity to matters of general welfare, such as the extension of the colonies into Canada, the construction of the Erie Canal system, the establishment of a national bank, and the upholding of the national honor no matter at what cost. In quiet seasons they took little interest, and seldom engaged, in the game of politics. They made good soldiers and landed proprietors, and were gentlemen of culture. Where they had power over ten ants they never abused it, and never were arbitrary or tyrannical. During the Revolution, tradition says, they incurred the displeasure of some of the patroon class by waiving all rents from tenants. They did this from pure philanthropy, and probably did not realize that in so doing they were making the stepping-stone from the then existing conditions to the anti-rent and anti-quarter sale agitation, which was to revolutionize the rural system of New York.

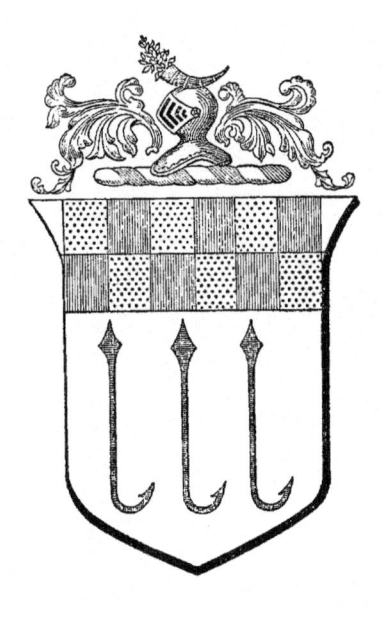

Smith

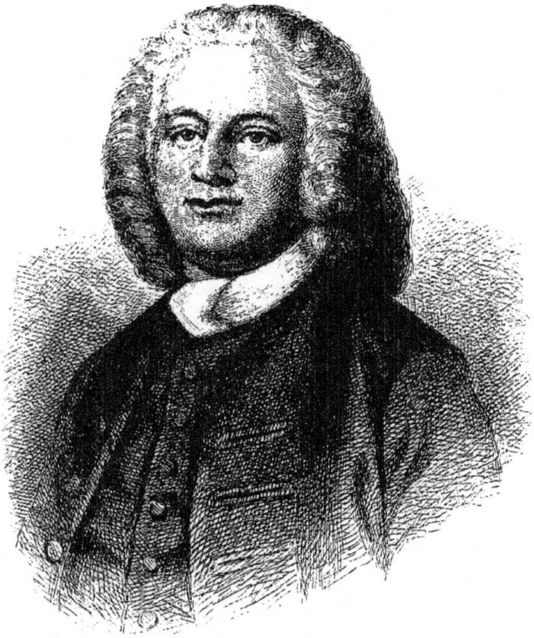

XXXIII

SMITH

FIVE generations of college men, whereof each has supplied distinguished lawyers to the community, is the simple but magnificent record of the Smith family of New York. Through professional ability, it has enjoyed the advantages of wealth; through marriage, it has become connected with many of the old Knickerbocker bloods, and through legal, literary, and medical services, it has stamped itself upon the chronicles of the State.

Its most prominent ancestor was William, a stalwart soldier in the army of Oliver Cromwell. He was one of the praying and pious soldiers of that period, who taught the world the impressive lesson that a religious devotee was more than a match in the tented field for the *William the Soldier and Puritan* conscienceless free-lance or the rovstering swashbuckler. His was the type which, after the Restoration, supplied the New World with so much of its best material. The emigrants brought with them across the seas the high moral purposes and the indomitable patience which had marked them in the civil struggles at home. That nearly all were narrow-minded and intolerant, is often charged against them as a heinous fault. Such criticisms, however, overlook the fact that the conquest of the New World demanded the iron virtues, and not the pleasing courtesies of a refined civilization. The great colonies of the world have been founded by heroes and zealots.

William the soldier was born in the Isle of Ely, Cambridgeshire, England, but removed and settled at Newport Pagnell, Buckinghamshire, where he died about 1682. He married Elizabeth Hartley of Lancashire, by whom he had six children—five sons and one daughter: William II., James, John, Samuel, Thomas (from whom the New York branch descends), and Christiana. Of this generation, two left home for America. William II., the oldest, emigrated to Jamaica, W. I., and settled at Port Royal, from which he is known as "Port Royal" Smith. He married Frances Peartree, daughter of Colonel William Peartree, who was Mayor of New York in 1703. From him are descended the Peartree-Smiths, who played an important part in the Empire State in the eighteenth century.

"Port Royal" Smith

Thomas, the fifth and youngest son of William I., was born in 1675 at Newport Pagnell, married Susanna Odell, and came to the New World with his three sons in 1715. He had scarcely more than landed when he started a movement looking toward the establishment of a Presbyterian Church, there being none in the city at that time. Success crowned his efforts, and in 1716 the denomination in which he was an enthusiastic worker had its own place of worship. He died in 1745. He was a merchant and a man of large means.

Thomas the Merchant

Of the children of Thomas, Judge William was one of the great men of his period. When he arrived with his father in New York he was eighteen years of age. The same year (1715) he entered Yale, where he was graduated in 1719, and took the degree of A.M. in 1722. For the next two years he served as professor at that institution of learning, during which period he showed so much ability that in 1724, when but twenty-seven years old, he was asked to become the President of the college. He declined, as he had already taken up the study of law, and had pursued it with such assiduity in his leisure hours that he was admitted to the bar the same year. Two months

Judge William

afterwards he opened a law office in New York, and was shortly in the enjoyment of a good practice.

From this point on until his death, in 1769, he was a leading figure in colonial life. He appeared in nearly every litigation of importance, and was a leader in each political issue. In politics, he was a Whig; in his ideas, an advocate of the people against the Crown. When the British officials undertook the prosecution of John Peter Zenger, editor of the New York *Weekly Journal* (1735), William Smith and James Alexander defended the accused, and so offended the magistrates that their names were stricken from the roll of attorneys. In spite of the power of the Crown, Zenger was acquitted, and the liberties of the press preserved. Although his disbarment lasted two years, it only served to increase his power and influence in the colony. In 1736, he was made Recorder; in 1748, he was one of the incorporators of Princeton College, and is said by the historian of that institution to have drawn up the first charter and the draft of the second. To the end of his life "he was the earnest friend of the college, and one of the most honored and influential members of the Board."

The cause of higher education was neglected in New York in those years. Among the chief men of that period, only Judge Smith and Lieutenant-Governor De Lancey were college graduates. The first step toward a better condition was taken by Judge Smith, William Alexander, and three members of the Morris family, who in 1732 petitioned the Assembly to establish a free school for teaching Latin, Greek, and mathematics. This was done the same year, and proved a success. The experiment was so popular that the same men now, aided by other leading citizens, determined to have a college in their own city. Funds were collected by lotteries, and an annual grant promised by the Legislature. In 1751, trustees were appointed, and in 1754, the charter of the College of the Province of New York, known as King's College, was granted. Owing largely to Judge Smith's efforts, the new school started upon a liberal and almost non-sectarian basis. In the Board of Governors were the rector of Trinity Church, the senior minister of the Reformed Protestant Dutch

Church, the minister of the Ancient Lutheran Church, the minister of the French Church, and the minister of the Presbyterian congregation. In 1754, the Judge, with a number of distinguished friends, arranged plans for a public library, obtained the charter, and started what is now the New York Society Library.

The year 1751 saw the Judge appointed Attorney-General and Advocate-General. Two years later, he was made a member of the Council. The following year, he was chosen to be one of the four representatives from New York to the General Congress at Albany. In 1760, the office of Chief Justice was offered to him by Lieutenant-Governor Cadwallader Colden, but declined. Three years afterwards, he accepted the appointment of Judge of the Supreme Court of the Province, and held it with singular ability up to the time of his death. He was twice married, his first wife being Mary Hett, by whom he had fifteen children; his second, Mrs. Elizabeth Scott Williams, by whom he had no issue. He applied his educational ideas to the training of his children. All were good French and Dutch scholars, and thoroughly versed in English literature. The sons were familiar with Greek and Latin, and had a fair knowledge of Hebrew.

Thomas [1700?], the second son of Thomas and Susanna, was a merchant and real-estate owner of considerable wealth. He **Thomas II., Merchant** was one of the first to develop Orange County, where he had a great tract of land. He lived at Smith's Clove, now Monroe. John, the third son [1702], was a popular **Rev. John** clergyman, who spent the larger part of his life at White Plains. He married Mehetabel Hooker, by whom he had four sons and eight daughters.

In the fourth generation, William Peartree [1723] was a public-spirited citizen and patriot, who was very active in civic affairs.

Chief Justice William [1728], son of Judge William, was the great man of the generation. He inherited his father's character, **Chief Justice William** and was a brilliant student. He was graduated from Yale in 1745, when but seventeen years of age. So great was his precocity that he was an honor man in the classics,

William Smith
Chief Justice of New York and of Canada.   From a steel engraving

mathematics, Hebrew, and medicine — a wonderful record for a mere youth. He entered his father's law office, where he had as a fellow-student William Livingston, the future war-Governor of New Jersey. He was admitted to the bar in 1760, and formed a partnership with Livingston, the firm immediately building up a lucrative practice.

Up to the time of the Revolution, no man stood higher in the affections of the Colonials. His culture, eloquence, probity, gentleness, and breeding made him a universal favorite. He was conscientious to a fault, doing things that to the great world seemed ultra-chivalrous and even quixotic. He would not defend a cause which he knew to be wrong, and when he served as arbitrator, he refused any remuneration, on the ground that a judge should never have any fee. He declined speculative cases, and would not permit a man to come into his law office unless it was with "clean hands." He was a copious writer, wielding a pleasant and powerful pen. His chief work, *A History of the Province of New York,* is an eighteenth-century classic. From this work he takes the sobriquet of "William the Historian."

Yet his very conscientiousness plunged him into a sea of trouble. When the Revolutionary War broke out, his sympathies were with the people, and yet he believed the crime of rebellion to be unpardonable. He was bitterly opposed to the tyranny of the British Government, but he thought redress should be sought along peaceful channels. He had the courage of his convictions, refusing to take part in the rebellion, on the one side, or to fight against his countrymen on the other. As a result, he was named in the Act of Attainder, and his estates confiscated. When moderate counsels prevailed, the act was cancelled, and the Chief Justice invited to return to New York. In the meantime, he, with his son William, had gone to England on the evacuation of New York in 1783. In 1785, he was appointed Chief Justice of Canada, where he exercised the functions of that high office with honor to himself until his death, in 1793. He married Jennet Livingston, daughter of James Livingston of New York, by whom he had ten children.

Thomas [1734], the second son of Judge William, was graduated from Princeton (1754) and admitted to the bar in 1756. He was a patriot, and, unlike his brother, a Revolutionist. He was a member of the Committee of Safety and of the Provincial Congress. His law practice was lucrative, and made him a wealthy man, outside of the property which he inherited. He married Elizabeth Lynsen, by whom he had a large family.

Thomas the Lawyer

Dr. James [1738], the third son of Judge William, was graduated from Princeton (1757), and received the best medical education of the time in Europe, and especially at Leyden, Holland. He was instrumental in the organization of the medical department of Columbia College, and in 1768 was appointed to the chair of chemistry and materia medica. He was an active Whig, and both in this country and abroad argued manfully for the colonies. He was not alone a great physician, but so far ahead of his time as to be pronounced too theoretical and fanciful. What galled the practitioners of the period was that Dr. James would write his theses in Latin or else employ so much of that language in his medical papers as to render them unintelligible to the average practitioner. He married Mrs. Atkinson, a wealthy widow of Kingston, Jamaica, by whom he had issue.

Dr. James

Joshua Hett [1749], the youngest son of Judge William, was admitted to the bar in 1772. He was a successful practitioner, and during the Revolution pursued the same course as his oldest brother, the Chief Justice. He was involved in the Arnold episode, but appears to have been innocent of all complicity in that treachery.

Joshua Hett the Lawyer

In the fifth generation, William [1769], the son of the historian, was educated in New York and England. He accompanied his father to Canada, where he was made Clerk of the Provincial Parliament. In 1814, he was placed in the Executive Council. He was lieutenant-colonel in the Quebec militia and a successful lawyer and writer. His chief work was *A History of the Province of Canada,* similar to his father's *A History of the Province of New York.* He married Susan Webber, by whom he had five children. His grandson,

William the Historian of Canada

Lieutenant-Colonel William C. Smith of the British Army, is the present head of that branch of the family.

Of the children of Thomas of Haverstraw, second son of Judge William, the most important was Thomas, Jr. [1760?]. He was a lawyer of wealth, who devoted most of his time to the management of his estate. He married Mary Taylor, daughter of John Taylor, a merchant prince of the metropolis, by whom he had five children. *(Thomas, Jr., the Lawyer)*

In the sixth generation, the children of Thomas, Jr., deserve special mention. The oldest, John Taylor, was graduated from Columbia University in 1805, and admitted to the bar in 1810. He became District Attorney of Rockland County, and for many years was active in State affairs. *(John Taylor, District Attorney)* He was a stanch supporter of De Witt Clinton and the canal policy, as well as of all the liberal movements of his period. He married Willimina Stodart, by whom he had six children—three sons and three daughters.

The head of the seventh generation, and of the house, so far as America is concerned, is Charles Bainbridge, a prominent member of the New York bar. He is a son of John Taylor and Willimina, and was born in 1822. He studied law in the office of William Curtis Noyes, and was admitted to the bar in 1846. *(Charles Bainbridge, Lawyer)* He has been an active and successful practitioner up to the present time. He married twice, his first wife being Miss Keteltas, by whom he had issue.

In the eighth generation is Eugene Keteltas, son of Charles Bainbridge. He was educated in this country and in France, and resides in Vermont. He is represented in the ninth generation by two sons. *(Eugene Keteltas)*

Female descendants of William and Elizabeth Smith married into the following families: Bostwick, Budd, Delafield, Denning, Doyle, Gordon, Hay, Herbert, Keteltas, Livingston, Mackie, Mallet, Maturin, Roberts, Rose, Ross, Sewall, Stewart, Tallmadge, Temple, and Torrans.

To-day, when all are agreed upon the value of education, especially in its relations to professional and social life, it is difficult to appreciate the conditions which prevailed in the first century of the life of New York. Schools were few and poorly patronized, and such of the citizens as desired to give their children the benefits of the best mental training were compelled to send them to New England or to the old country. The change which the colony underwent during these one hundred years was largely due to the influence and activity of the descendants of William and Elizabeth Smith. They had big hearts, and endeavored not only to give their own children the best education which could be procured, but also to place educational opportunities within the grasp of the community. Their work in respect to Yale, Princeton, and Columbia, and, above all, the example which they themselves set for their neighbors, were two forces potent for good. That the family has sustained its own traditions, was to have been expected.

Stuyvesant

Peter Stuyves
After an engraving of the picture owned by the N. Y. Historical Society

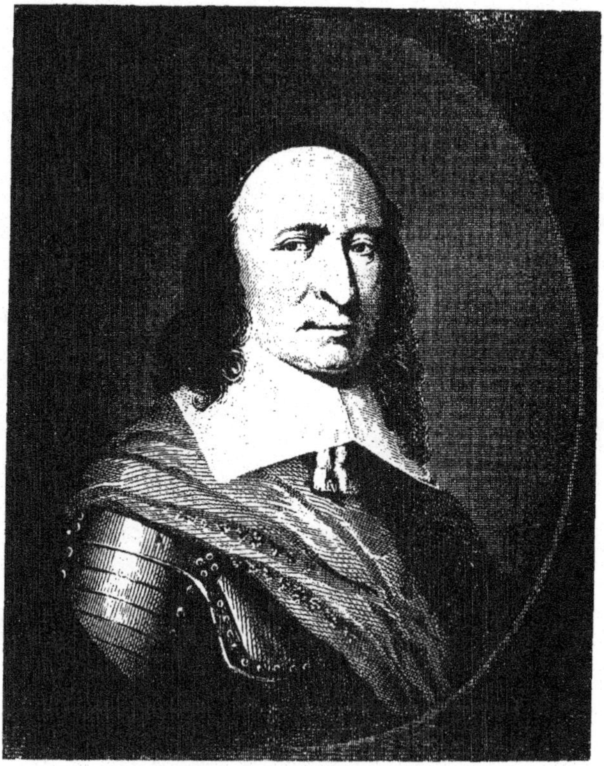

XXXIV

STUYVESANT

IN the early history of the New Netherlands, one man towers high over all the rest. A soldier, statesman, patriot, and philanthropist, he seems to have embodied the virtues of his age. Petrus, or Peter, Stuyvesant, the great Dutch Governor of New York, was born in 1602, in Friesland. **Petrus the Governor** His father was a clergyman, who gave the boy an excellent education, and developed the scholarly instincts which were to mark his subsequent career, but neither study nor the quiet life of Holland suited a youth whose vitality, physical and mental, was of heroic proportions. At an early age he had shown a love for military life, and to gratify it entered the service of the West India Company. This corporation represented the inordinate ambition of the Dutch leaders of that period. Upon it was conferred more power than had been bestowed by England upon the East India Company.

It had plenary rights to all the lands it might discover, occupy, or conquer. It had the right to make war and peace, enter into alliances, raise armies, build navies, construct fortresses, administer justice, impose tariffs and other forms of taxation, and its generals and admirals enjoyed an independence unlike anything known to either national or international jurisprudence. In return for these mighty prerogatives it was obliged to report its transactions from time to time to the States-General of Holland, and to apply to them for commissions for its chief officials. The object of the corporation was to build up a trade monopoly and a landed empire in the West, as had been done in the East, Indies.

The capital of the West India Company was about $2,500,000, which, in purchasing power, would equal about $25,000,000 to-day. These powers and wealth made it a quasi-political entity, stronger and better organized than many of the European nations of that period. Conducted by business-men, merit was the criterion of selection and advancement—more than in the administration of public affairs by the governments of the time. From the employees of the company were graduated many of the best soldiers and sailors of that century. Its service was the Mecca of adventurers from many lands. In the rosters which have come down to the present day may be found names of English, French, Swedish, Spanish, Italian, German, and even Russian officials.

Among its myriad servitors, Peter Stuyvesant was prominent within a few years after he had entered its employ. Of his exploits at this time, but little has come down from the past. Yet that little shows him to have been a fearless and even reckless fighter, a bold strategist, a powerful executive, and a stern disciplinarian, and by a seeming contradiction, a man of great kindliness and rare generosity. This combination of attributes made him popular if not beloved among the fighting men, who preponderated in the Company's service. He took part in the brilliant campaign against Spain which resulted in the conquest of several Spanish territories in the Antilles, and was thereafter made Governor of the island of Curaçoa.

Here, while occupying the gubernatorial chair, he led an expedition against the island of St. Martin, which belonged to Portugal, where, according to an ancient wit, he lost both the battle and his leg. He returned to Europe for surgical aid, and while convalescing was so eager for either vengeance or the carrying out of his plans that he secured a promise from the directors of the

Company to renew the attempt, which they did triumphantly four years later. In 1646, he was appointed Governor of the New Netherlands, and sailed on Christmas morning for his post. The sting of defeat must have been rankling in his bosom, because he did not proceed directly across the sea, but went to the West Indies and to Curaçoa, where he arrived early in 1647. Here he held many councils with his successor, and probably among the plans which the doughty veteran expatiated upon was the expulsion of the Portuguese from those seas.

He reached New Amsterdam in May of that year. With him were his wife, Judith Bayard, the daughter of a distinguished Huguenot divine, and his sister Anna, who had married Nicholas Bayard, his wife's elder brother, but who had been widowed and left with three infant sons. This group, the origin of two families, may be regarded as a genealogical unit. The Bayards had inherited the grace, intellectuality, and high moral sense of their clerical sire, while the Stuyvesants, brother and sister, seemed to have been made in the same mould of physical and mental power. The two women were to wield as potent an influence in the social sphere as the great Governor in the political. Even at home they would have been leaders of society. They were brilliant, cultured, and accomplished. Mrs. Stuyvesant, who was a Bayard, was beautiful, artistic, and gentle. Mrs. Bayard, who was a Stuyvesant, was massive, forceful, and proud. Each had a talent for business, and each acted as a tutor to her children, nephews, and nieces. They deserve special reference at this point because they exerted a profound influence upon the husband and brother. He consulted with them upon many, if not most, matters, and seemed to feel more confidence in their opinions than in those of his staff. To these women may be ascribed much of the moral force which prevailed during the Stuyvesant administration, and which was noticeable during that century.

The Dutch women were notably chaste and upright, but were, of course, apt to be influenced by those high in power. Mrs. Stuyvesant and Mrs. Bayard, occupying the highest official positions in the colony, set an example in both word and deed similar to that of the late Queen Victoria in the century just passed.

The Governor's administration may be called the golden age of the New Netherlands. He was no more than landed when he took up his work, and never wearied so long as he was in power. He organized a Council, established a court of justice, and instituted representative government. His Assembly was, of course, crude, consisting of eighteen delegates, elected by the people, from whom the Governor and Council selected a board of nine to act with them as advisers. He framed laws for the better government of the Indians, improved the revenue service, and increased the treasury receipts. He was wiser than his generation in disapproving the construction of poor and cheap houses and encouraging the building of those of a better type. Worthy of mention was his establishment of a town market and of an annual cattle fair intended to benefit the dairy and stock interests of the community. He took a large if not a chief part in founding the first public school. With remarkable foresight for that period, he perceived the necessity of accurate boundaries, and for a long time carried on a spicy controversy with Connecticut upon this topic.

As may be supposed, his career was stormy. He was a born commander, and brooked no opposition. According to modern standards, he was a genial, kind-hearted tyrant, who knew no law but his own will. He quarrelled with the patroons, merchants, and his own Council. When his enemies submitted reports against his course of action to the home Government, and the States-General commanded him to appear in person in Holland, he refused to obey in a tirade of Dutch eloquence which was long remembered by his hearers. In 1665, he sailed down the coast and up the Delaware, and took forcible possession of the Swedish colony of New Sweden, which he annexed to the New Netherlands, and called New Amstel.

In 1664, he signed the treaty of surrender to Great Britain, whereupon the town of New Amsterdam was rechristened New York. Circumstances connected with this surrender throw a clear light upon the Governor's character. The West India Company had come to neglect the colony, and, in spite of his repeated appeals for arms, munitions of war, and soldiers, had done nothing. He was not on friendly terms with the great patroons, whose estates lay between New Amsterdam and Fort Orange, and could not summon levies of men from their tenantry. New England was growing rapidly, and there was strong jealousy between the English settlers of Connecticut and Long Island and his own government. When, therefore, four English war-ships, with four hundred and fifty soldiers, arrived in the harbor, Stuyvesant had scarcely a hundred men and only a few small cannon to oppose them.

The English commander sent a summons to surrender promising life, liberty, and property to all who submitted to the royal authority. Stuyvesant read the letter, tore it to pieces, and set about making the best defence he could. Nicholas Bayard, his nephew, picked up the pieces of the letter and put them together. An anxious crowd had collected outside of the Council chamber, to whom the letter was read. Its tone was so kind and moderate that the people declared themselves in favor of surrender. A petition to that effect, signed by nearly all the leading citizens, was given to Stuyvesant, who, nevertheless, kept on preparing for battle. Everything was ready for action — the English fleet and soldiers, reinforced by Connecticut and Long Island troops, on the one side, Stuyvesant and a handful of men upon the other — when his favorite clergyman intervened, pointing out the folly and hopelessness of so unequal a struggle. Then, and not till then, did Stuyvesant yield.

His after-life was uneventful. He devoted himself to his cattle and farm, the latter running along what is now the Bowery well up to Harlem. His home was near what is now Eighth Street. A pear tree which he brought from Holland in 1647 was planted near the road, and lived and bore fruit until 1867. Its site at that time was the corner of Thirteenth Street and Third Avenue.

On the outer wall of St. Mark's Church is the tablet recording his death. He left two sons, Balthazar [1647] and Nicholas William [1648].

Balthazar Balthazar was a stanch Dutch patriot, and after New Netherlands became English he moved to the West Indies.

Nicholas William Nicholas William was a prominent citizen of early New York, who took a lively interest in church work and philanthropy. His first wife was Marie, only daughter of William Beekman, who died childless. His second was Elizabeth, daughter of Commander Slechtenhorst of Rensselaerwyck, by whom he had three children, Peter, Anna, and Gerardus or Gerard.

Of this generation Peter died unmarried, Anna espoused the Rev. Dr. Pritchard, a popular Episcopal clergyman of the period, **Peter** and Gerard, his second cousin, Judith Bayard. They had four sons, of whom only one, Peter [1727], left issue.

The latter married Margaret, the daughter of Gilbert Livingston. He occupied a leading place in New York society, his wealth being great from the growth in value of the Stuyvesant estate. He had six children, two sons and four daughters. This generation was probably the most important, socially, in the family career, both sons and daughters occupying eminent positions in the colonial world. Judith married Benjamin Winthrop; Cornelia, Dirck Ten Broeck; and Elizabeth, Colonel Nicholas Fish; while Margaret died unmarried.

Peter Gerard Peter Gerard [1778], was graduated from King's College (1794), was admitted to the bar, and practised law a short time. He gave up the profession in order to devote himself to the care of his large estate. He was twice married, but had no children by either wife. His first wife was Susan Barclay, and his second Helen Rutherfurd. He founded the New York Historical Society, of which he was President from 1836 to 1840.

Nicholas William II. Nicholas William II. married Catherine Livingston Reade, daughter of John Reade and Catherine Livingston, by whom he had nine children, six sons and three daughters. Peter, the oldest, married Julia Martin.

The Residence of Nicholas W. Stuyvesant

Which stood in 8th Street, between First and Second Avenues. From a print in *Valentine's Manual*, 1857

Nicholas William III. married Catherine A. Cheeseborough; John Reade married, first, Catherine Ackerley, and secondly, Mary A. Yates. Gerard married Susan Rivington Van Horne, Robert Reade married Margaret A. Mildeberger, Joseph Reade married Jane Ann Browning; Catherine Ann, the oldest daughter, married John Mortimer Catlin; Helen C. married, first, Henry Dudley, secondly, Francis Olmsted, and thirdly, William S. Mayo. Margaret Livingston married Robert Van Rensselaer. This was a generation of scholarly, well-to-do men, who devoted themselves to their estates, to study, and to social relations, but who took little part in the great world of affairs.

In the seventh generation Julia Helen married Rudolph C. Winterhoff; Catherine S., Edward M. Neill; Rosalie, Aristede Pillot; and Gertrude, Raymond P. Rogers, U. S. N.; Caroline Augusta, Benjamin A. Onderdonk; Margaret L. J., Howard Wainwright; Helen Mary, Robert Sandford; Catherine L., Francis R. Butler. Of the male members, Van Rensselaer Stuyvesant did not marry; Henry married Caroline Hoppock; Robert, Fanny J. Gibson; John Reade, Elizabeth T. Kendall; Robert R., Amelia Schuchardt; A. Van Horne, Harriet Le Roy Steward.

To this generation, on the maternal side, belongs Lewis Morris Rutherfurd, a great scientist. He was a grandson of Judith Stuyvesant, who married Benjamin Winthrop. Born in Morrisania [1816], graduated from Williams College (1834), admitted to the bar (1837), in 1849 he gave up law for science. Perceiving the importance of specialization in astronomical research, he took up astronomical photography, spectroscopy, and spectrologic analysis. With an intellect of extraordinary power, and with enough wealth to experiment upon a lavish scale, he made remarkable progress. In 1863, he started a series of papers on spectroscopic astronomy in the *American Journal of Science* which attracted great attention. His greatest work was the construction of differential gratings and of machines for ruling lines upon glass. So delicate were these instruments that they are said to have ruled ten and even fifteen thousand parallel lines to the inch. He succeeded in dividing space with the same accuracy as the most modern balance divides and weighs matter. Honors came upon him thick and fast both at home and abroad.

For more than a quarter of a century he was a trustee of Columbia College and a member of scientific associations. He was an Associate of the Royal Astronomical Society, and the recipient of more than a hundred medals, titles, degrees, resolutions, and other marks of esteem from the governments, colleges, and scientific institutions of the world. As physicist and astronomer, he held high rank. He died in 1892, at the age of seventy-six. His wife was Margaret Stuyvesant Chanler, and his oldest son, Stuyvesant Rutherfurd, who, by act of Legislature, transposed his two names.

Genealogically, the latter is now the most notable member of his race, being descended from Governor Stuyvesant of New Amsterdam, Governor Winthrop, of Massachusetts, Governor Dudley, of Connecticut, Governor Morris, of New Jersey, Robert Livingston, Balthazar Bayard, Walter Rutherfurd, and Lewis Morris, the signer of the Declaration of Independence. He was graduated from Columbia in 1863, and is a prominent member of the American Geographical Society, the American Museum of Natural History, the National Academy of Design, and a trustee of the Metropolitan Museum of Art. The other male members of the generation are the children of Robert R. Stuyvesant, F. Schuchardt Stuyvesant, who married Cornelia U. Bergen; Gerard, who married Mildred N. Floyd, and Van Horne, the son of A. Van Horne Stuyvesant.

Rutherfurd

The career of the Stuyvesant family, since the time of Peter the Governor, has been marked by scholarship and social prestige rather than by political, military, or commercial genius. It has been wealthy from the first generation, and has used its wealth wisely and well. Its members have been religious, and identified with charitable, educational, and other public-spirited movements. They have attended to all social duties, and from the landing of the bluff Governor to the present time have dispensed hospitality to all who came within their circle. Through marriage they have become related with many colonial families, but these relations have

that the name is essentially a New York
tropolis their name is stamped indelibly;
hall, and the Battery are mute witnesses of
Stuyvesant Square of his ancient country-

Tappen

Frederick D. Tappen
From a photograph

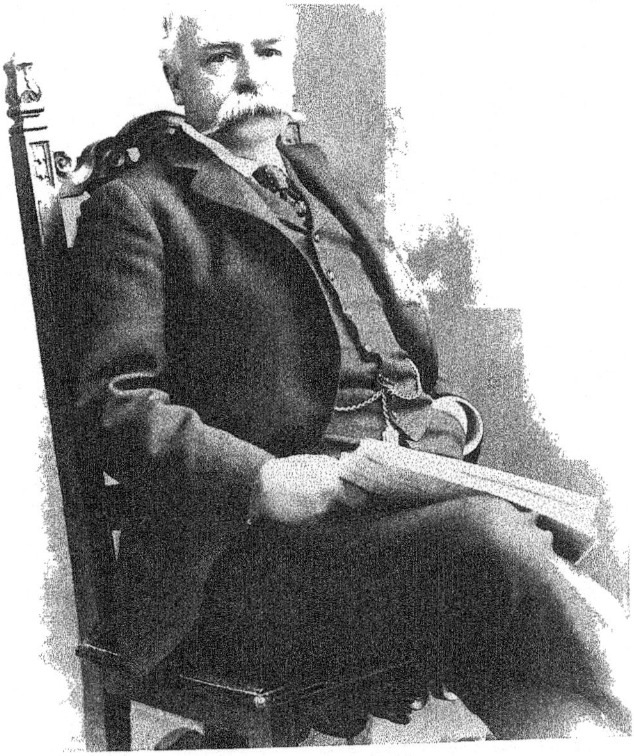

XXXV

TAPPEN

AMONG the families of the Empire State the Tappens or Tappans, as the name is also spelled, hold a curious position. Their renown rests upon achievement, probity, and public performance, but it has been largely increased by the attainments of another family of the same name. It is probable that the Tappans and Tappens of Massachusetts and of New York are of the same race. From the time of Henry VIII. up to Charles I., there was a small but constant migration of sturdy Hollanders into England. The superiority of the Dutch in spinning, weaving, bleaching, dyeing, and other industrial arts made them desirable acquisitions to any country; and in spite of the jealousy of fellow-craftsmen in Great Britain, they received in the main a hearty welcome from the English Government and people.

The New York Tappens, at least, were artisans of great ability. In the old records they are referred to as weavers, glaze-makers, shipsmiths, and builders. The records of the sixteenth and seventeenth centuries are incomplete and oftentimes untrustworthy. Of their origin nothing is known. The name has been derived from the Dutch and also from the old English patronymic of Topham. It is, however, more probable that the English family of Tappan brought its name from the Netherlands rather than that it changed the good Saxon patronymic of Topham into Tappan. No other branch of the Tophams is known to have made such an alteration, and it is difficult to conceive of an English family discarding or modifying their own name to "Dutchify" it. To complicate the problem still further, there was in the New Netherlands a Flemish family from Luxembourg which spelled its name Tapin, Tappin, or Tappen, and pronounced it Tappan, and in later years one of the offshoots spelled it to conform to the pronunciation.

The Massachusetts race has been pre-eminent for intellectuality, philanthropy, and practical Christianity; the Luxembourg for professional attainments; while the Knickerbocker stock has gained renown by its sturdy manhood, its high character, public spirit, and mental attainments. The distinction of each branch has been shed upon the other two. The New York family of Tappen came to the New World about 1630, and, after remaining a brief time in New Amsterdam, went to Fort Orange, where it settled and remained for two generations. It then broke asunder, the main line removing to Kingston, where it became distinguished in matters of the State and nation. The junior line remained in the neighborhood of Albany and sent out shoots to the West, which took root and grew into stately growths in the course of the years.

The founder was Jurian Teunisse, who married a daughter of Wybrecht Jacobse. Jurian must have brought considerable property with him from the Old World, as he appears to have been in easy circumstances, if not affluence, from the first. He was popular with the people and on terms of warm friendship with the patroons and leading merchants. He was a devout member of the Dutch Church and during the inclement winters devoted a certain number of hours every week to visiting and caring for the sick poor. The same kindly spirit actuated him in his dealings with the Indians, who called him "The Good Chief." His married life was happy and uneventful. In the latter part of his life (1654-1677) he seems to have operated largely in

Jurian the Founder

real estate, buying, selling, and exchanging upon a scale indicating the possession of large means.

In the second generation the leading figures were Tunis and Jurian II. They were well-to-do farmers and traders, Tunis seeming to have had the larger mercantile talent. He carried on commerce with New Amsterdam and afterwards New York; and on several occasions seems to have done business directly with Holland. At that time most of this trade was in the hands of the Dutch West India Company, the patroons, and the high officials. The few private citizens who engaged in it were men of means, prominent position, or of influence with the authorities. During the Indian troubles, the two brothers were enrolled in the militia, and probably took part in the fighting which occurred at that time. Like their father, they were devout and charitable, and were active members of the group which made Albany at that time the rival, if not the superior, of New York.

Tunis

Jurian II.

The wife of Tunis was Sarah Schepmoes, a Dutch belle of the time. The wedding, which occurred in 1695, was one of the most notable social events of the year. The wealth and social position of the parties, the beauty of the bride, and the popularity of the groom brought together a very distinguished assemblage from all the settlements, even from Breuckelen and Staten Island. The wedding-feast, tradition says, was a seven days' talk. Beside the luxuries in food and drink imported from the old country, there was an unusual supply of game, which had been purchased from the Indians, or had been contributed by the redmen and hunters. It lasted two days, during which time every friend and neighbor was expected to come and help himself. In middle age, Tunis removed to Kingston, which he made his permanent home.

In the third generation, the great personality was Christoffel who was born in Albany, but whose life is identified with Kingston, the whilom capital of the Empire State. He received an excellent education as well as a handsome patrimony from his father, Tunis, and on the latter's death

Christoffel

inherited the larger part of the paternal estate. He married Cornelia Vas or Vos, a handsome heiress, by whom he had a large family of vigorous and able children. Upon his farm he built a fine homestead, where he entertained generously. He held many minor offices, both in the public service and church administration.

In the fourth generation, Christopher the patriot was the leading figure. A man of marked ability, he became prominent in early life, and during a long career held many offices of honor and importance. Chief of these was membership in the First, Third, and Fourth Provincial Congresses, where he took strong grounds in favor of colonial liberty and independence. He was a trustee of Kingston, speaker of the Board, a magistrate, and President of the Board of Magistrates. He was deputy county clerk from 1759 to 1812 and county clerk from 1812 to 1821. His home was destroyed on the burning of Kingston by the British. At this juncture he displayed a gallantry and patriotism worthy of notice. When the attack began it was evident that there was no hope of successful resistance and there was barely enough time for the citizens to save their private property. Christopher had before him the alternative of preserving either the public records or his own personal belongings, including family heirlooms, deeds, and other evidences of wealth. He did not hesitate a second, but took his own horses and wagons to the court-house and removed the public records in safety, leaving his home to the torch of the foe. After the evacuation he rebuilt the family home, constructing it of stone and brick, and making it as fire-proof as the resources of that century would permit. Here he kept open house, as had been the habit of his father and grandfather. The mansion was the favorite resting-place of Governor George Clinton, who was Christopher's brother-in-law, as well as of the State and national leaders. Catey, a sister of Christopher, married Gilbert Livingston. Dr. Peter, a younger brother, was a distinguished physician, whose courtesy and attainments made him beloved in private life, and whose bravery and patriotism during the Revolution made him an idol of the public. A letter is preserved from Gilbert Livingston to Dr. Peter, which gives in pleasant fashion an account of the year 1775:

"NEW YORK, June 29, 1775.

"DEAR BROTHER—You will see by the warrants who are nominated officers for your County; it is very likely we shall raise an additional number of troops beside the three thousand now raised. We expect all diligence will be used in Recruiting, that the regiments may be formed immediately. Last saturday about two o'clock the Gens. Washington, Lee and Schuyler arrived here; they crossed the North River at Hoback and landed at Col. Lispenards. There were eight or ten companies under arms all in uniforms who marched out to Lispenards, the procession began from there thus, the Companies first, Congress next, two of Continental Congress next, general officers next and a company of horse from Philadelphia who came with the General brought up the rear: there were innumerable Company of people, Men, Women and Children present. In the evening Gov. Tryon landed as in the newspapers. I walked with my friend George Clinton, all the way to Lispenards, who is now gone home. I am very well, hope all friends so. The Tories Catey writes are as violent as ever, poor insignificant souls, who think themselves of great importance. The Times will soon show I fancy that they must quit their Wicked tenets at least in pretense and show fair, Let their hearts be black as Hell. Go on, be spirited and I doubt not success will crown our Honest endeavors for the support of our just rights and privileges."

Cornelia, another sister of Christopher, married Governor George Clinton, so that the family in this generation became allied with the two houses of Livingston and Clinton, then the great war leaders of the State.

Two sons in the fifth generation continued the prestige of their name. Christopher, Jr., the lawyer, was a man of marked ability and oratorical and literary power. He married Cornelia Kiersted.

Christopher, Junior

More conspicuous was John [1766]. He received a good education, studied law, and was admitted to the bar. His tastes were literary and journalistic, rather than forensic, and he began contributing to the press even before he attained his majority. He entered journalism, and became a popular and influential editor. His best-remembered work was done while he was editor and proprietor of the *Plebeian,* which afterwards became the *Ulster Gazette.* The paper was, anti-Federalist, and through its epigrammatic and argumentative power exerted great influence upon the political arena in the early part of the nineteenth century.

John the Editor

Colonel Charles Barclay [1796] represented the sixth generation. He was a son of John, the editor, and was an artist by taste and an architect by profession. Intensely patriotic, he volunteered in the War of 1812, and served with great gallantry throughout the conflict. After the war his military instinct kept him in touch with the militia, and in 1833 he was made Colonel of the Two Hundred and Thirty-sixth Regiment of the National Guard of New York State. He was deeply interested in the development of New York City, of which many of the finest buildings were the products of his brain. From 1835 to 1838 he was the City Superintendent of Repairs, a post equivalent to a modern municipal department of public works. He was happily married and had a numerous family. He lived to the extraordinary age of ninety-seven, and left behind him eleven children and more than thirty grandchildren and great-grandchildren.

Colonel Charles B.

Here belongs the famous educator, Rev. Henry Philip [1805]. Graduated from Union (1825), he entered Auburn Theological Seminary, where he took orders in 1827. Five years later, he accepted the chair of moral philosophy in the University of New York City. In 1852, he was elected the first chancellor of the University of Michigan, which he held for eleven years, during which he made that institution famous for its efficiency and excellence. He was a strong and fluent writer, contributing to the periodical press and publishing at least seven books of more than ephemeral value.

Tappen

Of the seventh generation, Frederick D.[1] [1829] is the head. He was educated at the Columbia Grammar School and the New York University (1849). Attracted by financial science, he began his career in the National Bank of New York, which afterwards became the Gallatin National Bank. In 1857, he rose to be cashier, and in 1868 president, which position he has held ever since, being probably the oldest of the great bankers of the nation. He is one of the few Americans who, beside mastering ordinary banking, have attained renown in the fields of high finance. His ability in this direction has given him national and international fame. In times of commercial panic or general depression, he has been instrumental in steering the ship of credit through the shoals of adversity.

Frederick D. the Financier

In the panics of 1873, 1884, 1890, 1893, and 1901 he was a leader in the movement of the great banks which checked the headlong fall of prices in Wall Street, and prevented the forced insolvency of hundreds and even thousands of responsible business concerns. He has the confidence of the banking world and of the vast business community which depends upon banks for the transaction of the enormous trade of the United States. In honor of his services in this field the great banks of New York presented to him, as a token of affection and esteem, a silver tankard which in itself was an epitome of financial history. It was made more than two hundred years ago, and was first presented to Sir John Houblon, Lord Mayor of London, and first Governor of the Bank of England, who, in a monetary crisis in 1693, took such prompt and decisive measures as to restore confidence to the business world and end disasters which were

---

[1] Frederick D. Tappen passed away in March, 1902. In his death the banking world lost one of its leading figures. His funeral was attended by representatives of nearly all of the financial interests of the metropolis and a public meeting of the bankers of the city was held at the clearing-house on Cedar Street to honor his memory.

Addresses, describing and commending his life-long services, were delivered by George G. Williams, president of the Chemical National Bank, J. Edward Simmons, president of the Fourth National Bank, Joseph C. Hendrix, president of the National Bank of Commerce, Thomas L. James, president of the Lincoln National Bank, Alexander Gilbert, president of the Market and Fulton banks, and Vice-President Hepburn of the Chase National Bank.

Nearly all of the banks of the city half-masted their flags, and similar action was taken by bankers in other cities of the Union.

threatening British credit, both public and private. Upon it is an inscription which tells in quaint language the story of that famous year. In the course of the centuries this tankard passed from the hands of the family, which is now believed to be extinct, and came into the possession of a New York collector of antiques. From him it was secured by Mr. Tappen's colleagues and presented to him just two hundred years after its first presentation for exactly similar reasons.

Mr. Tappen has been President of the Clearing-house Association twice, Vice-President of the Metropolitan Trust Company, a director of the Astor National Bank and Queen Insurance Company, and a trustee of the Royal Insurance Company. He married Sarah A. B. Littell.

The Tappens of New York have been characterized from the first by vigor, executive ability, and conservative patriotism. The founder was one of the greatest real-estate operators of his period, and the present head, seven generations afterwards, is one of the leaders of the financial world. The intervening links have been men of similar tastes and tendencies. They have cared little for the pomp and glory of life, but have possessed a deep faith in the great gospel of work, and the fruits of their labor have usually been dispensed in the forms of hospitality, philanthropy, and charity.

Van Buren

From a steel engraving.

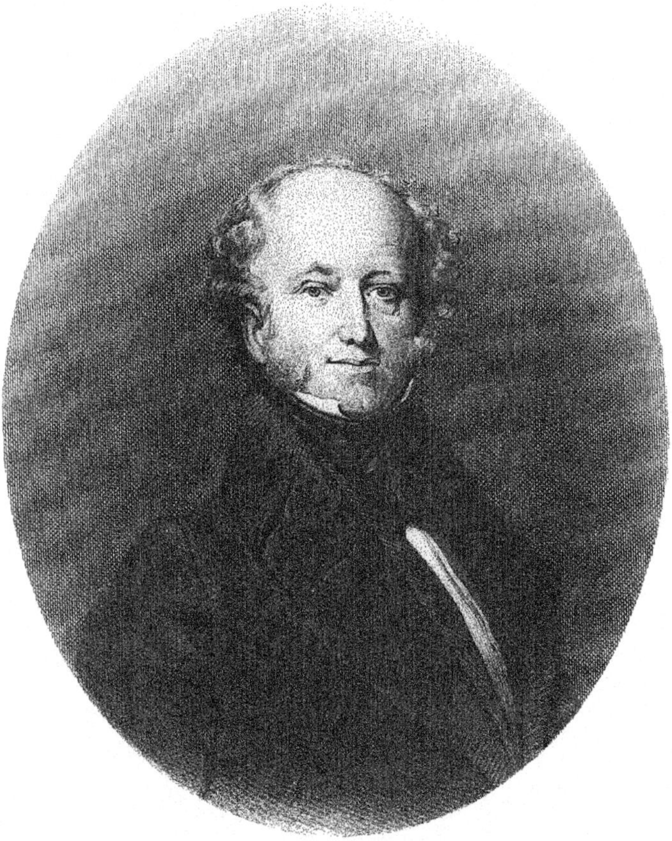

XXXVI

VAN BUREN

WHEN the patroons had secured the magnificent grants of virgin territory which, according to their hopes and ambitions, were to become populous and opulent feudal estates in years to be, their first care was to obtain settlers in the Old World to constitute a vassal yeomanry in the New. According to the means, the influence, or ability of these landed proprietors, or their agents, were the numbers and quality of the colonists whom they thus secured. While nearly all of those who crossed the sea in the middle of the seventeenth century were of the same general class, namely, vigorous and intelligent peasantry or artisans, there was considerable difference in their character and accomplishments. They varied from stern, religious, and energetic Scotch and Huguenots, to easy-going and unambitious Dutch farmers. It must be said that nearly all of the tenantry were admirable morally. In many cases, we know that they were certified to by their pastors at home; in other instances, we find allusions in the archives to instructions to agents to secure agriculturists of probity and good name. Further evidence is shown by the infrequency of crime and vice in the early Knickerbocker years.

In this respect, the Dutch West India Company and the patroons are entitled to the gratitude of prosperity. In securing good men and women, they builded better than they knew, and assured to the new community beyond the ocean a moral, mental, and physical strength which is seldom found in colonies, based more or less upon commercial considerations. Here Kiliaen Van Rensselaer is entitled to special consideration. He appears to have taken greater precautions in the selection of his tenants than any other of the leading men of the time. As far as possible, he chose young men, especially young married men.

Cornelius Maessen the Founder He had an eye for the future as well as for the present. Among his colonists was Cornelius Maessen, who emigrated from Buren, a village in the western part of Gelderland, lying a few miles from the River Rhine.

Unfortunately, the records do not show whether he was a native of the place. At that time such names as Van Buren were not family names in our sense of the word, but adjective phrases, indicating nativity or accidental or legal connection with a place. Cornelius himself did not use the name Van Buren, so far as is known, but signed himself Cornelius Maessen, which in English would be Cornelius, the son of Maes. It was his son, Martin, who seems to have first used the geographical name, and who signed himself Martin, or Marten, Cornelissen Van Beuren.

The founder sailed from the Netherlands in 1631, bringing with him a young wife, Catalyntje Martense, and a son, Marten, or Martin, who, according to an ancient legal document, was born in Houten, a village not far from Buren. On the voyage a second son, Hendrick, was born. This fact he used in later life to claim the honor of being the first Dutchman born in the New World. The family came over in the stout craft *Rensselaerswyck,* which, as the name indicates, was employed by the great patroon for the transportation of his tenants, servants, and supplies.

On reaching the New World, he stopped a brief time at New Amsterdam, where probably he looked with amazement at the funny little fort which Governor Pieter Minuit had improved, and at the wigwams which were to be found a short distance from the settlement. He proceeded up the river to a point a little below Greenbush, which was then known as Papsknee. Here he settled on a farm leased from Kiliaen Van Rensselaer. The few glimpses which the student is able to obtain of this period show a wise administration on the part of the patroon. He charged little or nothing for bringing over the colonists, and when they settled upon his land, he gave them all the necessary supplies and aided them in clearing the soil and making a home. In return, he asked one-tenth of the product of the soil and a quasi-feudal allegiance to him in his capacity as patroon. Compared with the Factor's Agreements of the Southern States, where the landlord and tenant divide the produce of the land equally, or those of the West, where the owner takes one-third and the tenant two thirds, Kiliaen's system seems to have been singularly generous.

Cornelis was not a poor farmer, like many of the emigrants of his time. He brought with him some property and a man servant or farm-hand, Cornelis Teunissen, who afterwards became a trader and commissary. The career of the first Van Buren was quiet and uneventful. His land was fertile, and under his management yielded large crops. One year the records show that he paid a tithe-rent of one hundred bushels of grain and a small amount of garden produce, which would indicate a total crop of over one thousand bushels of grain alone. He invested his money in real estate, one tract of which was a farm on the Island of Manhattan, next to the land belonging to Governor Wouter Van Twiller. His farm lay between Christopher and Fourteenth streets, and ran from a line west of Broadway down to the North River. Cornelis left four sons and one daughter. The latter married Dirck Wesserse (Ten Broeck), merchant, who afterwards became Recorder and Mayor of Albany, and a major in Colonel Pieter Schuyler's famous regiment.

One of the sons, Maes, for some unknown reason, adopted the family name of Bloemingdael, which probably represented the poetic title of his farm. From him comes the Bloomingdale family of New York, who genealogically are Van Burens. [Maes Bloemingdael]

Martin [1629] was a substantial citizen, who, after he came of age, settled at Albany. He was active in local affairs, and in 1700 was captain of a military company in Colonel Pieter Schuyler's regiment. He married twice: first, Maritje Quackenbosch, and, second, Tanneke Adams, widow. He was the ancestor of the President.

Captain Mattin

Hendrick [1631] remained in the neighborhood of the paternal home. He was a rich farmer and a devout member of the Dutch Reformed Church. During the Indian outbreak of 1663 he proved himself a brave soldier. He died leaving five children.

Hendrick the Devout

The third generation found the family well established at Albany, near Greenbush. Cornelius, son of Martin, married Ariaantje Gerritse Vandenberg, by whom he had one son. Cornelia, his sister, married Robert Teunise Van Deusen, who was the head of the family of that name. Peter married Ariaantje Barentse Meindersen. Martin, the most prominent figure of this generation, was a freeholder of Rensselaerwyck in 1720, and a leading member of the Dutch Church in Albany. He was twice married.

Martin the Deacon

The fourth generation repeated the experience of the third. The Van Burens grew in numbers, influence, and wealth. Among the more conspicuous members were the following: Tobias [1690], son of Cornelius, who became the ancestor of the Ulster County branch; he inherited a fortune from his father and a small estate from his grandfather, Martin. Marritje [1701], daughter of Martin, married Johannes Vosburgh, a prominent member of the family of that name. Barent [1702], her brother, was a wealthy farmer, who married twice: first, Margrietje Van Vechten, and, second, Mrs. Catalyntje Van Buren Schermerhorn, and had issue by both. Martin [1705], another brother, married Thenotje Vanderberg. Tobias [1710] married Marritje Hun, by whom he had one son. Other sons of Martin in this generation by his second wife, Maria Vandenberg, were Petrus [1723], who married Marritje Vanderpoel; Johannes, or John [1725], who married Marritje Briesch; Benjamin [1731], who married Cornelia Salisbury;

Barent the Wealthy

Tobias [1737], who married Catalyntje Witbeck. The children of Peter in this generation were Cornelius [1693], who married Maria Litner; Barent [1695], who married Maria Winne, and Tobias [1697], who married Anna Goes or Hoes.

In the fifth generation several members are noteworthy. Peter [1733], son of Martin, married Catharine Quackenbosch. They had a large plantation near Kinderhook, and were the godparents of President Van Buren. Abraham [1737] married Maria Goes Van Alen. They are best known as the parents of the President. *Captain Abraham* Abraham was a fine type of a revolutionary patriot. He was a strong advocate of popular rights before the Revolution, and upon the breaking out of hostilities was among the first, if not the first in Kinderhook, to enlist under the colonial banners. He rose to be a captain in the regiment commanded by Colonel Abraham Van Alstyne, a maternal relative.

Of the sixth generation, the most eminent was Martin [1782], eighth President of the United States. A remarkable memory, great physical and mental vigor, and infinite patience combined to make him successful in life. He took advantage of such educational facilities as were to be found in Columbia County in the latter part of the eighteenth century, and began to read law when a boy of fourteen years. *Martin the President* He worked tirelessly for seven years, serving as office-boy, messenger, clerk, copyist, practitioner in constables' courts, and collector.

In the evening he spent his time at debating clubs, and before he attained his majority had become noted for his logical power as well as eloquence. He displayed a love for politics from youth, and at eighteen was a member of a political convention. He was admitted to the bar when coming of age, and opened a law office at Kinderhook with his half-brother, James I. Van Alen. The same year he was a vigorous speaker in the gubernatorial campaign, and had the satisfaction of seeing his candidate, General Morgan Lewis, elected to the executive chair. He at once became prominent in State politics; in 1807, he was a leader of the movement in favor of Daniel D. Tompkins against his former friend, Lewis, and was again with the victors. Shortly afterward, as a reward for his services, he was appointed Surrogate of Columbia County by Governor Tompkins, displacing his half-brother, who belonged to the Lewis faction. In 1813, the balance of power shifted, and Van Alen replaced him in turn.

By 1811, he had become one of the State leaders of his party, and the following year he was elected to the Senate as a Clinton Republican, defeating Edward P. Livingston, who was supposed to be invincible. In 1815, the Attorney-Generalship was awarded to him, and the following year he was re-elected to the Senate. He removed to Albany, where he formed a partnership with Benjamin F. Butler. In the same twelve-month he made himself a foremost advocate of the Erie Canal. Politics at this period was in a chaotic state, the main parties being broken up into factions, which were more bitter toward one another than toward the opposition. Yet, out of these conditions, with a masterly skill for organization, Martin so manipulated personal and political forces that in 1821 he was elected to the United States Senate, being only thirty-nine years of age.

His course at the Federal capital was marked with the same tact and shrewdness as at Albany. He seemed to divine what the people wanted, and was in nearly every instance at the head of each successful measure. He had the rare genius of knowing when to keep silent. Re-elected to the Senate in 1827, he resigned to become Governor of New York in 1828. The same year he was the most distinguished advocate of General Andrew Jackson, who, when elected, made the New York diplomat his Secretary of State. In 1832 he was elected Vice-President, and as such was President of the Senate. Here he astonished his enemies by displaying imperturbable suavity and absolute fairness, treating friend and foe with equal consideration. In 1836, he was elected President of the United States. In this campaign may be seen the best evidence of his matchless craft. He was championed in the South as "a Northern man with Southern principles," while in the North he was heralded as "the apostle of progress and enlightenment." In 1840, he was renominated, but his star was now descendant, General Harrison being elected by an electoral vote of almost four to one. During the forty years after his retirement, he took a deep interest in public affairs, and exerted an appreciable influence upon the policy of his party, if not of the nation. He married Hannah Hoes, a kinswoman of his mother, by whom he had four children.

John Dash, the merchant [1811], was graduated from Columbia (1829), became a lawyer, and afterwards a successful importer. He retired from business when about forty with a large fortune, and led a life of study, in which he paid great attention to political topics, financial legislation, and the theories of taxation. He was one of the first to enunciate the modern theories of currency and to argue for a gold basis for all money. Lawrence [1783], a brother of the President, was a Kinderhook farmer, who, during the War of 1812, won distinction as a soldier and rose to be a major. *John Dash, Financier*

Major Lawrence

In the seventh generation the chief personage was Abraham [1807], son of the President. He was graduated from the United States Military Academy at West Point (1827), and made an enviable record as a soldier. He resigned in 1837 to become the President's secretary, but took up arms during the Mexican War, where he was brevetted for bravery. He married Angelica Singleton of South Carolina, who acted as mistress of the White House during her father-in-law's Administration. *Colonel Abraham*

John [1810], another son of the President, better known as "Prince John," from his manners and appearance, was graduated from Yale (1828), and admitted to the bar in 1830. A year afterwards he was *attaché* of the United States Legation at the Court of St. James, and Attorney-General of New York State in 1845. Eminent as a lawyer, orator, and politician, he was also a society leader up to the time of his death. He married Elizabeth Vanderpoel, by whom he had one daughter. *Prince John*

John Dash, Jr. [1838], was educated at Harvard and the

Rensselaer Polytechnic. He entered the Engineer Corps of the United States Navy in the Civil War, and served in that branch of the service until 1868. In 1876, he was State Engineer and Surveyor. He has written many valuable works upon mechanical science and other technical topics.

John D. II., Engineer

Robert [1843], son of John A., was graduated from the Rensselaer Polytechnic (1864) with honors. He served as an expert mining engineer in the Lake Superior copper district, and in 1866 entered the service of the city of Brooklyn as assistant engineer of the water works. In 1877, he became chief engineer, which position he still holds.

Robert, Engineer

The eighth generation was well represented by Singleton [1840], who was graduated from Columbia Law School (1865) and died in 1879; Frank Roe, who was graduated from Columbia College (1863) and thereafter received the degree of A.M.; Martin, who was graduated from Columbia College (1866); and Howard, who was graduated from Columbia Law School in 1878 and settled in Nyack, N. Y.

The Van Burens, outside of their great son, Martin, may be compared with many other Knickerbocker families, being marked by the same probity, thrift, patriotism, piety, and valor. Martin was a singular blossom of his race. He was one of the greatest politicians the United States ever produced, and understood the difficult art of managing human beings so well that he may be classed with such historical personages as Richelieu and Mazzini, but, unlike these great masters, he does not seem to have had any high ideal or master passion, unless it were the love of power or the aggrandizement of self. To him more than to any other political leader, belongs the onus of having made the doctrine of " to the victors belong the spoils " an organic part of the American political system. Careless writers have charged it to General Jackson. It was, of course, applied on a large scale during the latter's Administration, but the real actor was the keen-eyed intellectual Secretary of State, and not the bluff, big-hearted President. Beneath his graceful tact there was much fun and sterling humor. His best *bon mot* was that which tradition says he delivered to Queen Adelaide at a royal reception at the Court of St. James. She had the tactlessness to ask him how far back he could trace his ancestry. He bowed with the grace of a courtier as he responded "As far back as Kinderhook, your Majesty."

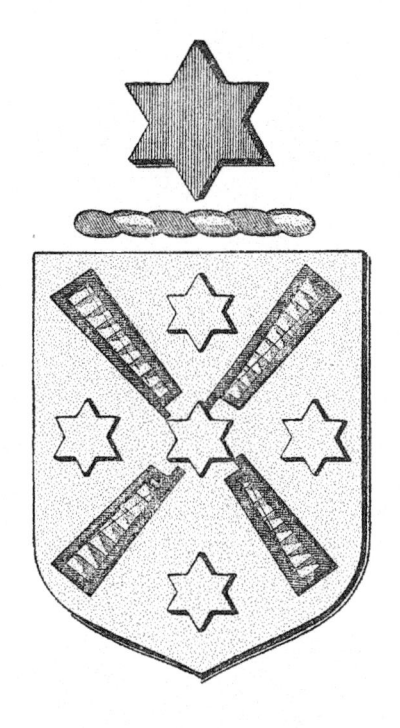

Van Cortlandt

Pierre Van Cortlandt
From the painting by J. W. Jarvis

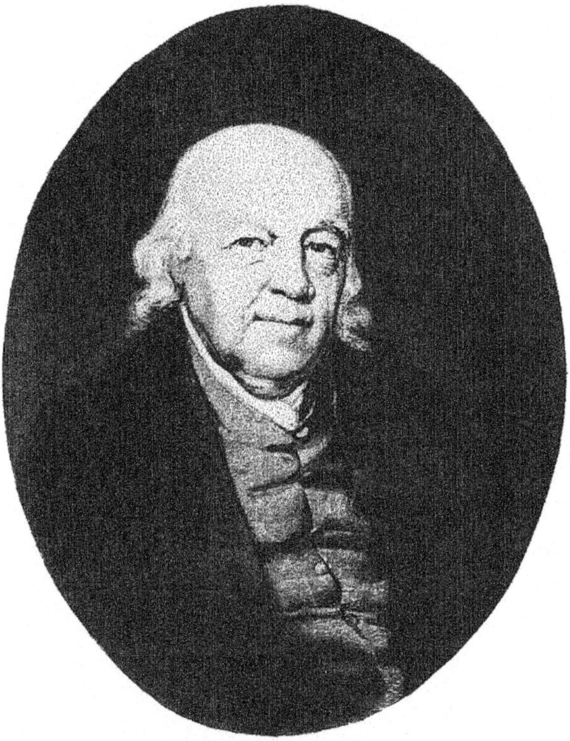

XXXVII

VAN CORTLANDT

THE sixteenth century was a period of disorder in Europe. Beside the religious and dynastic disturbances in the West, there were national and political struggles in the East. Sweden, Russia, Poland, Livonia, and the smaller principalities were constantly at war and undergoing the ravages of hostile armies. The Duchy of Courland was at one time a portion of Livonia, and enjoyed a semi-autonomous constitution. In 1561, it was ceded to Lithuania, and thereafter it became a part of Poland by the amalgamation of this kingdom with the former.

The population was a mixture of Letts, Russians, Lithuanians, Poles, Germans, and Scandinavians. Racially, it was Slav, Teuton, and Norseman. The people were brave, intelligent, and progressive, but bound by feudal customs and laws, necessitated by their surroundings. The Courland Dukes were on friendly terms with the Netherlands and frequently exchanged courtesies with the latter land in times of both peace and war. They had representatives equivalent to the consuls of to-day at the Dutch capital and leading cities. These were either relatives of the Ducal family, or gentlemen of their court. Unlike consuls, they had a quasi-military character, corresponding to the military *attachés* of the present age. Frequently these representatives became attached to the land to which they were accredited, and settled there permanently. One of this type was the Right Honorable Steven Van Cortlandt.

<small>Right Hon. Steven</small>

The name Van Cortlandt was the Dutch equivalent of Courland, referring to the land which Steven or his ancestor represented. Steven's oldest son, Oloff Stevense, was brought up as a gentleman of the period, and thoroughly trained in the profession of arms. When a young man he had become so expert a soldier that when he applied for service in the Dutch West India Company, he was engaged as an officer. In 1638, he was detailed to accompany Governor William Kieft, who had been appointed to succeed Wouter Van Twiller in the administration of the government of the New Netherlands. He arrived in New Amsterdam in March of that year, and in the following year was appointed "commissary of cargoes," or collector of customs. Four years afterwards he was made Keeper of the Public Stores, one of the most responsible posts of that time. In 1648, he resigned his office, became a freeman of the city, and began business as a merchant and brewer.

<small>Oloff the Founder</small>

In both callings he was remarkably successful, becoming before he died one of the wealthiest men on Manhattan Island. His military knowledge was so great that in 1849 he was elected Colonel of the City Guard. In 1645, he had been appointed one of the "Eight Men" (or Town Council), and, in 1649, one of the "Nine Men." In 1654, he was made schepen, and in 1655 Burgomaster or Mayor. He remained chief magistrate until the English conquest in 1664. His high abilities soon gained him the respect and confidence of the English Government, for which he acted as councillor and advisor up to his death in 1684. He married Annetje Loockermanns, by whom he had two sons and five daughters.

The two sons inherited their father's civic and commercial talents. Stephanus, the elder [1643], was the most eminent man of the province after it had become English territory. He was educated by the learned clergymen of New Amsterdam, and when he came of age was a fine scholar and a

<small>Judge Stephanus</small>

capable merchant. From this time on until his death his career was busy and brilliant. Among the positions he held were those of Judge, Ensign (1668), Captain, Colonel, Mayor (1677), Privy Councillor, Chief Justice, Judge of the Court of Common Pleas, Justice of the Supreme Court, Commissioner of Revenue, Deputy Auditor-General, and Deputy-Secretary of New York. The fortune which he inherited he increased by his own exertions, and invested it in real estate. In 1683, he bought 83,000 acres on the east side of the Hudson, which in 1697 was erected into the lordship and manor of Cortlandt. He also purchased great holdings on the west side of the Hudson, on Long Island, and in Sussex County, N. J.

At the time of his death he must have been seized of more than two hundred thousand acres, valued at over a million dollars. Upon the manor his son Johannes built a fort which was converted into a dwelling-house by Stephanus. *Johannes* The walls were of stone, nearly three feet thick, pierced with loop-holes for fire-arms. It stood near the mouth of the Croton River and has been the centre of social and intellectual life from that time to the present day. It is still in the possession of the founder's descendants. Stephanus married Gertrude Schuyler, by whom he had fourteen children. Five of his daughters made brilliant marriages, and became the maternal heads of many distinguished families: Anne wedding Stephen de Lancey; Margaret, Samuel Bayard; Maria, Killian Van Rensselaer; Gertrude, Henry Beekman, and Cornelia, Colonel John Schuyler.

Jacobus [1658], the youngest son of the founder, was a New York merchant and man of affairs. He had an estate at Yonkers, which was continuously held by his descendants until *Jacobus the* 1889, when it was purchased by the City of New York *Merchant* for public purposes, and appropriately named "Van Cortlandt Park." He was Alderman, Assemblyman, and, in 1719, Mayor of the City of New York. He owned a large estate at Bedford, Westchester County, of which a portion descended to John Jay, who built upon it a handsome mansion. Jacobus married Eva Philipse, by whom he had one son, Frederick [1698].

Three sons in the third generation were famous. Johannes, oldest son of Stephanus, married Anne Sophia Van Schaack, by whom he had a daughter, Gertrude, who married Philip Ver Plank. Johannes was a merchant and landed proprietor and active in benevolent work.

Philip [1683], the third son of Stephanus, was prominent in mercantile and public life. He was made a Councillor of the Province by Governor Montgomerie in 1730, which office he retained until his death, in 1746. He was made a Commissioner for the Crown in nearly all the important issues of his time. His wife was Catherine de Peyster, by whom he had five sons and one daughter.

Philip the Councillor

Frederick [1698], the son of Jacobus, was a man of great promise, who died in early manhood. According to the records, he was winning, learned, charitable, and devout. He married Frances Jay, by whom he had two sons.

In the fourth generation occurred the American Revolution, a political event of such far-reaching power that it turned father against son and brother against brother. Nearly all the old families of the State were affected, and among them the Van Cortlandts.

Stephen [1710], the oldest of the family, was marked by strong Royalist tendencies, which he transmitted to his children. He married Mary Walton Ricketts, by whom he had two sons, Philip and William Ricketts. Of these, Philip [1739] became a British soldier, rising to the rank of colonel. He married Catherine, daughter of Jacob Ogden, by whom he had twenty-three children. Five of his sons joined the British Army.

Colonel Stephen

Pierre [1721], the youngest son of Philip, inherited the manor, and early in life became prominent in the province. He served seven years in the Assembly, and while there was an eloquent and dauntless advocate for the rights of his people against those of the Crown. He was a member of the Provincial Convention, Council of Safety, and the Provincial Congress. When the province of New York organized

Pierre the Lieutenant-Governor

its own State Government in 1777, he was chosen Lieutenant-Governor, and held that office for eighteen years. He could have been re-elected, but declined on the score of age and ill-health. He presided at the Convention which formed the first State Constitution, and in every way stamped himself upon the political and social events of the time.

Pierre's course must have been difficult and painful. His favorite nephew, the head of the family, was an officer in the British Army, and many of his friends and relatives were enthusiastic Royalists. Their influence and that of many of the society leaders of the time were brought to bear upon Van Cortlandt to induce him to change his political views. In 1774, Governor William Tryon went from New York to Croton to call upon the "rebel Van Cortlandts," as they were then termed, Pierre having just been elected to the Colonial Assembly, and his son Philip having just completed his professional studies. To the former the Governor offered large grants of land and a probable title; to the latter, a commission as major in the royal army. Both father and son refused the offers, and Tryon returned disappointed to New York.

During the war Pierre entertained Washington, Franklin, Lafayette, Rochambeau, and other generals at the Manor-house; when the place was threatened by the British Army in New York, he removed his wife and children to one of the Livingston farms at Rhinebeck. The stout-hearted commoner was acting-marshal of the "Equestrian Provincial Congress." This body, during the Revolution, was frequently obliged to change quarters, and made the necessary journey upon horseback. Several times while marching they received dispatches from General Washington requiring official action. The bugler would sound halt; they would wheel their horses into a hollow square; there put through legislation in approved parliamentary style, and announce adjournment by the bugle call, when they would break into fours and proceed on their way. Pierre married Joanna Livingston, his second cousin, by whom he had eight children.

The two sons of Frederick, of the junior branch, were Colonel James, the patriot, and Augustus, the loyalist. Colonel James was a bluff, kind-hearted land-owner, who was as gentle in peace as he was terrible in war. He was idolized by the people of his district, especially by the poor, in whom he took a paternal interest. He married Elizabeth Cuyler. Augustus was a student and bookworm, who in early manhood became a clerk of the Common Council of New York City, and held that office for many years. At the outbreak of the Revolution he foresaw the chaotic conditions that were to ensue, and to preserve the city records he built, upon his own responsibility, and at his own expense, a great vault, in his own garden, of stone and brick, laid in cement so as to be water- and air-tight. To this he removed three cart-loads of official documents, and kept them unharmed during the war, and returned them in excellent condition after peace was declared in 1783. Of him a wit of the time said: "While other men were quarrelling about their duty to liberty and to the King, August Van Cortlandt saw only his duty to his books." He married Helen Barclay, by whom he had two daughters.

Col. James the Patriot

Augustus the Bookworm

In the fifth generation two of the sons of Lieutenant-Governor Pierre rose to prominence: General Philip [1749] and Pierre II. [1762]. Philip enlisted in the American Army in 1775, when he was commissioned lieutenant-colonel. The following year he was made colonel, and for his brilliant services during the Revolution a brigadier-general. He took part in the two decisive battles of the struggle, Saratoga and Yorktown, witnessing the surrender of Burgoyne at the one and of Cornwallis at the other.

Gen. Philip

His greatest exploit was the part he played in the Indian campaign in 1779. For this style of fighting, so different from that which prevailed among civilized people, he seemed to have an especial genius. For days he could remain with scarcely any sleep or food. He was a wonderful shot, and possessed a singular knowledge of woodcraft. He either knew or divined Indian strategy, and before he had been in the Indian territory thirty days was called by the redskins "The Great White Devil." Strangely enough, among the Indians he fought and routed were levies which had been brought from the far West by his cousin, Colonel De Peyster. Upon the return of peace he went into public life, and was successively Assemblyman, Senator, and Congressman from Westchester, holding the last office from 1793 to 1809. He never married.

Pierre, his brother, was graduated at Rutgers in 1783, studied law with Alexander Hamilton, but relinquished practice to attend to public affairs and the management of his property. He was Congressman, 1811–1812; Major-General of militia, a Presidential elector for Jefferson in 1800, and for William Henry Harrison in 1840. He took a deep interest in local matters, and for fifteen years was President of the Westchester County Bank. He was strenuous in developing trade and manufactures in that county, and used his influence and wealth to favor that end. He married, first, Catherine, daughter of Governor George Clinton, and, second, Ann, daughter of John Stevenson, by whom he had one child, Pierre. *Major-Gen. Piette*

Colonel Pierre [1815], the head of the family in the sixth generation, was a landed proprietor, a society leader, gifted with a splendid physique. During his long life of seventy years he was one of the most prominent men in Westchester and Dutchess counties. He administered the Manor-house according to its traditions, and entertained nearly all the leading people of the county within its portals. He married Catharine, daughter of Dr. Theodoric Romeyn Beck, the founder of Medical Jurisprudence. The issue of this happy union comprised Catharine Teresa Romeyn, who married the Rev. John Rutherford Mathews; Pierre Van Cortlandt, who died 1879; Romeyn Beck, who died 1843; Captain James Stevenson; Theodoric Romeyn, who died in 1880; Ann Stevenson, and Philip, who died 1858. *Col. Pierre*

Captain James Stevenson [1843], the head of the seventh generation, inherited the patriotic character of his ancestors. At the breaking out of the Civil War, though *Captain James S.*

but eighteen years of age, he volunteered, and served brilliantly through the entire conflict. He became aide-de-camp to General Corcoran, and afterwards served in the New York One Hundred and Fifty-fifth, and lastly in the New York Twenty-second Cavalry. He was with the last-named body during Sheridan's historical campaign. He was admitted to the Society of the Cincinnati in 1885, upon the death of his father, Colonel Pierre.

Catharine T. R. Van Cortlandt Mathews, who now occupies the Manor ferry-house, which is converted into a handsome home not far from the Manor-house, is an historical and genealogical student of note, and has contributed largely, as did her mother, to the biographical literature of the State. She has preserved many relics of the race, some of which run back to Oloff, the founder in America.

The Van Cortlandt family belongs to a rare type. From its foundation in the New Netherlands, it has owned great holdings of real estate and enjoyed the advantages of wealth, education, and social prestige. None of its members have entered trade, and but a few have been merchants or professional men. They have produced many men of public affairs, of whom a majority have been statesmen of rare ability. Their lives have been devoted to the management of estates, and to the performance of their duties as parents, citizens, and Christians. From the time of Oloff down, they have brought to the New World the finest products of European art, paintings, miniatures, jewels, tapestries, elegant furniture, marvellous products of the loom, beautiful apparel, fine books, the choicest glass, porcelain, and household decorations. These have served as object-lessons to a community, whose growing wealth required some directing influence to confine it to the channels of good taste, and prevented its departure into those of vulgar luxury and ostentatious display. With the material side of art has gone the spiritual side. They have cultivated noble literature, the best music, the finest manners, and the broadest religious thought. These admirable features of modern life can only be brought into a new community by those who have wealth and wisdom. In this respect, the

hold a high place in the annals of the Empire they may not have impressed themselves upon high finance as other families have done, they first in fostering the development of the civic and f New York life.

Van Cott

XXXVIII

VAN COTT

AMONG the early settlers of New Amsterdam was Claes Cornelise Van Cott, who came to the New Netherlands in 1652. He belonged to Northern Holland, the name being taken from the village of Cott or Catt, both forms being employed by the family, one branch of which has contracted it to Catt. Here for many generations it had prospered, supplying numerous sons to the Dutch navies and armies. In the blood ran a strong love for adventure which, added to a superb physique, made them famous in that part of the country. Their maritime and martial prowess was theirs by descent, as the family originally had come from Scandinavia, where it had made its record among the fierce Vikings of the early centuries.

The old Dutch records give the names of many Van Cotts in the rosters of its navies and armies, but in the latter part of the sixteenth and seventeenth centuries the only reference that has been found indicates that they were among the brave men that fought the Spanish rule, and that they gave many of their sons upon the altars of religious and political liberty.

Claes crossed the ocean to New Amsterdam in 1652. He was a young man with but little money, his family having lost largely in the wars which preceded that time. He staid a few years on Manhattan Island and then crossed the East River to the village of Brooklyn and took up a large farm, which he worked, with more or less profit, until about 1680. Allured by convenience of access to New York, he removed to Bushwick, which he made his final residence and where he died about 1692.

In the second generation, Cornelius, Jr., was the chief figure. After coming of age, he removed to Flushing, where he founded the Queens County branch of his race. His wife was Antie Sprung, a wealthy Dutch belle, who brought him an estate that, added to his own, made him a wealthy man. His brother Jan remained upon the paternal homestead and led the life of an industrious and thrifty farmer.

In the third generation, Cornelius of Flushing was notable for his public spirit and enterprise. He was active in road building and the development of local commerce. He perceived the future importance of Long Island Sound as a mercantile highway, and either owned or was interested in a number of sloops whose home port was Flushing, and which traded with New York, Connecticut, and the eastern end of Long Island. Many offices of honor were held by him both in civil and ecclesiastical matters. He was a devout churchman and was famous for his charity and generous hospitality.

David [1720], of the fourth generation, bore a substantial resemblance to his distinguished uncle Cornelius. He was a farmer, trader, and public-spirited citizen. During the Revolution, he rendered many services to the Colonial armies and was one of the sturdy Dutch burghers who went down to defeat in the Battle of Long Island. The war destroyed his property, and the privations he endured broke down his constitution. He died a few years after the conclusion of peace. His wife was Nellie Praa.

In the fifth generation, Cornelius was a busy and progressive agriculturist, and took a deep interest in local and national affairs. He was also a revolutionist, like his father, and was wounded by the British during the campaign of Long Island.

At the conclusion of the war he returned to Brooklyn, where he passed the remainder of his days. He was popular in church circles, and his daughter Cornelia was the belle of Brooklyn in the latter part of the eighteenth century. She married John Debevoise, the head of the Debevoise family.

Gabriel [1780] was the chief member of the sixth generation. He received an excellent education and on reaching manhood's estate he gave up farming and went to Manhattan, where he entered commercial life. He was an excellent business man and built up a large trade and handsome fortune. He established business connections with different places in this country, Nova Scotia, New Brunswick, and Great Britain. A man of the highest honor himself, he gave almost unlimited credit to those with whom he was on friendly business relations. This worked very well in peace, but proved ruinous in time of war. The breaking out of the conflict with Great Britain in 1812 taught him the stern lesson that private rights and obligations have little or no meaning when nations are engaged in fierce combat. What with the blockade and embargo, the refusal of correspondents to honor drafts or pay just debts, he saw his business destroyed and his fortune swept away. The worry and strain proved too much for him, and, with the little money he had remaining, he removed to Smithtown, Long Island, and there started a new career. There is something pathetic in his sense of duty. He labored long and well with only one ambition, and that was to pay off his own debts which had been contracted during, and prior to, 1812. With remarkable resolution, he toiled until this was accomplished, and thereafter accumulated enough to leave fortunes to his children. If credit is to be bestowed upon the Revolutionary Van Cotts, much more belongs to this stern, upright man, who consecrated his life to the performance of what he regarded as a duty. Gabriel was twice married, the sons by his first wife being Richard [1805], Joshua [1815], and Cornelius, and by his second wife, Thomas and Gabriel. All of these reached manhood's estate, married, and had issue. Richard, the oldest, was a New York merchant who was prominent in the first half of the nineteenth century. His wife was Caroline Case, by whom he had four children.

The leader of the generation was the Hon. Joshua M., who was educated in New York, and at Yale, and after graduation from that University was admitted to the bar. He made a specialty of Admiralty cases. In this important branch of the law, he became one of the great masters and was retained in many of the most important litigations of his time. Though a man of great public spirit and a polished speaker, he cared little for office and refused many nominations and positions that were tendered to him by the political leaders of the State. The only exceptions he made to this rule were when he accepted the position of Corporation Counsel of Brooklyn, and again in 1868, when he was a Delegate-at-large to the Constitutional Convention. Up to his death, in 1896, he was a leader of the New York bar.

The eighth generation produced many men of distinction. Of the main line, the leader was Hon. Cornelius [1838], at this writing Postmaster of New York. He was educated in the city schools and in early life took up the insurance business, where he rose quickly and became Vice-president of the Ætna Insurance Company. From 1859, when he came of age, he took an active part in public affairs. In 1873, he was made a member of the Board of Fire Commissioners, serving from 1873 to 1875, and from 1879 to 1885; a larger part of the period being President of the Board. His administration should be long remembered by the many valuable reforms which he introduced; so progressive were his ideas that they aroused the antagonism of grasping property-owners and ultra-conservative citizens. His design of compelling the owners of all large buildings to use improved and convenient fire-escapes was emasculated by the politicians to the present unworthy system. He advocated larger and more numerous exits to the large stores, theatres, and churches, so as to prevent the blocking of people in a crisis or panic, which is usually produced by the outbreak of a conflagration, and insisted upon the prohibition of the ancient practice of having church and other doors which opened inward and were fastened during the hours of service.

Nearly all of his propositions were adopted in the course of time and many of the new reforms of to-day are restatements of his suggestions made twenty-five years ago.

To him belongs the credit of having called attention to the danger of fire, lightning-stroke and accident from non-insulated or poorly insulated electric wires, and the peril as well as unsightliness of large telegraph poles in the great city. Within ten years after he officially called attention to these facts, the poles were removed, the wires buried and insulated so thoroughly that the conditions as to which he gave the alarm ceased to exist. In 1887, he was elected to the State Senate, where he made an enviable record. In 1889, he became Postmaster of New York. He served his term and was reappointed to the position, which he still holds. He married Fanny Thompson, by whom he had issue.

Dr. Joshua Marsden [1861] was educated at the Brooklyn Polytechnic Institute and the Long Island College Hospital, being graduated from the latter institution in 1885, and receiving the position of interne upon graduation. In 1886, he was appointed adjunct to the chair of histology and pathologic anatomy. In 1888 he went to Europe and studied under Professor Koch in bacteriology, and Professor Rudolph Virchow in general pathology. Upon finishing his studies, he visited all the important medical laboratories in Germany and Austria, the Pasteur Institute in Paris, and the Medical Institute of London.

In 1891, he was appointed to the chair of pathology at the Long Island College Hospital. Many distinguished medical and scientific societies claim him as a member, and in several he is an officer and leader.

Alexander H. is a prominent member of the New York bar, and resides in Brooklyn. He is conspicuous in political and social circles and has served as Assistant District Attorney of King's County.

David H., another brother, was a lawyer, litterateur, and a poet. He contributed freely to the press and had begun to make a name in the world of letters, when he was suddenly stricken by death. Other members of this generation were Thomas [1834],

Wickfield [1840], and Gabriel [1844], all of whom married and had issue.

In the ninth generation Richard [1864], son of the Hon. Cornelius, took an active part in New York life. In 1897, he was elected to the Assembly, where he displayed rare ability and fidelity to duty. He married May Richardson, by whom he had issue.

Another member of this generation was Lincoln, who was graduated from Columbia in 1884 and entered the railway calling. He rose to be travelling auditor of the New York Central Railroad.

The Van Cotts have been typical Knickerbockers of the democratic type. From the first, they have been opposed to privilege and in favor of liberty, and home rule. The first of the race in the New World, Claes Cornelise, was opposed to doughty Governor Stuyvesant and on the side of the patroons and merchants. In the Revolution the race was for the colonies and against the Crown. In 1812, they were on the side of the Republic, and during the Civil War the Hon. Joshua was one of the great leaders of the Union Republican organization. In their politics they have been nearly always identified with the more progressive of the parties, but within their own organization they have been allied rather to the conservative than the radical elements. Their motto has been progress, but never haste. They have manifested a sound mind in a sound body, and in law, medicine, politics, official life, agriculture, science, and commerce, have made their mark by patient energy and indomitable will power. The family has grown with the years, and is now well distributed in New York State, with branches in four other commonwealths. Though of Dutch ancestry, they are Americans of the most pronounced type.

Vanderbilt

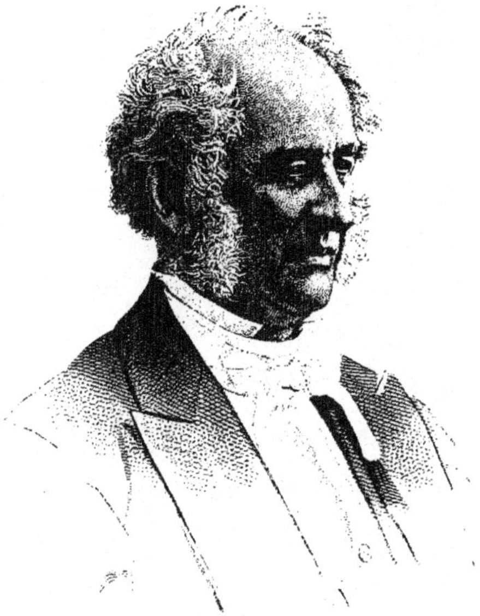

XXXIX

VANDERBILT

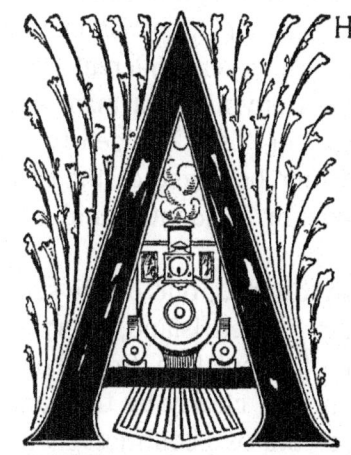

A HALF-CENTURY ago the railways of the United States were in the same condition as the coral polyp. They were a congeries of separate units — alive, but uncontrolled and unorganized. To-day they may be compared to a highly developed mammal, so thoroughly correlated that each fibre of its being is in touch and sympathy with all the rest. This change from what Herbert Spencer would call heterogeneity to homogeneity was, of course, unavoidable, and would have come about in due season, no matter who the men or what the forces that might have been involved in the operation. Had the metamorphosis been slow, the country would be now in the same state as it was in 1875. The difference between existing conditions and those of a quarter-century ago are due to the swiftness of the transformation. In this evolution one man, Cornelius Vanderbilt, stands out above the rest like a giant in an ancient army of foot-soldiers.

The Vanderbilts are of Dutch origin. The first of the race in this country was Jan Aertsen Van der-bilt, a Holland farmer, who came to the New World in the first half of the seventeenth century, and who settled in the neighborhood of Brooklyn about

1650. As the name indicates, the family belonged originally to either the village of Bilt, a suburb of Utrecht, or the parish of Bilt in Frisia. Family names in old Holland were very different from those of the present time. The true patronymic of a man was the father's Christian name, with "sen" or "son" added to it. The name of the place to which the father belonged or the calling which he practised was descriptive or incidental, and not appellative.

In the second generation the family divided, one of the sons removing from Brooklyn to New Dorp, Staten Island, in 1715. There was at that time a movement of population from Long Island to Staten Island, which is shown very clearly by the same family names appearing in the records of the two counties. The separation of the Vanderbilts was soon attended by religious differences, the New Dorp branch being converted to the Moravian Church. In this, the eighteenth century, both branches increased in numbers and prosperity. They were successful farmers and pursued industrious and godly lives. Their names are found in the old church records, and at times in the civil lists of the period. Here belong John and Jeremiah Vanderbilt, stalwart members of the Provincial Congress.

In the fourth generation of the Moravian branch the leading member was Cornelius Vanderbilt. Like his forbears, he was a farmer, tilling a large amount of land on the northeast side of Staten Island. His chief farm was near the Quarantine ground, and as early as 1780 he had established a ferry to New York. He started it in order to carry his own produce to the city markets. By degrees he built up a good business in carrying freight for his neighbors, and at last made it a daily enterprise, his stout sloop leaving his wharf in the morning and returning from the city early in the evening. Among his quiet neighbors he was looked upon as a prodigy of ability and wealth. Before middle age he had acquired a competence, and when he died he left what was regarded as a fortune. He was blessed with a wife of remarkable wisdom and thrift. She took charge of the dairy, and probably the garden, and con-

Cornelius, Father of the Commodore

William H. Vanderbilt
From a steel engraving

ducted business on her own account. She invested her profits wisely, and when she died, at the age of eighty-seven, she left $50,000. From her youth, tradition says, she was a leader of Staten Island society. According to the records of the time, she attended all the weddings, christenings, funerals, and other functions, and is everywhere alluded to as "kindly, generous, loving, and extremely wise."

The characteristics of both husband and wife were transmitted to their son Cornelius, better known as "The Commodore." Born in 1794, he was the oldest of a family of nine children. He was endowed with a superb physique, and from his boyhood was a champion in all out-door sports. He had an aversion to school and to books, and a hearty love for farming, sailing, driving, and travel. His dislike of study was doubtless due to the school system in New Dorp, which was of the most conservative and repressive nature. The children were obliged to sit erect and silent upon uncomfortable wooden seats, and were punished rigorously for the slightest infraction of the rules. For a boy of superabundant health and strength, the schoolroom must have been a purgatory. At ten, the youth began to aid his father, and at twelve was a valued assistant. Before he was sixteen, he desired to go into business on his own account, and to become a boatman. Even here his common sense manifested itself. There were many watermen at the time, and he noticed that those who had the handsomest craft did the best business. He therefore applied to his mother for the loan of a hundred dollars with which to get the finest boat that he could secure. He made this request on the first day of May, 1810, twenty-six days before his birthday. His mother replied: "If by your birthday you plough, harrow, and plant with corn that lot (one of eight acres) I will advance you the money."

It was seemingly an impossible job, but the boy was equal to the emergency. He called together all his juvenile friends, told them of the conditions of the task, and agreed that if they would help him he would give them sailing excursions in return.

The youngsters were only too glad to accept the offer. They turned to, and for a fortnight that field was an ant-hill of boyish activity, every one working, and young Vanderbilt easily excelling all his companions. Not only was the work done, but in addition the boys removed every stone from the soil, and with them built a wall which is said to have increased the value of the property by $200. Young Cornelius got his boat, and the boys had their excursions. His success was immediate. He was soon the most popular boatman in the harbor, and that summer cleared $1000. In the spring of 1814, he obtained a contract from the Government for the transportation by water of supplies to the nine military posts around the city. The work was so severe that at times he was on his feet twenty-four and thirty-six hours consecutively, but he carried it through without a complaint, and made enough money to build in the fall a fine schooner, and the following year, with his brother-in-law, a still larger and swifter craft.

His success emboldened him to larger efforts, so that in 1818 he was the owner of three vessels, a comfortable home, and $9000. He astonished his friends at this point by giving up his former business and becoming the captain of a steamboat. There was a bitter prejudice against steam at the time, and the wiseacres of the day regarded his move as the height of folly, but he, with extraordinary foresight, saw the magnificent future of the new system of navigation, and went into it with characteristic energy. For twelve years he retained his position and incidentally conducted a hotel at New Brunswick, the terminus of his steamboat route. By the time he was forty years old his fortune was estimated at $500,000. When the gold excitement broke out in California, he established a passenger line to the Pacific via Nicaragua. This with his other enterprises netted for him $10,000,000 in the course of eleven years. In the meantime, he had anticipated the importance of the great trunk lines running into New York, although it may be questioned if he contemplated their unification. He bought New York and New Haven stock in 1844 by disposing of the Sound Steamboats he

The Obelisk in Central Park
Brought from Egypt by Wm H. Vanderbilt

then owned, and in 1863 he purchased a large part of the shares of the New York and Harlem Railroad, and began acquiring Hudson River shares. His next move was to consolidate the Hudson River and Harlem Railroads. In 1867, he was elected president of the New York Central Railroad. Into this road he introduced the reforms which he had applied with so much success to the other two lines. The year 1869 saw him consolidate the two companies, and also secure a controlling interest in several small roads. He died in 1877, leaving a fortune estimated at $100,000,000. He was a man of great generosity, but never allowed his name to appear in connection with giving. The chief exception to this rule was his gift of a million dollars wherewith to establish Vanderbilt University in Tennessee. He was twice married: to Sophia Johnson in 1813, and to Frances Crawford in 1869. There were twelve children by the first union, but none by the second.

Of the daughters, Phebe [1815] married James M. Cross; Ethelinda [1818], Daniel B. Allen; Emily [1823], William K. Thorn; Eliza [1828], George Osgood; Sophia [1830], Daniel Torrance; Maria Alecia [1831], N. La Bau; Catherine [1834], first, Smith Parker, and afterwards, Gustave Lafitte ; Marie Louise [1835], first, Horace Clark, and second, Robert Niven.

Of the three sons, only one married and had issue. This was William Henry [1821]. He began commercial life at the age of seventeen, and attracted notice in the business world by his singular success in the management of the Staten Island Railroad, of which he was made receiver by the court. This may be regarded as his education in railroad finance. His next step forward was when he was chosen vice-president of the Harlem and Hudson River Roads in 1864, and thereafter of the New York Central. His management of these corporations was marked by tact and wisdom. He secured control of the Canada Southern and the Michigan Central Roads. Between 1877 and 1880 he obtained control of the Chicago and Northwestern, and of the Cleveland, Columbus, Cincinnati, and Indianapolis Railroads. The year 1879 witnessed the formation of the largest railroad syndicate which had yet been organized. To it he sold 250,000 shares of his New York Central stock. He died in 1885. He increased the wealth of Vanderbilt University by nearly $400,000; he gave to the College of Physicians and Surgeons (Columbia) a new building, costing $500,000; he paid the expenses ($103,000) incurred in removing the obelisk from Egypt to Central Park, and distributed large amounts of money among many charities and church works. His wife was Maria Louise Kissam, whom he married in 1840, and by whom he had eight children.

Of the daughters of William Henry, Margaret Louisa married Elliot F. Shepard; Emily, William D. Sloane; Florence Adele, H. McKay Twombly; and Eliza Osgood, W. Seward Webb. Of the four sons, Cornelius [1843] married Alice Gwynne; William Kissam [1849], Alva Smith; Frederick W. [1858], Mrs. Alfred Torrance; George [1864], Edith Stuyvesant Dresser.

All of the male members of this generation have been active in New York society and commerce. Cornelius, the oldest, was carefully trained for business by his father. He was placed in the offices of the New York Central, and rose from clerk to be president. His life was exceedingly busy; he was a director in thirty-four railways, and a trustee of many institutions. He was a generous contributor to the Protestant Episcopal Church and to numerous charities and philanthropies.

Cornelius III.

The other three sons are prominent in railway affairs. Two tributes from this generation to their father deserve mention: one, the Vanderbilt Clinic, which was presented by the four sons to the College of Physicians and Surgeons, and the other, the Sloane Maternity Hospital, presented to the same college by Emily, the wife of William D. Sloane

In the next, or present generation the great-grandchildren of the Commodore are: Cornelius [1873], who married Grace Wilson; Gertrude [1876], who married Henry Payne Whitney; Alfred Gwynne [1877], who married Elsie French; Reginald [1880]; Gladys [1885]—these being the children of Cornelius; Consuelo [1877], who married the Duke of Marl-

Cornelius IV.

Residence of the late Cornelius Vanderbilt, 57th Street and Fifth Avenue

Vanderbilt

borough; William K. [1880], who married Virginia Fair; and Harold [1882] — the three being the children of William Kissam. Of this group, Cornelius has displayed high talent as a physicist, mechanical engineer, and inventor. The fact is notable, because he seems to be the first in ten generations to manifest this type of mentality

Among the descendants of the Commodore who through marriage bear other names may be mentioned members of the families of Horton, Wilmerding, Wallace, Schieffelin, Morris, Fabbri, Burden, Thorn, King, Baring, Parrish, Post, Kissell, Anthony, Hadden, Dyer, Blois, Aymar, Barker, Collins, and Souberbille.

The Vanderbilt record represents the triumph of constructive over destructive finance. The great head, the Commodore, had from his Dutch ancestry all the slow and conservative qualities which are needful in the world of moneyed affairs. To this he added an ambition, will-power, and force which were monumental. The larger part of his life was a fierce battle against rival capitalists, many of whom lived by the death of others. This was true in the world of shipping, and especially true in the railway sphere. His chief competitors were men who will go down in history as "wreckers." They owned railroads, not for the benefit of the stockholders, but of themselves. They used their position to control the stock market, and, after fleecing every person possible, they usually wound up by destroying the properties they were supposed to protect, and out of the ruins carving additional fortunes. The history of American railways for many years was the story of misappropriation and malappropriation. It is painted in the darkest colors, and to few of the figures which occupy its scenes can the historian look with pride or sympathy. Against this motley crew the old Commodore stands out in magnificent relief. In his rugged Dutch heart he knew that honesty paid in the long run, and that the greatest reward came to him who best did his duty. He made his millions not at the expense of others, but by helping others to make thousands where before they had made hundreds.

By reducing the rates for travel and traffic, by diminishing the peril, wear, and tear of railway life, by utilizing every new invention and discovery, by employing men with regard to their fitness and merit, by organizing railways as a general organizes an army, he estabished a new precedent and standard for American financiers. His descendants have but followed in his foot steps. Scores of other financiers have taken up the work, and, following the same lines, have met with the same success. The giant operations of to-day are merely repetitions on a larger scale of what the old New York Central President did forty years ago. He was the first American railway king in the true sense of the word. His kingdom was small, compared to the empires whose capitals now dot Wall Street, and his army of employees insignificant beside those which serve the huge corporations of the present year, but their systems are his system applied to new conditions, and their success is based upon the principles he laid down for his own guidance. As the prosperity of the Empire City and State is so largely a consequence of its matchless railway facilities, his name will go down to the future as one of its most useful citizens.

Van Rensselaer

Kiliaen Van Rensselaer
First Lord of the Manor

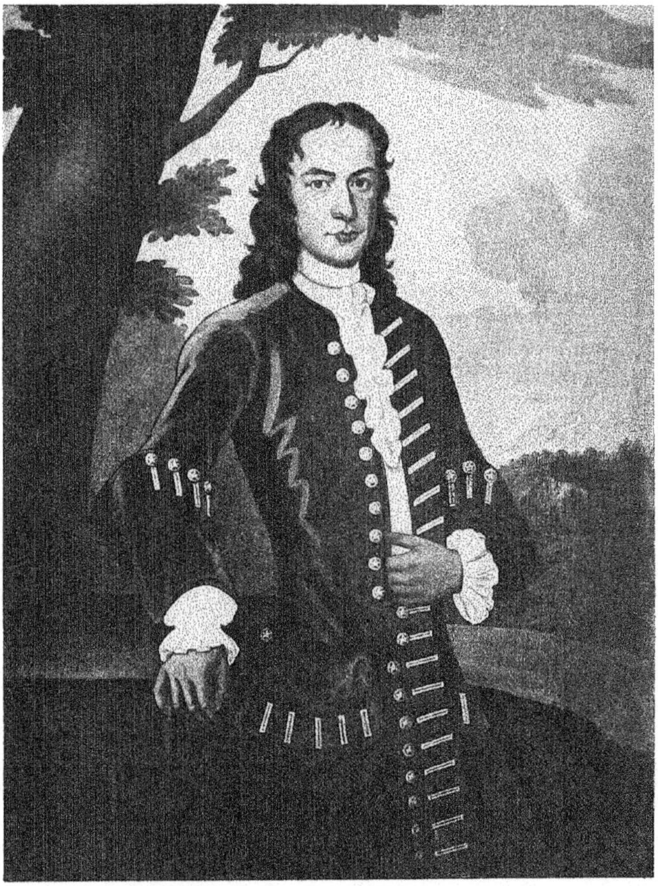

XL

VAN RENSSELAER

IF the greatness of a family is to be measured by the number of distinguished public servants it has given to the State, the Van Rensselaers are entitled to a high place on New York's roll of fame. From the first Dutch settlements to the present time, a period of thirteen generations, they have always been represented by one or more members of ability and social position in public affairs. The family will be long remembered because it was identified with the movement for establishing a landed aristocracy of the New World. It enjoyed the ancient Dutch title of Patroon, and, after the supersedure of the Dutch by English authority in America, of Lord of the Manor. They were a stalwart race and fought strenuously for their ideas. Their titles vanished in the Revolution, but their real-estate system was not abolished until the middle of the nineteenth century.

The founder of the family in America was Kiliaen Van Rensselaer, who was a wealthy Amsterdam merchant, and a leader in the famous guild of trading princes which at that time played so prominent a part in the commerce of the world. He owned large estates in the Netherlands, and was a director of the Dutch West India Company. He must

Kiliaen

have been shrewd and far-sighted. When the company took possession of land around the Hudson River, he, with his colleagues, instituted a college of nine commissioners to take charge of the new enterprise, and practically to become an *imperium in imperio*. It is needless to remark that Kiliaen was a member of this smaller body, and before a year had passed was apparently its active head. As a member of the company, he voted in favor of a liberal charter to the college, which created a number of patroons with feudal power and jurisdiction, of whom he was one of the most prominent. He was fair and just in his dealings. He might have followed the example of the Puritans and Pilgrims, and seized land without recognizing the rights of the redmen. This was too common a course in those years, and had he done it, it would have provoked neither censure nor comment.

But he sent out agents and bought the land from the Indians in 1630, and paid the owners even more than they demanded. Then with mercantile thrift he had the sale sanctioned by the college and the company under their great seal. He kept on securing other bits of choice land for seven years, when he concluded that his property was as large as he could handle with his surplus wealth. It was a magnificent estate. His agents with fine judgment had chosen a territory which composed a tract twenty-four miles wide and forty-eight miles long, containing more than seven hundred thousand acres, which now constitutes the counties of Rensselaer, Albany, and the northern part of Columbia. If the record is to be believed, he never came out to take charge of his colony, although he sent out colonists and stores with generous hand. According to tradition, however, he visited Rensselaerwyck, as he styled the colony, once or twice, but if he ever made the trips, they must have been of brief duration.

Kiliaen's wisdom was shown in another point — the selection of his colonists. As far as he could, he picked out young farmers—strong, healthy, intelligent, and married. To keep them from growing homesick, he dispatched regularly shipments of

Margare Schuyler
Wife of Stephen Van Rensselaer III.

Philip Van Rensse ae
Mayor o A bany

various goods and merchandise from home, taking care to include little articles of comfort or pleasure-giving quality, which would appeal to the better nature of his tenants. One cargo, sent in 1643, and consigned to his colony for its own use, was valued at twelve thousand eight hundred and seventy guilders—about as many dollars, according to the purchasing value of the guilder at that period. The great merchant was working not for himself, apparently, but for his children. Rensselaerwyck was to be a petty principality, of which his descendants were to be the feudal lords. At the very start he built a fort and went to the expense of equipping it with the best cannons of the time. He organized a court which dispensed justice, civil and criminal, and from which appeals were allowed to a higher tribunal. Even here the forethought of the man was well displayed. On the face of the old documents it does not appear whether these appeals lay to the college, the company, or to the highest court of the Netherlands.

As all his colonists were required to take an oath of allegiance to him, it may be inferred that the indefiniteness as to appeals was intentional, and was put there with a view to denying in the future any jurisdiction of a superior power outside of the Netherlands. This would have avoided any claim of suzerainty by the college or the company. The colony grew in prosperity and numbers, and was a formidable rival for many years to New Amsterdam. The superintendents were generally, if not always, blood relatives of the first Patroon, and men of strong personality and executive power. Two of them, Jan Baptist Van Rensselaer and Jeremias Van Rensselaer, carried the estate through all the storms and troubles of those *Jan Baptist* exciting times, and increased its value to handsome proportions. The latter possessed a chivalrous nature of the highest type. After the New Netherlands were transferred to England, there was some legal trouble in securing the *Jeremias* confirmation of the Van Rensselaer grants. Partly to evade the legal difficulties, and partly, perhaps, to tempt the man, several people of prominence advised Jeremias to take out the patents in his own name. At the time he had a large interest in the property, both as agent and as heir, and could have obtained the patent in his own name without deceit or trouble. But it is recorded that he refused the offer with the simple remark: "I am only a part heir, and I cannot defraud my sisters and brothers."

In 1695, the great Kiliaen Van Rensselaer estate was divided, the American part going to Kiliaen of Albany, son of Jeremias, for himself, his brothers and sisters, and the Holland possessions to the heirs living in that country. In 1704, Queen Anne confirmed Kiliaen's estate. This made him the first Lord of the Manor of Rensselaerwyck, of which he was also the fourth Patroon. From Kiliaen, and his brother Hendrik, have sprung all the American Van Rensselaers. The other relatives of the three generations preceding them either died childless or else remained in the Old World. Kiliaen married his cousin, Maria Van Cortlandt, by whom he had six sons and four daughters. His oldest son, Jeremias, who died unmarried, was the fifth Patroon, and his second son, Steven, the sixth. The latter's son, Stephen II., became the seventh Patroon, and married Catherine Livingston, daughter of Philip Livingston, signer of the Declaration of Independence. He built the Van Rensselaer manor-house, which in the last century was regarded as the finest colonial mansion in the Empire State. Like his ancestors, Stephen was a royal host. He entertained in a style which would have been extravagant for other citizens. To his tenants he was a kind landlord, aiding them to improve their property and the surrounding country, and often making improvements himself for their benefit. His very generosity proved paying investments. Thus he assisted several tenants in building sloops with which to navigate the Hudson. In the course of time they paid him back the loans, and with true Knickerbocker gratitude always carried his produce and freight for smaller rates than they charged other customers. The same policy marked his construction of wharves and toll bridges, limestone kilns and brickyards.

Maria Van Cortlandt
Wife of Kiliaen Van Rensselaer, the Fourth Patroon

Anna Van Wely
Second Wife of Kiliaen Van Rensselaer, the First Patroon

The next generation produced the flower of the family. This was Stephen Van Rensselaer III., fifth Lord of the Manor and eighth Patroon. His father having died, he was educated by his grandfather, Philip Livingston. Under *Stephen III.* such auspices he progressed rapidly, and in due course was graduated from Harvard with high honors. He married Margarita Schuyler, thus transmitting to his posterity the blood of five of the great colonial families — Schuyler, Van Rensselaer, Livingston, Van Cortlandt, and Ten Broeck. After graduation, he kept up his studies, and at the same time personally managed his large estates. Four years later, he became interested in military affairs, and received a commission as major of infantry. He was so active in his new position that in 1786 he was promoted to be colonel; thereafter he was made a major-general. He also entered politics, and proved an efficient Assemblyman, Senator, and Lieutenant-Governor. His first wife dying, he married Cornelia Paterson, daughter of Supreme Court Judge William Paterson, who was also Governor of New Jersey. In 1810, the General was appointed upon the commission to designate the route for the Erie Canal. In 1816, the law was passed for building that vast waterway, and he served as member of the board and then as president from 1824 until his death in 1839. In the War of 1812 he displayed rare gallantry and military skill.

Among his officers were many of his kinsmen, notably his cousin, Colonel Solomon Van Rensselaer, who was wounded at the battle of Queenstown Heights. In addition *Colonel Solomon* to his studies, his business, military affairs, and his political labors, Stephen Van Rensselaer still found time for a vast amount of outside work. From 1819 to 1839, he was a Regent of the State University, and, in the last years of that period, its Chancellor. From 1823 to 1829, he served acceptably in the House of Representatives. In 1824 he founded the first scientific school in the New World. His own words show how far ahead he was of the times: " A school to qualify teachers to instruct the application of experimental chemistry, philosophy, and natural history to agriculture, domestic economy, and to the arts and manufactures." This school, now known as the Rensselaer Polytechnic Institute, will always be a memorial to the philanthropy and statesmanship of its founder. In 1825, Yale conferred upon him the degree of LL.D.

The eighth Patroon left twelve children, three by his first and nine by his second wife. Of these, Stephen Van Rensselaer IV., usually referred to as the Young Patroon, was the eldest. To him had descended the bulk of the great Van Rensselaer estate or plantation, and by him, through political causes, it was dissipated for ever. The dream of the first Patroon came to naught in the lifetime of his ninth successor. The occasion was what is known to-day as the anti-rent war, and it was brought about by industrial rather than political forces. Under the old Dutch system the great plantation of seven hundred thousand acres had been split up in small holdings, and these leased in perpetuity for rent charges or services of the olden time. For one field, so many bushels of grain per annum was the rent; for another, so many skins and pelts; for a third, so much timber; and, for a fourth, so many head of cattle, or of sheep. This cumbrous system, well enough adapted to a primitive age, had become utterly opposed to the new conditions of the land. The Van Rensselaers were fine landlords, which cannot be said of all the Patroons of New York, but even with the kindest landlord there was always trouble. Besides this, no tenant desired to make improvements, whose benefit would revert to the landlord and not to himself. Opposition to the rent system developed into agitation, and this into social and political organizations. Conflicts occurred between the anti-renters and the authorities, and at one time it looked as if civil war or insurrection would devastate the fair land of the old manorial grants.

Stephen was a man of singularly sweet disposition, and rather than oppose the people in their desire for a change in the landed system, he gave up the traditions of his race, cutting his estate into farms and house lots, and selling them to the highest bidder. It was a losing transaction in every way. Worst of all, the country was agitated, the market was worse than stagnant, and most

Stephen Van Rensselaer III.
Patroon of the Manor of Rensselaerwyck.   Major-General of the United States Army

of his sales went, it is said, for a mere song. Although legally his father was the last of the Patroons, yet the people of his time, with poetic justice, called him by that title, and as "the last of the Patroons" he will go down to history. He married Harriet E. Bayard, by whom he had five daughters and three sons. The preponderance of female children has caused this branch of the family almost to disappear in other names, among which are the Douws, Thayers, Robbs, Andrews, Townsends, Barbers, Crosbys, and Berrys. In the web of life, the threads cross unceasingly The late Stephen Van Rensselaer Townsend, who was graduated from Harvard in 1882, was looking over the university rolls one day, and there found that his great-grandfather, after whom he was named, had been graduated in the class of 1782, just one century before.

Among those who have rendered public service in the present generation of the oldest branch of the family, are William Bayard Van Rensselaer, Dr. Howard Van Rensselaer, and the Rev. Stephen Van Rensselaer. A distinguished brother of Stephen was Brigadier-General Henry Van Rensselaer, who graduated at West Point in 1827, and served as lieutenant in the United States Army. He was sent to Congress in 1841, and during the rebellion was a colonel, inspector-general, and aide-de-camp to General Scott. He died just before the close of the war of typhoid fever, contracted while in the service.

Dr. Howard

Gen. Henry

Besides General Henry was his nephew, Kiliaen, who was born 1845, at Albany. He entered the Civil War a mere boy, and rose to be a captain in the Thirty-ninth New York Volunteers. He took part in some fourteen engagements, and served under Generals Grant and Hancock.

At the close of the war he travelled and entered business life, but after a few years came to devote most of his time to philanthropy and church work. Another hero of the civil conflict was William Van Rensselaer, of the Seneca Falls branch of the family. He was an officer of the New York Volunteer Engineers, and fought with distinguished gallantry in the Army of the Potomac.

Col. William

Of the eight other brothers and sisters of Stephen IV., there has been a similar preponderance of female descendants, and the absorption of their own in other family names. Here are found the Ervings, Pruyns, Coopers, Kings, Atterburys, Fairfaxes, Hodges, Grubbs, Screvens, Lorillards, Kennedys, Waddingtons, Delafields, Crosbys, Baylies, and Crugers.

Less distinguished, perhaps, than Stephen III., the eighth Patroon, were his kinsmen, Jeremiah, Colonel Kiliaen, Kiliaen K., and Solomon. Jeremiah was born in 1741, was graduated from Princeton College in 1758, and took part in the Revolution. Distinguished as a member of Congress, he represented New York from 1789 to 1791. He was Lieutenant-Governor from 1801 to 1804.

Col. Kiliaen Colonel Kiliaen Van Rensselaer, a grandson of Jeremiah III., son of the first Patroon, who succeeded his brother Jan Baptist as director of the Colony of Rensselaerwyck (1658), was an ardent patriot in Revolutionary days. At the outbreak of hostilities he joined the colonial forces and took with him three of his sons, leaving behind only those who were too young to go to war. He and his boys served with heroism, he being known as "Fighting Kiliaen" (or "Colonel Kiliaen") during the conflict and afterwards, as long as he lived. He was complimented by Washington.

Kiliaen K. Kiliaen K. Van Rensselaer, son of Colonel Kiliaen, was a Yale graduate, and in college he achieved a high reputation for scholarship. After graduation he became private secretary to General Schuyler, who had married his cousin. In his leisure he studied law. He entered the bar and belonged to a famous group of jurists, which included James Kent, De Witt Clinton, and Ambrose Spencer. He was elected to Congress in 1801, and was re-elected four times. Chief among his descendants

Dr. Maunsell may be mentioned the Rev. Dr. Maunsell Van Rensselaer, the Episcopal divine, President of De Veaux College, and thereafter of Hobart College, who was born in Albany, 1819.

In 1876, he resigned the presidency of Hobart College and went to Europe. He occupied the pulpits of Emanuel Church and the

Cornelia Paterson
Wife of Stephen Van Rensselaer III. From a miniature

American Chapel at Geneva, the corner-stone of which was laid by Gen. U. S. Grant. He was afterwards connected with many philanthropies.

Solomon Van Rensselaer was also a soldier in the eighteenth century. He enlisted when but nineteen years old, and served under General Wayne, in 1794. In 1799, he was promoted to be major, and was Adjutant-General of New York from 1801 to 1810. He fought bravely through the War of 1812, and ended his military career by becoming a Congressman, from 1819 to 1822.

A celebrated junior line from Jeremias, third son of the first Patroon, has added many names to the roll of honor. One of these begins with his great-grandson Major James Van Rensselaer, who fought bravely in the Revolution, enjoyed the confidence of Washington, and at one time served under Gen. Montgomery. From him comes the line marked by Philip, Gratz, and Cortlandt Van Rensselaer, formerly United States District Attorney in this city. The records of the eighteenth century show at least seventy members of the family besides those enumerated.

Major James

Mention should be made of Colonel Stephen, son of Brigadier-General Henry, a brilliant soldier on General Scott's staff during the civil conflict, whose heroism has adorned the history of that giant struggle; of Rev. Cortlandt, son of Rev. Cortlandt, a noted Presbyterian divine, a war chaplain and an efficient secretary of the Presbyterian Board; of Philip Livingston, another son of Rev. Cortlandt who made a laudable war record· of William, son of William P., an officer in the U. S. Volunteers; and of Stephen Van Rensselaer Cruger, a brilliant soldier. The five were grandsons of Stephen and his wife, Cornelia Paterson. To this generation belongs James Tallmadge (son of Philip S. and his wife Mary B. Tallmadge), who was U. S. Assistant District Attorney for New York.

Reverend Cortlandt

The Van Rensselaer fame will rest more upon political than upon personal grounds. Were every member of the race annihilated the story of the family would be preserved by all students of jurisprudence. Many attempts were made toward establishing aristocracies of various types in the New World. In Maine, when it **was** Acadia, the French endeavored to reproduce upon a small scale the social features of the *ancien régime*. In Mexico, both Church and State essayed the creation of ecclesiastical and Castilian tenures. The experiments of Lord Delaware and other English nobles are well known. None of these came to any notable success, but the plans of the great Kiliaen Van Rensselaer were made with consummate skill and executed with magnificent power. He and his descendants ruled with wisdom and justice. If ever a feudal aristocracy could have been perpetuated in the New World, they were the men to perform the task. The abolition of the double title of Patroon and Lord of the Manor was the first blow which the spirit of the New World administered to their cherished designs. Though the titles were abolished by the Revolution, the system remained unchanged. Even as late as 1812 it looked as if the Patroon system were to become a factor in the social development of the Empire State. The anti-rent agitation, followed by the legislation which was enacted in Albany between 1845 and 1860, was the second blow which put an end to the last relics of feudal Europe. The Van Rensselaers made a brave fight for the cause with which they were identified, and the last of the Patroons went down in defeat like a gentleman. He himself lived to see the day when his representatives at Albany and Washington were the descendants of the oath-bound underlings of his ancestors. It took two hundred years for John Smith to take the Patroon from the manorial chair, and to carve the manor into ten thousand independent little farms. Yet in this change the heroic qualities of the Van Rensselaers were developed and made greater. Those who fought in the Revolution were a higher and finer type than those who first ruled the poor farmers of Rensselaerwyck, and with the final crash the newer generation took up the great work of life with a zeal and manhood worthy of any race.

Van Siclen

XLI

VAN SICLEN

THE consolidation of Brooklyn with New York was merely the legal recognition of a very ancient fact. From the founding of New Amsterdam the two boroughs have been organic parts of the same community. Indeed, Brooklyn up to the middle of the nineteenth century was more intimately associated with New York proper than were Haarlem and the settlements beyond that river, which now make a continuous city from the Battery to Yonkers. Nowhere is this better evidenced than in the history of the old families. Both boroughs have equal claims upon the Livingstons, Schermerhorns, Remsens, Kings, Schencks, and Vanderbilts. To this class belongs the ancient Dutch race of Van Siclen, which crossed the ocean to the New Netherlands in the middle of the seventeenth century, and has been an influential element in the development of the community up to the present time. Like most of the old Holland names, the orthography of the patronymic has varied considerably. Among the forms which it has assumed may be enumerated Van Sicklen, Van Sichlen, Van Siclen, Van Sickelen, Van Siechelen, Van Sychlen, Van Scyklen, Van Syckle, Vansyckel, and Van Sickle. Several branches have dropped the Van and simplified the name to Sickel and Sickles.

In Holland, the family belonged to the agricultural class, and held many positions indicative of importance in the State. They were Syndics, Burgomasters, elders and deacons, lieutenants and captains, merchants and divines. Anthony van Sicklen was one of the Protestants who emigrated from Catholic Belgium (from Ghent), in 1566, to Protestant Holland, where he became a Councillor from the province of Zeeland, representing that province and signing the Pacification of Ghent, with William the Silent and the other Dutch representatives. For three centuries at least, in the Old World, they were noted for their physical vigor and soldierly qualities. They seemed to enjoy war for its excitement and glory rather than for ambition or gain. They took part in every war wherein the Netherlands were engaged, and supplied many free lances to other nations. They were in the armies of Gustavus, of the Duke of Burgundy, the Kings of France, and Charles V., the great Emperor of Germany. Military life is closely connected with the nomadic instinct. The soldier has no home and is called by both duty and inclination to march from camp to camp and country to country. This nomadic instinct appeared in the history of the Van Siclens in the New World. In the seventeenth century they seemed to have visited all of the settlements of the New Netherlands, and in the eighteenth to have been among the explorers and pioneers of the unbroken West.

The founder was Ferdinandus [1635], who at the age of seventeen came to New Amsterdam, where he stayed a year or more, **Ferdinandus the Founder** and then settled in Flatlands, Long Island. Here he soon had a large farm, and was doing a profitable business with Brooklyn and New Amsterdam. He married Eva Antonise Jansen, by whom he had three sons and five daughters. These children were strong and sturdy and must have been of invaluable service to their parents. In the Dutch families at that time the boys aided the father upon the land and with the live stock, while the girls helped the mother in the care of the house, the management of the poultry-yard and dairy, and in spinning, weaving, and dyeing.

The father of Eva, the wife of Ferdinandus, was Antony

The Old Van Sicklen House in Ghent, Belgium
Built about 1338, and still standing

Jansen, known as Antony Jansen van Salee, and sometimes as Antony Jansen van Fez, from his having lived for some time in Morocco at the cities of Salee and Fez; he had carried out practically the motto of his Beggars' Badge: "Liver Turc dan Paus," (literally, "Rather Turk than Papist"), becoming a freebooter and capturing Spanish and other Catholic ships. This Beggars' Badge, which is in the possession of Mr. George W. van Siclen, was one of the most famous coins or badges of Europe, being in the shape of a crescent, and having on the obverse the other motto: "En tout fidelle au Roi" (In all things faithful to the king). This was the motto of the Dutch Protestants who rebelled against the Spanish Inquisition, yet claimed to remain faithful to Philip II. The crescent was the badge of the "Beggars of the Sea," while the badge of the "Gueux" or Beggars of the Land had for motto, "En tout fidèle au roi jusqu' à porter la besaçe" (In all things faithful to the king, even to carrying a beggar's sack), because a Spanish count, when Brederode and the Dutch nobles came to King Philip's representative with a petition against the Inquisition, said, scornfully· "Here come those beggars." The latter badge had the portrait of Philip II. on one side, and on the reverse a beggar's sack with two hands clasped through the strap, and pendant from the sides of the metal badge two metal gourds or bottles, and from the bottom, a cup; at Mr. van Siclen's suggestion this was adopted as the badge of the Holland Society of New York, and is made by Tiffany from a model sent by the Numismatic Society of Amsterdam. Antony Jansen van Salee was called "The Turk," and received from Governor William Kieft a grant of land where Bensonhurst now stands; it is known to this day in the abstracts of title as "The Turk's Plantation." A brazier of his is in the possession of Mr. Robert Bayles, president of the Market & Fulton National Bank, of New York, to whom it descended from Johannes Gulick, who married a daughter of Ferdinandus van Sicklen. From Ferdinandus [1635] and his wife Eva are descended all the Van Siclens in America. Before 1566, the Van Sicklen family were living in Ghent continuously from A.D. 1338, and prior, often serving as *échevins,* or members of the city council. George van Sicklen was abbot of St. Bavon, A. D. 1405. The family were Normans and came to Ghent from Amiens. A stone residence is standing in Ghent to-day (1902) which was standing there in A. D. 1338, and is and always has been known as "De Groote Sickele" and "La Grande Fauçille," belonging to the Van Sicklen family; it has lately been purchased by the municipality of Ghent and is to be used as a museum of antiquities; it is built of rough-hewn stone, "Belgian pavement," and is about one hundred feet square.

Not far from the Van Siclen homestead (near Van Siclen Station on the Brooklyn Elevated) was the settlement of the Canarsie Indians, who proved kind neighbors, and a warm friendship sprang up between them and the family. The children used the camp as a playground, and picked up a knowledge of the Indian tongue. This idle accomplishment had singular consequences. In each generation during the following century at least one Van Siclen was the official interpreter of the Dutch, and afterwards of the British Government. Several of them became so much attached to the redmen that they left their homes and lived with and ruled the latter. One of them, tradition says, became a titular chief, and transmitted his complimentary title through several generations.

The three sons played prominent parts in their time. They and their father were among the moving spirits in the establishment of a market and fair in Brooklyn. This was patterned after the jovial town-fairs of Holland, and proved a thorough success. On fair days the grounds about the market were covered with booths, tents, and Indian wigwams, the farmhouses held open hospitality, and in the afternoon and evening music and dancing gave pleasure to the young, and pipes, beer, and wine to the old. It was the first collective attempt on the part of the community to cater to the social side of life in this part of the New Netherlands. These fairs must have been a pleasant spectacle. The rosy-cheeked girls, fresh from the farms, attired in gayly-colored dresses, with heavy jewelry and voluminous linen petticoats, the stalwart young farmers in their traditional Dutch garb, soldiers and sailors, merchants and their families from neighboring towns, with a sprinkling of Indians through the crowd, must have made a picturesque ensemble. The records show that many visitors came from New York, some of whom took part in the dancing and festivities.

Of the three sons, Reinier [born about 1659] remained at home; Johannes, the scholar, became a schoolmaster in Flatbush; and Ferdinandus, Jr., settled upon a farm in the neighborhood, and became a notable Indian interpreter and farmer.

Johannes was a popular pedagogue, and enjoyed the respect and affection of his townsmen. To be a teacher in those days meant much more, in view of the environment, than it does to-day. He was second only to the pastor, and in some respects played a larger part than the latter. A fair idea of his duties, as well as of the social conditions of the latter part of the seventeenth century, may be obtained from the Flatbush schoolmaster's agreement of 1682:

<small>Johannes the Schoolmaster</small>

"(1.) The school shall begin at eight o'clock, and goe out at 11; shall begin again at one o'clock and ende at four. The belle shall be rung before the school begins.

"(2.) When school opens one of the children shall reade the morning prayer as it stands in the catechism, and close with the prayer before dinner; and in the afternoon the same. The evening school shall begin with the Lord's prayer and close by singing a psalm.

"(3.) Hee shall instruct the children in the common prayers and questions and answers off the catechism, on wednesdays and saturdays, too enable them to saye them better on sunday in church.

"(4.) Hee shall be bound to keepe the school nine months in succession from September to June, one year with another, and shall always be present himself.

"(5.) Hee shall bee Chorister of the Church, ring the belle three times before service, and reade a chapter of the Bible in the Church between the second and third ringinge of the belle; after the third ringinge hee shall reade the ten commandments, and the twelve articles of Ffaith, and then sett the Psalm. In the afternoon, after the third ringinge of the belle, hee shall reade a short chapter or one of the Psalms of David, as the congregation are assemblinge; afterward he shall sett the psalm.

" (7.) Hee shall provide a basin of water for the baptisme, for which hee shall receive 12 stuyvers in wampum for every baptisme Ffrom parents or sponsers. Hee shall furnish bread and wine Ffor the Communion att the charge of the Church. Hee shall also serve as Messenger Ffor the Consistorie.

" (8.) Hee shall give the Funerale invitations and toll the bell, and Ffor which hee shall receive Ffor persons of 15 years of age and upwards 12 guilders, and Ffor persons under 15, 8 guilders, and if hee shall cross the river to New York, hee shall have four guilders more.'

The school money was paid as follows:

" (1.) Hee shall receive Ffor a speller or reader 3 guilders, and Ffor a writer 4 guilders Ffor the day school. In the evening 4 guilders Ffor a speller and reader, and 5 guilders Ffor a writer per quarter.

" (2.) The residue of his salary shall bee 400 guilders in wheat off wampum value delivered at Brookland ferry, with the dwelling, pasturage, and meadow appertaining to the school."

Johannes, after several years' service, moved to Jersey, where he was followed shortly afterwards by his nephew, Jan. Here he established the New Jersey branch, which was to become one of the great families of that State.

In the third generation the leading figures were Cornelius of Gravesend, who in middle life bought a large tract of land in Amentrem, Huntingdon County, N. J.; Ferdinand of Gravesend, who was a prosperous farmer and real estate owner; Reinier of Flatbush, who was a farmer, merchant, and public official; Ferdinand of Flatlands, who married Mary

Reinier of Flatbush

Van Nuyse, increased the ancestral estate, and had property at Canarsie and in Queens County; Jan of Raritan, who was the possessor of a large estate, and was a leading man in that part of Jersey. All married and had large and vigorous families.

The fourth generation witnessed the continuation of the prosperity enjoyed by the third, and a wider distribution of the members. Reinier [1716] was a leader of Gravesend and Flatlands. Gysbert [1718] was a large landed proprietor in Gravesend. Johannes [1722] had a fine establishment at New Lots, and Cornelius [1728] was one of the wealthiest farmers at Wappinger's Falls, N. Y. Reinier was a selectman in Huntingdon County, N. J. Andries [1718] was a justice at Raritan, N. J. Johannes [1720] was an influential farmer, soldier, and trader at Brunswick. Abraham [1723] founded a family in Philadelphia. Jacobus settled in Albany, and Peter began life in New York City. *Judge Andries*

The fifth and sixth generations covered the most important event of the eighteenth century, the War of Independence, and afforded opportunity for many of the family to display military skill and patriotic virtue. One of these was Peter, son of Peter, who served under General George Clinton. *Peter the Pioneer* He was wounded several times, but invariably reported for duty before his wound had completely healed. On one occasion he was sent back because he was still unable to use a gun. At the close of the war he joined a party of adventurous soldiers who went West and established settlements along the Ohio River. Here he made a record as a pioneer, and founded a branch in the "Buckeye" State. Ferdinand of Wappinger's Falls, N. Y., was a well-to-do patriot, who contributed largely to the Revolutionary cause. He belonged to the militia of the place, and is said to have taken part in the battle of Saratoga.

Lieutenant Abraham [1775] was a soldier, farmer, and musician. He served in the War of 1812, where he displayed great valor. He settled in Orange County, N. Y., where he established a local branch of his race. Captain James [1790], of the Jacobus line, also served faithfully in the same war. *Lieutenant Abraham*

Captain Joseph [1797], of the Reinier branch, enlisted, when a mere lad, in the army, where he rose to be captain. In later life he removed to Michigan, where he made a permanent home, and where his descendants are now quite numerous. He was Captain of the Belvedere Rangers, and when receiving his honorary discharge from General Jackson was highly praised by that great soldier.

<small>Captain Joseph</small>

The seventh and eighth generations supplied many soldiers to the armies of the Union. More than one hundred appear upon the rolls. Of these, the more conspicuous were: Richard Henry [1827], of the Abraham branch, who served in the Forty-second Illinois; Sergeant De Witt Clinton [1816], of the Andrew branch, who was a brilliant soldier in the Black Hawk War, where he made himself famous as an Indian fighter; Lieutenant Moses E. [1815], his brother, who won the military laurels of the family. When seventeen years old, he enlisted in the Black Hawk War; in 1846, he marched to Mexico and served through that struggle, and, in 1861, he was one of the first to offer himself to the national Government. He inherited the Van Siclen talent for Indian languages, and served as Government interpreter for many years. Lyman, of the Peter branch, a cavalryman from Michigan during the Civil War, was captured by the Confederates, and died from jail fever in Andersonville.

<small>Sergeant De Witt Clinton</small>

<small>Lieutenant Moses E.</small>

John Sydney [1827], son of De Witt Clinton, was another hero of the great conflict, where his career was altogether unique. He was captured at the beginning of the war, and taken to Selma, Ala. Here he contrived a plan of escape, which was discovered. He was forthwith removed to Meridian, Miss., where he with other prisoners built a tunnel and fled to the woods. He was recaptured and returned to his former place of captivity. Here he designed another jail escape, but was transferred to Cahaba, Ala. Twice again did he try to break his confinement, and was each time transferred, first to Selma and thence to Vicksburg. Here at last he was exchanged, and immediately went back to the front. His boast was that he "had

<small>John Sydney the Pioneer</small>

done time in seven Southern prisons." George Washington [1841], of the Peter branch, enlisted in 1862, and was discharged at the end of the war with the rank of corporal. He was one of the company which captured Jefferson Davis after the fall of Richmond.

At the present time the family is represented by the eighth and ninth generations. Of these, the chief is George West [1840], who was graduated from the College of the City of New York (1857) and the Columbia Law School (1867), and was admitted to the bar, where he achieved success in real-estate law. He was the founder of the Title Guarantee and Trust Company of New York; founder and first Secretary of the Holland Society of New York and the first Secretary of the Holland Trust Company of New York. He married Sarah Gregory, by whom he has issue. Three years after her death, in 1901, he married Grace C. Hogarth.

George West

Arthur, son of George West, was graduated from Columbia Law School [1891] and was admitted to the bar; Matthew, his other son, is a senior at Amherst. James Cornell, of the Reinier branch, was graduated from the Columbia Law School in 1892. Judge Bennett Van Syckel of the Supreme Court of New Jersey is a jurist of the highest rank. And John T. Van Sickle, manager of the Morgan S. S. line to New Orleans, is long known for his executive ability.

At the present time the family is represented by numerous branches in the Empire State and elsewhere. It has members at its old homesteads in Flatlands, Gravesend, and Brooklyn, as well as in Queens, Manhattan, and the Bronx. It is uniformly marked by the old Dutch virtues — patience, industry, resolute probity, and a deep love for education.

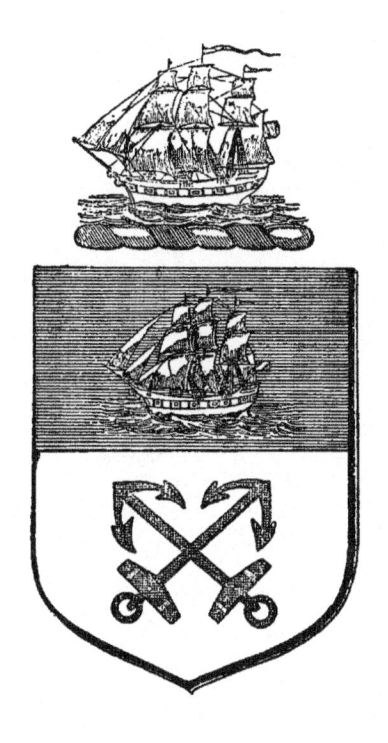

Wendell

XLII

WENDELL

IN the first century of the Hudson River settlements, it was rare for either Knickerbocker or Englishman to move eastward and invade the sterile territory of the Puritan. To the stout burghers of New Amsterdam, New England was a rocky land peopled by wild Indians, wild beasts, and wilder Englishmen. It was rarer still for a Dutch family to become identified with New England life, and to attain as much celebrity in Massachusetts as the main branch did in New York. Yet this is what occurred with the great Dutch family of Wendell, one of the most distinguished of the colonial stocks of the Empire State. Not alone under their own name did they make history in the Bay State, but in their two immortal descendants, Oliver Wendell Holmes and Wendell Phillips, they added two great stars to the heavens of American intellectuality.

The founder of the race in the New World was Evert Janse, who was born [1615] in the little city of Embden in East Friesland, then belonging to the Netherlands, but now part of the province of Aurich, in the kingdom of Hanover, Germany. Embden was not the home of his race. Not many years before, his family had lived in the district of Rhynland or

Evert Janse the Founder

Delftland, from which they fled to escape the sword and rack of the Duke of Alva. In Rhynland the family owned several farms and possessed considerable property, much if not most of this being lost when they departed for the North. Nevertheless, enough remained to give Evert a good education, and to enable him in 1639-1640 to cross the ocean to the New Netherlands. He arrived in 1640, during the administration of Governor William Kieft.

New Amsterdam, though small, was a busy community, with galleons coming and going, and Indian traders arriving and departing by both land and water. Most of the population were busy upon farms or converting the wilderness into arable fields. Another group were trading with the redmen, from whom they purchased the fine furs and peltries which were so prized by the nobility and the well-to-do classes of Europe.

Evert seems to have been a trader at first. Five years were spent in New Amsterdam, and then he joined in the prevailing movement of population from Manhattan Island to the great Van Rensselaer settlements around Fort Orange. He did not settle at Rensselaerwyck proper, but made a comfortable home almost under the guns of Fort Orange. He took title to property, and obtained a trading license, pursuant to the custom of the period. Gifted with pleasant manners and a fine sense of justice, he quickly became popular with the sachems, and within a year was among the leading merchants of the place. He won the esteem of his neighbors at the same time, who honored him with many positions of dignity and profit.

In 1652, he, with other burghers, had a dispute with the great war-horse, Petrus Stuyvesant, Governor of the New Netherlands. The latter, a keen-eyed soldier, when visiting Fort Orange saw that the houses around the fort weakened the latter from a strategic point of view, as they were in the line of gunfire from the fort, and offered protection to an advancing enemy. He, therefore, under the provision of some ancient documents, claimed title to all land around the fort, for a distance of 250 Dutch rods, and ordered the burghers to remove their property, their homes to be destroyed, and the land converted into an open space, according to the military tactics of the time. The sturdy burghers, aided by Evert, rose up in immediate protest, and, like their descendants of to-day, held a mass-meeting, in which they denounced the Chief Magistrate in round terms. A delegation was appointed which waited upon the Governor, who so enjoyed their belligerent attitude that he compromised the matter by paying them handsomely for their houses and improvements, and gave them patents for land further away from the fort, of larger extent than the farms which they surrendered.

The incident is a pleasant one, and shows both Governor and colonists in very favorable light. Wendell's new farm was on the south side of the present city of Albany. Later he removed to a site now the corner of James and State streets. Here he passed the remainder of his life, and here his son Thomas lived in the first part of the eighteenth century. Among the offices which Evert held were ruling elder of the Dutch Church (1656), Orphan Master (1657), and Magistrate (1660-1661). Evert was twice married, his first wife being Susanna de Trieux, daughter of Philip de Trieux, the Marshal of the province; and his second, Maritje Alrahamise Vosburgh, of Beverwyck. He had issue by both wives.

His children inherited his fine appearance and unusual ability. Thomas, the eldest, took as his patrimony the paternal mansion, where he acted as a father to his many nieces and nephews. He was never married, having, **Thomas the Hospitable** according to a family tradition, been jilted in young manhood, and thereupon become a confirmed misogynist. His favorite amusement, tradition says, was to entertain a lot of Indian friends, who, according to the critics of the Dutch age, invariably grew "beastlie drunken" at the most interesting part of the banquet. The fame of his hospitality crossed the seas, so that nearly all newcomers of any social position at home made their first visit upon "Uncle Thomas" at Albany. Abraham, the trader and soldier, married Maryken Van Nes of Albany. John [1649], the third brother, married, first, Maritie Jillisse Meyer, and, secondly, Elizabeth Staats, of Albany. Jeronimus [1655] married Ariaantje Harmense Visscher. Philip [1657] married her sister,

Maria Harmense Visscher. Evert, Jr. [1660], married Elizabeth Sanders, of Albany. He had one son and two daughters by his second wife.

Next to Abraham, John [1649] was the most conspicuous member of this generation. He was a devout member of the church and received his education from the minister. Manifesting great aptitude for business, he accumulated a large estate, and after arriving at the age of thirty, devoted much of his time to public affairs. He was a Justice of the Peace in 1684, captain in the Albany militia in 1685, an alderman in that city the following year, and in 1690 was one of the Commission which negotiated a treaty with the Five Nations and superintended the defence of Albany against a threatened attack of the sons of the forest. Both his wives brought him large fortunes in their own right, so that in middle age he was not only rich in money and warehouses, but also in large tracts of land in the Mohawk Valley, in what is now Saratoga County, and in other districts of the province. His daughter Elsie married Abraham Staats, Jr., a leading man of the time, while Marritie married Jan Johannse Oothout of Albany.

John the Public Spirited

The third generation was marked by many members of unusual energy and ability. Abraham [1687], son of John, removed from Albany to New York not long after he came of age, and started a commercial house, which grew to large proportions. He established relations with prominent houses in Holland, England, and New England, and shipped great quantities of furs to Europe, which netted him profits, sometimes of great amounts. He married Katrina De Kay, great-granddaughter of Anneke Jans, who brought him a large dowry and afterwards a handsome fortune by inheritance. His mercantile relations with Boston increasing, he established a branch house there, which, proving very remunerative, caused him to remove to that city and make it his permanent home.

Abraham the Merchant

Here his son John [1703] married Elizabeth Quincy, daughter of the Hon. Edmund Quincy, and his daughter Elizabeth married Edmund Quincy, Jr. This founded the

John, of Boston

alliance between the Wendell and Quincy families which was to play an important part in the social history of Massachusetts, and reinforce through its wealth and prestige the influence of his younger brother Jacob [1691], who also removed to the capital of the Bay State.

This brother became identified with New England even more thoroughly than did Abraham. He married Sarah Oliver of Cambridge, by whom he had twelve children. His daughter Sarah married the Rev. Dr. Abiel Holmes, and their fourth child was Dr. Oliver Wendell Holmes. Margaret, the twelfth child, married William Phillips, and their grandson was Wendell Phillips, the reformer and orator. *Oliver Wendell Holmes* *Wendell Phillips*

Hermanus [1678], the son of Jeronimus, was a leading citizen of Albany. He was an Alderman (1714-1720), Indian Commissioner (1728-1732), and again an Alderman (1726-1727). He incurred some opposition on account of his strenuous endeavors to open roads into the Indian country. During these years there was always a commercial conflict between the trading element and the governing element. The former desired to preserve their industry, and objected to any change which would decrease the supply of furs or alter the modes of collection and distribution. The latter, with an eye to the development of the country, desired to clear the wilderness and construct roads, not only for commerce, but also for military purposes, in the event of an Indian uprising or a war with France. *Alderman Hermanus*

Hermanus married Anna Glen, by whom he had issue. He was the head of three of the most distinguished lines or branches of his house.

Ephraim [1685, or 1688, as is given in some of the records] was a rich landowner and influential churchman of his community. He contributed "largely to the Gospel," and was often an officer in assemblies, synods, and other convocations of his faith. *Ephraim the Elder*

Harmanus [1714], son of Hermanus, was a leader of his time. Enjoying independent means, he devoted himself to study, and to public affairs. He was an Alderman at *Judge Harmanus*

Albany for many years, and an Associate Judge of the Court of Common Pleas (1752-1758). He was the possessor of a fine library in both Dutch and English, which he generously put at the service of his neighbors and of the lawyers who attended his court. He married Catharina Van Vechten, by whom he had numerous children.

Abraham, brother of Harmanus, was enterprising and ventursome. On coming of age he moved to Schenectady, from which **Captain Abraham** he is known in the family records as Abraham of Schenectady. During the old French war (1744-1748) he was active in organizing the military company which was formed in that neighborhood to resist any possible attack. He married his cousin, Elizabeth Wendell, by whom he had issue.

Hendrick, or Henry, was one of the Albany patriots who so ably aided the Revolutionary cause. As early as 1770 he was a **Hendrick the Sheriff** forcible speaker against the new imposts which had been laid upon the colonies, and the exasperating restrictions upon their trade. In 1774, he was one of the Committee of Safety and Correspondence which was appointed by the Freeholders of Albany. Along with his name upon the list are those of John Barclay, John R. Bleecker, Stephen de Lancey, Abraham Ten Broeck, Abraham Yates, Jr., Cornelius Van Santvoordt, John H. Ten Eyck, Henry L. Bogert, Jacob C. Ten Eyck, and Robert Yates. In 1777, he was elected Sheriff of Albany, which office he held until 1786, often acting as Provost Marshal, as well as Court Executive. He married Maria Lansing, by whom he had issue.

The fifth generation supplied many brave sons to the Revolution. Captain John Harmanus [1744], son of Judge Harmanus, **General John H.** was a lawyer, in active practice, when the mutterings of the coming storm of war were heard. He was a warm friend and supporter of his cousin, Sheriff Henry, and aided the latter materially in the period immediately preceding the Revolution. He took arms in 1775, when he was appointed lieutenant and quartermaster of the Second Albany Battalion. In 1776, he was promoted to be captain, and served in the First New

York, under Colonel Goose Van Schaick, until 1781. After the war his gallantry was recognized by his appointment as brigadier-general of militia. In 1796, he was elected to the Assembly from Albany County, and, in 1812, he was made Surrogate. His wife was Cathalina Van Benthuysen.

Lieutenant Jacob Henry [1754], son of Judge Henry, had just come of age when the Revolution broke out. He promptly joined the colonial forces, and fought with high gallantry until the restoration of peace in 1783, having risen during that period to the rank of adjutant. He was thrice elected to the New York Assembly (1796, 1797, 1798). His wife was Gertrude Lansing, daughter of the Honorable Peter Lansing. <small>Lieutenant Jacob H.</small>

Sheriff Harmanus [1767], son of Sheriff Henry, was one of the wealthy men of Albany and devoted the larger part of his time to public affairs. He served upon many committees and held numerous positions of honor and trust. He was made Sheriff in 1803. <small>Sheriff Harmanus</small>

John [1731] was the scholar of the family. He was graduated from Harvard in 1750, and married Dorothy Sherburne. He established a branch, of which the most important member has been Professor Barrett [1855], his great-grandson. The latter was graduated from Harvard (1877), and became assistant professor of English literature and thereafter professor in that university. He married Edith, the daughter of William Curtis Greenough. <small>John the Scholar / Professor Barrett</small>

John Lansing [1785] was the most prominent member of the sixth generation. He studied law with his brother Garritt Wendell, a distinguished real-estate lawyer of the time, and became a member of the Albany bar. He was elected judge of Washington County for one term, but made his fame as a reporter of the New York Supreme Court. His great works are *Reports of Cases in the Supreme Court* (twenty-six volumes), and the *Digest of Cases, Supreme Court of New York.* He also edited Starkie's *Law of Slander* and Blackstone's *Commentaries* with rare judicial ability. <small>John L. the Jurist</small>

Dr. Peter, son of Adjutant Jacob Henry, was a distinguished

physician of Albany in the early part of the century. From him
has descended an important branch, which included
Dr. Harman and Benjamin Rush, his sons, and Burr
and Benjamin Rush, Jr., grandsons. The last-named was graduated from Yale (1878), and from the Columbia Law School (1882).

Dr. Peter

Harmanus C. [1781] was a landed proprietor who inherited fortunes from both his father, Cornelius [1745], and his grandfather, Hermanus [1714]. He was a magistrate for twenty years, and an active participant in public affairs during his entire life. His wife was Cathalina Hun. He is represented in the seventh generation by William, who married, first, Sarah Kip, and, second, Frances Roberts.

Judge Harmanus C.

The sixth generation from Evert, Junior, was represented by William Henry, of Ballston Spa, N. Y. To him the public is partially indebted for the development of that beautiful community. He was for many years supervisor and a member of many progressive local organizations. He married Anna Melvin.

William Henry

From Abraham [1791], of the Harmanus branch, came the members of the family who were the pioneers of Kansas, Michigan, Minnesota, and Wisconsin. They were stanch free-soilers, and carried into the West the public schools and the liberal laws of the Empire State. This branch supplied Adelbert Chauncey [1848] to the Union Army, where he made a brilliant record, closing his military career as a staff officer of Major-General Granger. The branch was represented in the ninth generation by William Fuller [1873], who was graduated from the University of Minnesota in 1892.

Colonel Adelbert C.

The career of the Wendells in both Massachusetts and New York has been marked by business ability, intellectuality, social grace, and patriotism. They have served in every conflict, from the old French wars to the late struggle with Spain. Their sons are upon the rolls of the great universities, and their names are found in the lists of eminent lawyers, writers, scientists, and pedagogues.

INDEX

A

Abeel (Beekman), Magdalene, i., 29
Abercrombie, Colonel, i., 23
Alburtis (Barclay), Louisa, i., 29
Alexander (Duer), Lady Catharine, i., 129
— William (General), i., 129
Allen, Margaret De Lancey, i., 95
Allen, William, i , 95
Allyn (Gardiner), Elizabeth, i., 149
Alsop, John, i., 69
Ames, Fisher, i., 140
Andrews, W. (Rev.), i., 16
Anthon (Fish), Marion G., i., 142
Armstrong (Astor), Margaret, i., 7
Ashdoer, i., 3
Ashton (De Peyster), Frances, i., 111
Aspinwall (Renwick), Anna L., ii., 88
William H., ii., 88
Astor, Ava Willing, i., 9
Battery, i., 9
& Broadwood, i., 3
Charlotte A. Gibbes, i., 8
(Langdon) Dorothea, i., 5
Eliza, i., 5
Family, i., 3-10
Henry, i., 4
House, i., 7
Jacob, i., 3
John Jacob, the founder, i., 3, 38
John Jacob III., i., 8
John Jacob IV., i., 9
Laces in Metropolitan Museum, i., 8
Library, i., 7
(Bristed) Magdalen, i., 5
Margaret A. Armstrong, i., 7
Mary D. Paul, i., 8
Military Company, i., 9
Regiment, i., 9
William, i., 8, 9
William Backhouse, i., 5
William Waldorf, i., 8

B

Baker (Delafield), Ann, i., 84
Baldwin (De Peyster), Christianna, i., 109
Bancker (De Peyster), Anna, i , 105
— — Mary, i., 105
Barber (Delafield), Elsie, i , 85
Barclay, Adelbert E. E. W., i., 20
(Robinson) Anna D., i., 19
Anna M., i., 20
Anthony, i , 19
Anthony, i., 20
Catherine Cochrane, i., 20
(De Lancey) Cornelia, i., 19, 97
Cuthbert (Rev.), i., 20
David (Colonel) the founder, i., 13
David, i., 16
Dentie Lent, i., 19
Fanny, i., 21
Frederick W., i., 20
George, i., 20
Harold, i., 21
Henry (Rev.), i., 16
Henry, i., 20, 21
Henry A., i., 20
Henry A. W., i., 20
House, the, i., 16
James L., i., 20
John, i., 16
John O'C., i., 20
J. Searle, i., 20
J. Searle, i., 21
Mary Rutgers, i., 19
(Rives) Matilda A., i., 20
Olivia Mott Bell, i., 20
Robert (Governor), i., 15
Robert C., i., 21
Sackett M., i., 20
Susan De Lancey, i., 19, 97
Thomas (Colonel), i., 19, 97
Thomas (Rev.), i., 16
Thomas (Captain), i., 20

Index

Barclay, Thomas III., i., 20
    Walter C., i., 20
    Wright, i., 21
Bard (Delafield), Eliza, i., 83
— William, i., 83
Barnwell (Cruger), Mary, i., 73
Bayre (Fish), Clemence S., i., 141
Beam, Catherine A., i., 131
— John, i., 131
Beasley (Delafield), Margaretta, i., 85
Bedlow (Beekman), Mary E. G., i., 31
Beekman, Abian Steele Milledoler, i., 32
    (De Peyster) Ann, i., 109
    Catherine B., i., 32
    Catherine Peters de la Noy, i., 29
    Catherine Sanders, i., 31
    Catherine Van Boogh, i., 28
    Cornelia, i., 32
    Cornelius, i., 26
    Elizabeth de Peyster, i., 29
    Family, i., 25
    Gerard, the scholar, i., 26
    Gerard (Dr.), i., 28
    Gerard, i., 31
    Gerard, i., 32
    Gerardus, i., 29
    Gerard W., i., 31
    Gertruyd Van Cortlandt, i., 29
    Henry (Colonel), i., 28
    Henry II. (Colonel), i., 29
    Henry R., i., 32
    Henry R. II., i., 32
    Isabella Lawrence, i., 32
    Jacobus, i., 29
    Jacobus, i., 29
    James, i., 30
    James William, i., 31
    James William II., i., 32
    Jane Keteltas, i., 31
    Janet Livingstone, i., 29
    Joanna de Loper, i., 29
    John, i., 29
    John, i., 31
    Josephine, i., 32
    Magdalene Abeel, i., 29
    (Livingston) Margaret, i., 30
    Mary Duyckink, i., 31
    Mary E., i., 32
    Mary E. G. Bedlow, i., 31
    Street, i , 27
    Swamp, i., 27
    Wilhelmus, the founder, i., 25
    William (Dr.), i., 29
    William F., i., 32
Bell (Barclay), Olivia M., i., 20
Bellomont, Governor, i., 28
Benjamin, Julia K. Fish, i., 141

Benjamin, Samuel N. (Colonel) i., 141
Benson, Dirck, i., 117
    (Duane) Eve, i., 117
Berkeley (original or older form of Barclay), i., 13
— Lord, i., 15
Blair (Cruger), Elizabeth, i., 71
Blake, John L. (Rev.), i., 45
Blealsley (Cruger), R. A., i., 74
Bleecker, Jan., ii., 106
— Margaret Rutgers, ii., 106
Bogart (Delafield), Anita, i., 85
Boke, Jaquemyntje, i., 38
Bowers (Duane), Marianne, i., 123
Bowne, Robert, i., 4, 5
Boyd, Harriet Delafield, i., 85
    Robert, i., 85
Breck, Charles D., i., 132
    Mary Duer, i., 132
Brevoort, Annetje Bastiaense, i., 37
    Catherine Delamater, i., 39
    (Hicks) Charlotte, i., 39
    Elizabeth Dorothea Lefferts, i., 41
    Elizabeth Schermerhorn, i., 42
    Family, i., 35
    Hendrick Jansen, i., 35
    Hendrick II., i., 37
    Hendrick III., i., 39
    Henry i., 39
    Henry II., i., 39
    Henry (Captain), i., 40
    Henry Leffert, i., 42
    James Carson, i., 41
    James Renwick, i., 42
    Jan Hendricksen, i., 37
    John, the goldsmith, i., 39
    (Bristed) Laura, i., 42
    Mary Ren Van Couwenhoven, i., 37
    (Astor) Sarah Todd, i., 38
    Sarah Whetten, i., 39
Briggs (Cornill), Rebecca, i., 56
Bristed, John (Rev.), i., 5
    Margaret Astor, i., 5
Broadwood (Astor &), i , 3
Brogan (De Peyster), Elizabeth i., 109
Brooks (Delafield), Anna O., i., 85
    Frederick W., i., 85
Buchanan, Thomas, i., 69
Bunner (Duer), Anna B., i., 131
    George, i., 131
Burgwm, J. Pollock, i., 21
Burke, Edmund, i., 70
Burns, Robert, i., 108
Burr, Aaron, i., 49

C

Carrick (Barclay), Lavinia, i., 20
Carter (Cruger), Sarah E., i., 74

Index

Carteret, Sir George, i., 15
Chandler (Gardiner), Sarah, i., 149
Chew, Beverly, i., 130, 131
    (Duer) Lucy, i., 131
    Maria T. Duer, i., 130
Church (Cruger), Catherine, i., 173
Clark, Joseph, i., 132
    (Duer) Josephine, i., 132
    Wilhelmina B. De Lancey, i., 98
Clarkson, Alice Delafield, i., 84
    Howard, i., 84
    (De Peyster) Susan M., i., 111
Clinton, Alexander, i., 46
— Alexander (Dr.), i., 52
— Alexander James, i., 52
— Catherine Jones, i., 52
— Charles, i., 45, 46
— Charles, son of James, i., 49
— Cornelia Tappan, i., 49
    De Witt, i., 48, 49, 50–52
    Elizabeth Denniston, i., 46
    Family, i., 45
    George (Admiral,) i., 93
    George (Governor), i., 31, 45, 47–49
    George, Jr., i., 49
    Henry, Sir, i., 45
    James (Brig.-General), i., 45, 46, 121
    Mary De Witt, i., 47
    Maria Franklin, i., 52
    Mary Little Gray, i., 47
    Spencer, i., 52
    William, i., 45
Clive, Lord, i., 127
Cochran (Barclay), Cornelia, i., 20
Colden, Cadwallader (Governor), i., 94
— Elizabeth De Lancey, i., 94
College, Columbia, i., 17, 18
— Kings, i., 17, 18
Colles, Christopher, i., 49
Collet (Barclay), Ann Wilkes, i., 20
Cook, Anna L. Delafield, i., 85
— William G., i., 85
Cooper, Susan A. De Lancey, i., 97
— James Fenimore, i., 97
Cornbury, Governor, i., 28
Cornehill (for Cornell), i., 55
Cornewall " " i., 55
Cornewell " " i., 55
Cornell, Abigail B. Hicks, i, 59
    Alonzo B. (Governor), i., 57, 61, 62
— Charity Hicks, i., 57
    Charles, i., 59
— Edward Everett (Dr.), i., 62
    Ezekiel (General), i., 58
    Ezra, i., 57, 59, 60
    Family of, i., 55, 56, 63
    George, i., 59

Cornell, George, brother of John Black, i., 60
    George Birdsall, engineer, i., 63
    Isaac Russell, i., 60
    Jacob, i., 59
    Jacob Squire, i., 57
    James Lefferts (Dr.), i., 63
    John (Colonel), i., 57
    John (Lieutenant), i., 58
    John, evangelist, i., 62
    John, merchant, i., 59
    John Black, inventor, i., 60, 61
    John Henry, composer, i., 62
    John M., philanthropist, i., 62
    Mary Katherine Osterburg, i., 62
    Rebecca Briggs, i., 56
    Richard (Deputy), i., 56, 57
    Richard II., i., 57
    Robert Clifford (Judge), i., 63
    Sarah Cortilyou, i., 61
    Thomas, i., 56
    Thomas, of Portsmouth, i., 56
    Thomas [1620?] i., 57
    Thomas (Squire), i., 57
    Thomas (Assemblyman), i., 57
    Thomas (Captain), i., 58
    Thomas, inventor, i., 59
    William, i., 56
    William (Captain), i., 57
    William W., manufacturer, i., 60
    William Mason (Dr.), i., 61
    Whitehead, i., 58
    Whitehead II., i., 59
Cornhill (for Cornell), i., 55
Cornill " " i., 55
Cornwall " " i., 55
Cornwallis, Lord, i., 46
Cornwell (for Cornell), i., 55, 56
Cortilyou, Sarah, i, 61
Couwenhoven, Johannes, i., 37
— Maryken, i., 37
Covington, E. M., i., 83
— General, i., 83
— (Delafield) Harriet B., i., 83
Cox, Ann De Lancey, i., 97
    John, i., 97
Cressen (Cruger), Henrietta, i., 71
Cromwell, Oliver, i., 14
Crosby, Frederic V. S., i., 85
    Julia R. F. Delafield, i., 85
Cruger, Alfred, i, 73
    Ann Markoe, i., 72
    Ann Trezevant Heyward, i., 73
    Anna de Nully, i., 72
    Anne de Lancey, i., 70
    Bertram Peter, i., 73
    Bertram, i., 74
    Caroline M. Shepherd, i., 74

250

Index

Cruger, Caroline Smith, i., 71
    Catherine Church, i., 73
    Eliza Kortright, i., 73
    Eliza L. C. Dyckman, i., 73
    Elizabeth Blair, i , 71
    Elizabeth Harris, i., 69
    Elizabeth Roberts, i., 73
    Elizabeth Van Schaack, i., 70
    Euphemia W. Van Rensselaer, i., 73
    Eugene, i., 73
    Eugene [1836] i., 74
    Family, i., 67, 75
    Frances A. Jones, i., 73
    Frances E. Rusher, i., 75
    George Ehninger, i., 74
    George Seymour, i., 73
    Gouverneur, (Rev.), i., 74
    Hannah Slaughter Montgomery, i., 69
    Henry Gressen, i., 72
    Henry (Councillor), i., 69
    Henry II , the M.P., i., 70-71, 72
    Henry III., i., 73
    Henrietta Cressen, i., 70
    Henry Harris, i., 72
    Henry Mortimer, i., 75
    Henry Nicholas, i., 73
    Henrietta Julia, i., 73
    Harris [1795] i , 73
    Harriet, i., 73
    Harriet D , i., 73
    James Hamilton, i., 73
    James Henderson, i., 75
    John, the founder, i., 68
    John Church, i., 73
    John Harris (Colonel), i., 70, 72, 94
    John, the merchant, i., 72
    John Peach, i., 73
    John Whetten, i , 75
    Julia Grinnell Storrow, i., 75
    Laura A., i., 74
    Lewis Trezevant, i., 73
    Louise E. Ancrum Williamson, i., 73
    Mary, i., 69
    Mary Barnwell, i., 73
    Mary Boynton, i., 75
    Maria Cuyler, i., 69
    Mary Romaine, i., 73
    Martha Ramsay, i., 72
    Matilda Caroline, i., 72
    Melville Wood, i., 73
    Melvin S., i., 74
    Nicholas, i., 71
    Nicholas, Jr., i., 73
    Nicholas III., i., 73, 74
    Nicholas IV., i., 73, 75
    Nicholas V., i., 75
    Peter Cornee, i., 75

Cruger, Philip, Sir, i., 68
    Randolph, i., 74
    Robert, i., 74
    R. A. Blealsley, i., 74
    Sarah E. Carter, i., 74
    Sarah J. Maxwell, i., 73
    Stephen Van Rensselaer, (Colonel), i., 74, 75
    Susan Matilda Whetten Rathbone, i., 73
    Telemon, i., 71
    William Hyde, i., 73
    William R., i., 75
Cuyler (Cruger), Maria, i., 69

D

Davenport, John (Rev.), i., 146
De Kay (De Peyster), Frances, i., 109
Delafield, Albert, i., 84
    (Clarkson) Alice, i., 84
    Anita Bogart, i., 85
    Anna Baker, i., 84
    Anne S. Lloyd, i., 85
    Ann Hallet, i., 80
    (Cook) Anna L., i., 85
    Annie O. Brooks, i., 85
    Benjamin T., i., 85
    (Hall) Catherine C., i., 84
    Charlotte H. Wyeth, i., 85
    Clara C. Foster, i., 84
    Clarence, i., 83
    Clarence II., i., 85
    (Sturgis) Cornelia, i., 84
    (Woodbury) Cornelia, i., 85
    Cornelia V. R., i., 85
    (Krebben) Edith, i., 84
    Edith Wallace, i., 83
    Edward, i., 82
    Edward, i., 84
    Edward, i., 85
    Edward Joseph, i., 85
    Elinor E. Langdon, i., 82
    Eliza Bard, i., 83
    Eliza Bard II., i., 85
    Eliza Paine, i., 83
    Elizabeth, i., 85
    Elizabeth Breese, i., 85
    Elizabeth B. Moran, i., 84
    Elizabeth Ray, i., 85
    Elizabeth Schuchardt, i., 84
    Elsie Barber, i., 85
    Emily Prime, i., 83
    Eugene C., i., 85
    Family, i., 79
    Floyd, i , 84
    Francis, i., 84
    Frederick, i., 85

Index

251

Delafield, Frederick Prime, i., 85
   (Boyd) Harriet, i., 85
   Harriet Baldwin, i., 83
   Harriet Cecil, i., 84
   Harriet Coleman, i., 85
   Harriet W. Tallmadge, i., 81
   Helen Summers, i., 83
   Henry, i., 82
   Henry Parish, i., 84
   — John, the founder, i , 79, 80
   — John II., i., 81
   — John III., i., 83
   — John IV., i., 84
   Joseph (Major), i., 81
   Julia, i., 30
   (Longfellow) Julia, i., 85
   Julia Floyd, I., 82
   Julia Floyd II., i., 84
   Julia Livingston, i., 82
   Julia Livingston II., i., 83
   Julia R. F., i., 85
   Katherine Floyd, i., 84
   Katherine Van Rensselaer, i., 84
   Lettice L. Sands, i., 85
   Lewis Livingston, i., 83
   Lewis Livingston II., i., 85
   Lizzie H. Kamp, i., 84
   Louisa Eaton, i., 84
   Louisa Potter, i., 83
   Margaretta Beasley, i., 85
   Marguerite M. Dewey, i., 84
   Mary, i., 85
   (Sturgis) Mary, i., 84
   (Dubois) Mary Ann, i., 83
   Mary C. Livingston, i., 83
   (Neely) Mary Floyd, i , 83
   Mary P. Munson, i., 82
   Mary Roberts, i., 81
   Maturin Livingston, i., 83
   Maturin Livingston II., i., 85
   Nina M., i., 85
   Richard, i., 82
   Richard, i., 84
   Robert Hare, i., 85
   Rufus, i., 85
   Rufus King, i., 83
   Tallmadge, i , 83
   Tallmadge II., i., 84
   Wallace, i., 84
   Walter, i., 84
   William, i., 82
Delamater (Brevoort), Catherine, i., 29
De Lancey, Alice Izard, i., 97
   (Cruger), Ann, i., 70
   Anne Van Cortlandt, i., 91
   Anna, i , 95
   Anne, i., 92

De Lancey, Anne C., i., 97
   Anne Cox, i., 97
   Anne Heathcote, i., 93
   Cornelia Barclay, i., 97
   Edward Etienne, civil engineer, i., 98
   Edward Floyd [1795], i., 97
   Edward Floyd [1821], i., 97, 98
   Elizabeth C., i , 94
   Elizabeth E. H., i., 98
   Elizabeth F., i., 96
   Etienne (Stephen), i., 91, 92
   Family, i., 89, 90, 98
   Frances Jay Munro, i., 97
   Guy (Vicomte), i., 90, 91
   Hannah S., i., 95
   Jacques (Seigneur), i., 91
   Jacques II. (Seigneur), i., 91
   James (Judge), i., 92, 93, 94
   James II., i., 95
   Jane, i., 97
   John, i., 94
   John, i., 95
   John Peter, i., 95, 97
   John Peter II., i., 98
   John [1741] i., 96
   Josephine, i., 98
   Martha, i., 95
   Margaret A., i., 95
   Margaret M., i., 98
   Mary, i., 95
   Mary E., i., 97
   Oliver (General), i., 94, 95
   Oliver (Lieutenant), i., 96
   Oliver, i., 97
   Peter, i., 94
   Peter, i., 96, 97
   Phila Franks, i., 94
   Stephen (Etienne) the founder, i., 91 92
   Stephen II., i., 95
   Stephen (Captain), i., 95
   Stephen [1740], i., 96
   Stephen [1748], i., 97
   Susan, i., 92
   Susan Augusta, i., 97
   Susannah, daughter of Chief Justice, i., 95
   Susannah, daughter of Peter, i., 97
   Thomas J., i., 97
   Thomas J. (II.), i., 97
   Warren, i., 96
   Wilhelmina, V. C., i., 98
   William Heathcote (Bishop), i., 97
   William Heathcote II., i., 98
   William Howe (Sir), i., 97
De la Noy (Beekman), Catherine Peters, i., 29
Denning (Duer), Hannah, i., 130

Index

Denning, William, i., 130
Denniston (Clinton), Elizabeth, i , 46
De Nully, Anna, i., 72
De Peyster, Abraham (Captain), i., 109
    Abraham (Judge), i., 103, 104, 105
    Abraham (Treasurer), i., 105, 106
    Abraham [1742], i., 109
    Abraham [1753], i., 109
    Ann, i., 109
    Ann B., i., 109
    Anna Bancker, i., 105
    Anna Schuyler, i., 106
    Arent Schuyler, i., 108
    Arent II., i., 109, 110
    Augusta McEvers, i., 112
    Augustus (Captain), i., 110, 111
    Berthick H., i., 109
    Catharina, i., 105
    Catharine L., i., 109
    Catharine Schuyler, i., 106
    Christina B., i., 109
    Cornelia Lubbertse, i., 102
    Cornelius [1673], i., 105
    Elizabeth B., i., 29
    Elizabeth Brogan, i., 109
    Elizabeth Henry, i., 109
    Elizabeth Rutgers, i., 109
    Estelle Livingston, i., 112
    Family, i., 113
    Frances De Kay, i., 109
    Frances Goodhue Ashton, i., 111
    Frederick, i., 106
    Frederick (Captain), i., 109, 111
    Frederick J., i , 112
    Frederick the Marquis, i., 107
    Gerard, i., 106
    Gerard [1737], i., 109
    Helen Hake, i., 109
    Henry, i , 113
    Isaac, merchant, i., 105
    Jane Jansen, i., 109
    James [1745], i., 109
    James [1757], i., 109
    James Abraham (Colonel) i., 107
    James Ferguson, i., 111
    Johannes (Renteneer), i., 102, 103
    Johannes II., i., 105, 107
    Johannes (Captain), i., 106
    John [1731], i., 109
    John J. [1781], i , 113
    John Watts (Major-General), i , 112, 113
    John Watts [1841], i., 113
    Johnston Livingston, i., 113
    Joseph Reade, i., 109
    Julia Ann Toler, i., 113
    Margaret K., i., 107

De Peyster, Margaret Van Cortlandt, i., 106
    Maria Antoinette Kane Hone, i., 111
    Mary Bancker i., 105
    Mary Justine Watts, i., 111
    Mary Livingston, i., 113
    Mary O., i., 107
    Mary Van Baal, i., 105
    Nicholas, i., 109
    Pierre Cortlandt, i., 113
    Pierre Guilliaume [1707], i., 106-108
    Pierre Guilliaume II., i., 109
    Richard Varick, i., 113
    Robert Gilbert Livingston, i., 113
    Sarah R , i., 107
    Susan Maria C., i., 111
    William, i., 109
    William [1735], i., 109
    William [1792], i., 113
Detrich, George, i., 4
Dewey (Delafield), Marie, i., 84
De Witt (Clinton), Mary, i., 47
De Zeng, Josephine M. De Lancey, i., 98
    William S., i., 98
D'Hauteville, Elizabeth S. Fish, i., 141
    Frederick S. G., i., 141
Douglass (Barclay), Grace, i., 20
    (Cruger), Harriet, i., 73
Drawyer, Andrew (Admiral), i., 16
    (Barclay) Anna D., i., 16
Duane, Abraham, i., 123
    (Pell) Adelia, i., 123
    Althea Keteltas, i., 118
    Anthony, the founder, i., 117
    Cornelius, i., 123
    Eve Benson, i., 117
    Family, i., 117
    James, i., 118
    James Chatham, I., i., 123
    James Chatham, II., i., 124
    John, i., 123
-     (North) Maria, i., 123
-     Maria Livingston, i., 119
-     Marianne Bowers, i., 123
-     —— (Feathstonhaugh) Sarah, i., 123
Du Bois, Cornelius, i., 83
    (Delafield) Mary A., i., 83
Duer, Alexander, i., 131
·   (Irving) Anna H., i., 131
·   Anna Van Buren, i., 132
·   Anne B. Bunner, i., 131
·   Beverly Chew, i., 132
·   Caroline King, i., 131
·   Catharine Alexander, i., 129
·   (Beam) Catherine A., i., 131
·   Catherine Robinson, i., 131
·   Denning, i., 132
·   (Smith) Catherine, i., 132

Index 253

Duer, Edward Alexander, i., 132
  (Wilson) Eleanor J., i., 131
  (King) Elizabeth D., i., 131
  Elizabeth Mead, i., 132
  Ellen Travers, i., 132
  Family, i., 127
  (Robinson) Frances, i., 130
  (Hoyt) Frances M., i., 131
  George Wickham, i., 131
  Georgiana Huyler, i., 131
  Hannah M. Denning, i., 130
  (Robinson) Henrietta, i., 130
  (Gedney) Henrietta, i., 131
  James Gore King, i., 132
  John, i., 130
  John II., i., 132
  John Beverly, i., 132
  John King, i., 131
  Josephine Clark, i., 133
  Lady Catharine, i., 129
  Lady Kitty, i., 129
  Louise Suydam, i., 132
  Lucy Chew, i., 131
  (Chew) Maria T., i., 130
  Maria Westcott, i., 131
  (Breck) Mary, i., 132
  Mary A. Hamilton, i., 132
  Rufus King, i., 132
  (Smith) Sarah, i., 130
  Sarah Du Pont, i., 132
  Sophia Lawrence, i., 132
  William (Judge), i., 131
  William the founder, i., 127, 133
  William III., i., 132
  William Alexander II., i., 132
  William Denning, i., 131
Du Pont Henry, i., 132
— (Duer), Sarah, i., 132
Duyckinck (Beekman), Mary, i., 31
Dyckman (Cruger), Eliza L. C., i., 73

E

Ellison, Mary De Lancey, i., 97

F

Feathstonhaugh, George W., i., 123
  Sarah Duane, i., 123
Fish, Clarence S. Bryce, i., 141
  (Northcote) Edith, i., 141
  (Hauteville) Elizabeth S., i., 141
  (Morris) Elizabeth S., i., 139
  Elizabeth Sackett, i., 137
  Elizabeth Stuyvesant, i., 139
  Emily N. Mann, i., 141
  Family, i., 137

Fish, Hamilton, i., 139
- Hamilton II., i., 141
- Hamilton III., i., 141
- Hamilton IV., i., 141
- Jonathan the founder, i., 137
- (Benjamin) Julia K., i., 141
- Julia Kean, i., 141
- (Neilson) Margaret A., i., 139
- Marion Anthon, i., 142
- Marion G. Anthon, i., 142
- Nicholas (Colonel), i., 138
- Nicholas, ii., 141
- (Webster) Sarah, i., 141
- Sidney Webster, i., 142
- Stuyvesant, i., 139
- Stuyvesant (railway-president), 141
- Stuyvesant II., i., 142
- (Le Roy) Susan, i., 139
- (Rogers) Susan L., i., 141
Floyd, Elizabeth De Lancey, i., 96
  (Delafield) Julia, i., 82
  Nicoll, i., 82
  Nicoll (Colonel), i., 82
  Richard (Colonel), i., 96
  William, i., 82
Foster (Delafield), Clara C., i., 84
  Frederick, i., 84
Franklin, Benjamin, i., 93
  (Clinton) Maria, i., 52
Franks, Phila De Lancey, i., 94
Fraunces, Samuel, i., 92
Fulton, Robert, ii., 97

Gardiner, Abigail Worth, i., 152
  Abraham (Captain), i., 151
  Abraham (Colonel), i., 150
  Adele Griswold, i., 153
  Baldwin, i., 153
  Coralie Livingston, i., 153
  Coralie L. Jones, i., 153
  Daniel Dennison, i., 151
  David, i., 149
  David, i., 152
  David (the lawyer), i., 152
  David (4th Lord), i., 150
  David (6th Lord), i., 151
  David Johnson (8th Lord), i., 153
  David Johnson II., i., 153
  Deborah L. Avery, i., 151
  Elenor Groesbeck, i., 152
  Elizabeth Allyn, i., 149
  Elizabeth Coit, i., 150
  Elizabeth Hedges, i., 149
  Elizabeth Mulford, i., 151

Index

Gardiner, Eunice Otis, i., 151
    Family, i., 145
    Frances Mulford, i., 153
    Hannah Havens, i., 151
    Howell, i., 152
    Jeremiah, i., 151
    Jerusha Buel, i., 151
    Joanna Conkling, i., 151
    John, i., 151
    John (of Eatons Neck), i., 151
    John i., 153
    John, Jr., i., 151
    John (3d Lord), i., 149
    John (5th Lord), i., 151
    John (Dr.), i., 151
    John David (Rev.), i., 153
    John Griswold, i., 153
    John Lyon, i., 153
    John Lyon II., i., 153
    Joseph (Captain), i., 150
    Julia Havens, i., 152
    Juliana McLachlan, i., 152
    (Tyler) Juliana, i., 152
    Lion, the founder, i., 145
    Louise L. Veron, i., 153
    Lydia Dann, i., 152
    Lyon, i., 153
    Margaret Moore, i., 152
    Mary L'Hommedieu, i., 153
    Mary C. L'Hommedieu, i., 153
    Mary King, i., 149
    Mary Leringman, i , 149
    Mary Smith, i., 151
    Mary Thompson, i., 153
    Mary Wilemson, i., 146
    Nathaniel (Dr.), i., 151
    Phœbe Weed, i., 152
    Rachel Gardiner, i., 151
    Samuel (Captain), i., 150
    Samuel, i., 151
    Samuel Buel (10th Lord), i., 153
    Samuel Smith, i., 152
    Sara Grant, i., 150
    Sarah Chandler, i , 149
    Sarah Griswold, i , 152
    Susan Mott, i., 153
    William, i., 151
    Winthrop, i., 153
Gedney, David, i., 131
    Henrietta Duer, i., 131
Gibbes (Astor), Charlotte Augusta, i., 8
Gray, Mary Little (Clinton), i., 47
Gustavus Adolphus, King, i., 13

H

Hake (De Peyster), Helen, i., 109
Hall (De Peyster), Berthick, i., 109

Hall, Catherine C. Delafield, i., 84
    John J., i., 84
Hallett (Delafield), Ann, i., 80
    Joseph, i., 80
Hamilton, Adelaide, i., 163
    Alexander, i., 163
    Alexander, i., 71, 109, 121, 122, 138 157–161
    Alexander (Laird), i., 137
    Alexander II., i., 161
    Alexander III., i., 162
    Alice, i., 163
    Allen McLane, i., 163
    Charles Apthorp i., 163
    Charlotte Augusta, i., 163
    Charlotte Pierson, i., 163
    (Schuyler) Eliza, i., 162
    Elizabeth, i., 163
    Elizabeth Schuyler, i., 161
    Family, i., 157
    James, i., 157
    James Alexander, i., 162
    John Church, i., 162
    Juliet P. Morgan, i., 164
    Maria Eliza, i., 163
    Maria E. Van den Heuval, i., 162
    Mary Augusta, i., 132
    (Schuyler) Mary M., i., 162
    Philip, i., 161
    Philip, II., i., 162
    Schuyler (Major-General), i., 162
    Schuyler, Jr., i., 164
    William Gaston, i., 163
    William Pierson, i., 164
Harris (Cruger), Elizabeth, i., 69
Hauteville, Elizabeth S. Fish d', i., 141
    Frederick S. G. d', i., 141
Hayward (Cruger), Ann T., i., 73
Heathcote (De Lancey), Ann, i., 93
    Caleb, i., 93, 94
Hedges (Gardiner), Elizabeth, i., 149
Hicks, Abigail B., i., 59
    (Cornell) Charity, i., 57
    Charlotte Brevoort, i., 30
    Whitehead (Mayor), i., 39
Hitchcock, Lieutenant-Colonel, i., 58
Hobart, Bishop, i., 97
Hoffman, Abraham, i., 176
— Adrian (Dr.), i., 179
    Alida L. Hansen, i., 172
— Ann C., Stoutenburgh, i., 179
— Anthony (Colonel), i., 175
— Anthony (Judge), i., 173
— Anthony A. (Judge), i., 176
    Anthony N., i., 179
— Arthur Gilman, i., 184
— Beekman Verplanck (Captain), i., 179

Index

Hoffman, Beulah Murray, i., 177
 Cadwallader Colden (Rev.), i., 180
 Catharina van Gaasbeck, i., 173
 Catharine Douw, i., 175
 Catharine Verplanck, i., 175
 Charles Fenno, i., 182
 Charles Frederick (Rev.), i., 183
 Cornelia R. Vredenburgh, i., 175
 David Murray, i., 180
 Edward Fenno, i., 184
 Edy Silvester, i., 176
 Eleanor L. Vail, i., 183
 Elizabeth Baylies, i., 184
 Elizabeth Snedeker, i., 176
 Emily Burrall, i., 182
 Emmerentje, C. D. W., i., 171
 Eugene Augustus (Rev. Dr.), i., 182
 Eugene Augustus II., i., 184
 Family, i., 169
 Frances A. Burrall, i., 180
 Gertrude Verplanck, i., 176
 Glorvina R. Storm, i., 178
 Harmanus (Captain), i., 175
 Helena Kissam, i., 176
 Helena Van Wyck, i., 174
 Jane Hoffman, i., 176
 John Thompson (Governor), i., 183
 John White, i., 184
 Josiah Ogden (Judge), i., 177
 Josiah Ogden, II., i., 184
 Lindley Murray, i., 180
 Lindley Murray II., i., 184
 Lysbeth Hermans, i., 177
 Margaret Bayard, i., 176
 Maria Fenno, i., 178
 Martin, the founder, i., 170
 Martin (Colonel), i., 172, 173
 Martin (Captain), i., 176
 Martin, i., 177
 Martin, i., 180
 Mary Colden, i., 178
 Mary C. Elmendorf, i., 183
 Mary Frances Seton, i., 177
 Mary M. Ogden, i., 180
 Mary Rutgers, i., 175
 Matilda, i., 181
 Mills, i., 172
 Murray (Judge), i., 180
 Nicolaes (Captain), i., 171
 Nicholas (Captain), i., 171
 Nicholas, i., 174
 Nicholas Anthony, i., 176
 Ogden, i., 181
 Ogden (Judge), i., 184
 Philip Livingston, i., 176
 Philip Verplanck, i., 178
 Phœbe Pell, i., 179

Hoffman, Phœbe W. Townsend, i., 180
 Rachel Dubois, i., 176
 Richard Anthony (Dr.), i., 179
 Richard Kissam (Dr.), i., 179
 Robert (Colonel), i., 175
 Samuel Southard (Colonel), i., 184
 Samuel Verplanck, i., 178
 — — II., i., 184
 Sarah Ogden, i., 174
 Sarah Van Alstyne, i., 175
 Tryntje Benson, i., 172
 Virginia E. Southard, i., 182
 Wickham (Colonel), i., 184
 William (Dr.), i., 178
 Zachariah (Lieutenant), i., 176
 Zacharias (Captain), i., 171
 — — II., (Captain), i., 173
 Zecharias (Captain), i., 171
Holmes, Abiel (Dr.), ii., 243
 Oliver Wendell, ii., 243
 Sarah Wendell, ii., 243
Hone (De Peyster), Maria A. K., i., 111
Hoyt, Frances M. Duer, i., 131
 Henry S., i., 131
Hull, General, i., 40
Hunter, Elizabeth E. De Lancey, i., 98
 Governor, i., 28

I

Irving, Anna H. Duer, i., 131
 Pierre P. (Rev), i., 131
 Washington, i., 39, 40, 41
Izard, Alice De Lancey, i., 97
 Ralph, i., 97

J

Jansen, (De Peyster) Jane, i., 109
Jay (Balch), Anna, i., 199
 — (von Schweintz), Anna, i., 200
 . Anna Maria, i., 191
 — (Pierrepont) Anna Maria, i., 199
 — Anna M. Bayard, i., 191
 — (Robinson) Augusta, i., 200
 — Augusta McVickar, i., 198
 . Augustus, i., 200
 — Augustus II., i., 191, 192
 . Augustus the founder, i., 190
 — (Dubois) Catherine, i., 199
 — (Chapman) Eleanor, i., 200
 — Eleanor K. Field, i., 199
 — (Pellew) Eliza, i., 199
 — Emily Astor Kane, i., 200
 — Euphemia Dunscombe, i., 192
 — (Munro) Eva, i., 191
 — Family, i., 189
 — (Van Cortlandt) Frances, i., 191
 — Frederick, i., 191

Index

Jay, Harriette A. Vinton, i., 200
- James (Dr.), i., 191, 192
- John, i., 199
- John (Chief-Justice), i., 191
- John Clarkson (Dr.), i., 199
- John Clarkson II., (Dr.), i., 200
- Josephine Pearson, i., 199
- (Van Horn) Judith, i., 191
- Julie Post, i , 200
- (Wurts) Laura, i., 200
- Laura Prime, i., 199
- Lucy Oelrichs, i., 200
- Margaret Barclay, i., 192
- (Banyer) Maria, i., 197
- (Butterworth) Maria B., i., 199
- (Edwards) Mary, i., 200
- (Schieffelin) Mary, i., 200
- (Vallette) Mary, i., 191
- Mary Duyckinck, i., 192
- Mary R. Clarkson, i., 197
- (Prime) Mary Rutherford, i., 199
- Mary Van Cortlandt, i., 191
- Peter, i., 190
- Peter (Jr.), i., 191
- Peter II., i., 191
- Peter Augustus, i., 197
- II., i., 199
- III., i., 200
- Pierre, i., 190
- (Dawson) Sarah, i., 199
- (Bruen) Sarah Louisa, i., 199
- Sarah V. B. Livingston, i., 195
- (Clarkson) Susan Maria, i., 199
- William, i., 198
- William (Colonel), i., 200
Jefferson, Thomas, i., 49
Johnson, Samuel (Rev.), i., 17
Jones, Anne DeLancey, i., 95
- (Clinton) Catherine, i., 52
- De Witt Clinton, i., 52
- (Cruger) Frances A., i., 73
- Julia De Witt, i., 52
- Thomas (Judge), i., 95

K

Kamp (Delafield), Lizzie H., i., 84
- Richard, i., 84
Kean (Fish), Julia, i., 141
Keoncott (De Peyster), Margaret, i., 107
Keteltas, Abraham (Rev.), i., 118
- (Duane) Althea, i., 118
- (Beekman), Jane, i., 31
Kieft, William (Governor), i., 56
King, Adelaide L. Yorke, i., 213
- Adeline McKee, i., 212
- (Paterson) Alice C., i., 211

King, Archibald Gracie, i., 131, 212
- Caroline, i., 211
- Caroline, i., 222
- (Duer) Caroline, i., 131, 211
- Charles (General), i., 213
- Charles (President), i., 209
- Charles Ray (Dr.), i., 212
- Cornelius Low (Colonel), i., 212
- Cyrus, i., 206
- Edward, i., 211
- Edward II., i., 212
- (Halsey) Eliza G., i., 211
- Eliza Gracie, i., 209
- Elizabeth D. Duer, i., 131, 212
- Elizabeth Fisher, i., 212
- Elizabeth Lewis, i., 212
- (Van Rensselaer) Elizabeth R., i., 211
- Emily Post, i., 211
- (Paterson) Emily S., i., 211
- (Martin) Esther, i., 211
- Family, i., 205
- (McLane) Fanny L., i., 211, 212
- Frederic Gore (Dr.), i., 211
- (Davis) Frederica G., i., 210
- (Schuyler) Gertrude, i., 211
- Hannah Fisher, i., 212
- (Wilkes) Harriet, i., 211
- Henrietta Low, i., 210
- Isabella Bragdon, i., 206
- Isabella R. Cochrane, i., 212
- James Gore, i., 131, 211
- James Gore II., i., 131, 211
- Janet de Kay, i., 212
- John, the founder, i., 205
- John Alsop (Lieutenant), i., 208
- John Alsop II., i., 212
- Julia Lawrence, i., 211
- Maria Williamson, i., 213
- (Gardiner) Mary, i., 149
- (Nightingale) Mary, i., 211
- (Richards), Mary, i., 211
- (Waddington), Mary A., i., 211
- Mary Alsop, i., 206
- Mary Black, i., 206
- Mary C. Rhinelander, i., 212
- Mary Ray, i., 209
- Mary Stowell, i., 205
- Nancy Fisher, i , 212
- Richard, i., 206
- Richard II , i., 212
- Rufus, founder in New York, i., 206
- Rufus II. (General), i., 212
- Rufus III., i., 213
- Sarah R. Gracie, i., 211
- Sarah Worthington, i., 211
- Susan Elliott, i., 212
- William (Governor), i., 206

Index

King, William Gracie (Colonel), i., 212
Kip, Abraham, i., 221
   (Rhinelander), Adelaide, i., 226
   Anna de Sille, i., 219
   Anne C. Wilson, i., 225
   Brockholst Livingston, i., 224
   Catalina de la Noy, i., 221
   Catalina de Suyers, i., 219
   Charlotte M. Wells, i., 223
   Cornelia Brady, i., 226
   Cornelia Lewis, i., 223
   Elizabeth C. Kinney, i., 226
   Elizabeth Marschalk, i., 222
   (Storrs) Elizabeth, i., 224
   Eva K. M., i., 225
   Eva Lorrillard, i., 225
   Family, i , 217
   Francis M. (Rev.), i., 225
   George Goelet, i , 223
   Harriet L. Van Rensselaer, i., 224
   Hendrick, the founder, i., 217, 218
   Hendrick II., i., 219
   Hendrick III., i., 221
   Henri or, Henry II., i., 218
   Henry III., i., 223
   Henry IV., i., 223
   Isaac, i., 219
   Isaac, i., 221
   Isaac, i., 221
   Isaac, i., 222
   Isaac (Dr.), i., 222
   Isaac Lewis, i., 224
   Isaac Lewis (Dr.), i., 226
   Jacob, i., 219
   Jacob, i., 221
   Jacob, i., 221
   Jean Baptiste, i., 218
   John, i., 221
   Lawrence, i., 226
   Lawrence (Colonel), i., 225
   Leonard, i., 222
   Leonard II., i., 224
   Leonard III., i., 224
   Leonard IV., i., 225
   Leonard William, i., 224
   Leonard William, Jr., (Rev), i., 226
   Magdalena Van Vleeck, i., 221
   Margaret de Marveil, i., 218
   Maria E. Lawrence, i., 224
   Maria Ingraham, i , 224
   Maria Vermilyea, i., 219
   Marie de la Montagne, i., 219
   (Kane) Mary, i., 224
   Mary R. Bayard, i., 225
   Nicholas, i., 221
   Rachel Kip, i., 222

Kip, Rachel Swarthout, i., 221
   — Roeloff, i., 217, 218
   — Roeloff II., i., 218
   — Roeloff III., i., 222
   — Samuel I., i., 222
   — Samuel II., i., 223
   — Sarah de Mille, i., 221
   — Sarah Smith, i., 224
   — (Burgess) Sophia, i., 224
   — William F., i , 222
   — William Ingraham (Rev.), i., 224
   — William Ingraham II., i. 221
   — William Ingraham III., i., 226
   — William V. B., i., 226
Knickerbocker, Dietrich, i., 40
Kortnght (Cruger), Eliza, i., 73
Krebben, Christian C., i , 84
   Edith Delafield, i., 84
Kuyter Jochiem P. (Captain), i., 36

L

Langdon (Delafield), Elinor E., i., 82
   John, i., 82
   Thomas E., i., 82
Lawrence, Abraham Riker, i., 237
   Abraham Riker (Judge), i., 243, 244
   Adam, i., 233
   Albert Gallatin (General), i., 244
   Alfred Newbold, i., 244
   Alice W. Work, i., 245
   Amy Whipple, i., 234
   Andrew (Captain), i., 236
   Anna, i., 244
   (Delafield) Anna A., i., 83
   Anna Townsend, i., 236
   Augusta M. Nicoll, i., 240
   Catharine i., 246
   Catherine Farmer, i., 234
   Catherine Livingston, i., 234-235
   Catherine Remsen, i , 236
   Clement, i., 245
   Charles William, i., 243
   Christina Knell, i , 241
   Cornelia A., i , 242
   Cornelius Van Wyck, i , 240
   David, i , 234.
   Deborah Smith, i., 232, 234
   Deborah Woodhill, i., 233
   Deborah Woolsey, i., 233
   Edward Newbold, i., 244
   Effingham, i , 233
   —   —   i., 244
   —   —   II., i., 234
   —   —   III., i., 236
   —   —   (Judge), i., 236
   Eliza Miner, i., 244

Index

Lawrence, Elizabeth Little, i., 233
    Elizabeth Smith, i , 232
    Elizabeth Watson, i., 236
    Estell, i., 237
    Eugene, i., 241
    Family, i., 229
    Ferdinand, i., 241
    Hannah Bowne, i., 233
    Hannah Newbold, i., 244
    Harriet, i., 242
    Henry, i , 230
    Henry, i., 242, 243
    (Beekman) Isabella, i., 32
    Isabella E. Burgoyne, i., 241
    Isaphene C., i., 242
    James (Sir), i., 229
    James (Captain), i., 238-239
    John, i., 230-231
    John, i., 233
    John, i., 234
    John, i., 237
    John (Captain), i , 233
    John (Judge), i., 233
    John Burling, i., 244
    John L., i., 237
    John L., i , 243
    John L., i , 244
    John L , i , 244-245
    John Smith, i , 243
    John Watson, i., 240
    Jonathan, i., 233
    Jonathan, i., 236
    Jonathan (Major), i., 235
    Jonathan (Dr.), i , 243
    Jonathan (Jr.), i , 243
    Jonathan V., i., 233
    Joseph, i , 232-233
    Joseph, i., 234
    Joseph, i., 237
    Joseph, i., 241
    Judith Fish, i., 235
    Julia B., i., 242
    Julia Montandevert, i., 239
    Lavinia Oliver, i., 245
    Lydia A., i., 244
    Margaret S. Müller, i., 237
    Maria C. Prall, i , 240
    Maria E., i., 242
    Mary, i., 231
    (Whittinghame) Mary, i., 231
    Mary Betts, i., 234
    Mary A Jones, i , 237
    Mary K. Bowne, i., 240
    Mary Richardson, i., 243
    Mary Sackett, i , 237
    Mary Townley, i., 232
    Mary Woodbury, i., 233

Lawrence, Matilda Washington, i., 229
    Nicholas, i., 237
    Obadiah, i., 234
    Oliver, i., 245
    Patience Sackett, i., 233
    Rachel A. Hicks, i , 240
    Richard, i., 230
    Richard, i , 233
    Richard, i., 236-237
    Richard, i., 243
    Richard, i., 243
    Richard (Captain), i., 235
    Robert (Sir), i., 229
    Rosetta Townsend, i., 241
    Ruth, i., 245
    Ruth Riker, i., 235
    Samuel (Judge), i., 236
    Samuel Adams, i., 236
    Samuel Sterry (Dr), i., 241
    Sarah Smith, i., 237
    Sarah A. Smith, i., 237
    Sophy Tilley, i., 243
    Susanna T. Eaton, i., 234
    Sybil Sterry, i., 234
    Thamen Fisher, i., 236
    Thomas, i., 237
    Thomas (Captain), i., 234
    Thomas (Captain), i., 235
    Thomas (Major), i., 230, 231
    Thomas of Newton, i., 233
    Walter, i., 236
    Watson E. (Judge), i., 240
    William, i., 230
    William, i., 232
    William, i., 236
    William, i., 246
    Willlium (Dr.), i., 234
    William (Judge), i., 230, 231
    William Anderson, i., 243
    William Beach, i., 241, 242, 243
    William Miner, i., 245
    William T., i., 237
    William Thomas, i., 243
Lefferts (Brevoort), Elizabeth D., i , 41
    Lefferts, i., 41
Leisler, Jacob (Governor), i , 28
Lent, Abraham, i., 19
    (Barclay) Dentie or Dientje, i , 19
Le Roy, Catherine Rutgers, ii., 139
    Cornelia Rutgers, ii., 139
    Daniel, i., 139
    Jacob, ii., 109
    Susan Fish, i., 139
Lerringman (Gardiner), Mary, i., 149
Lewis, Ann, i., 253
    Elizabeth Annesley, i., 251
    Elizabeth Ludlow, i., 253

Index

Lewis, Family, i., 249–256
    Francis, Jr., i., 253
    Francis, the Signer, i., 82, 249, 250, 252–255
    Gertrude Livingston, i., 255
    Margaret (Delafield), i., 82
    Morgan (General), i., 82, 253-254-255-256
Library, the Astor, i., 7
— the New York Society, i., 18
Lincoln, Abraham, i., 140
Livingston, Abraham ii., 16
    Albert Gallatin ii., 14, 15
    Alida, ii., 11
    Anne Horne S., ii., 16
    Brockholst [1757], ii., 12, 13
    (Ten Broeck), Catharine, ii., 11
    Catherine, ii., 11
    Charles Carroll, ii., 13
    Cornelia Beekman, ii., 6
    Edward, i., 130; ii., 13, 14, 15
    Eliza, ii ,16
    Elizabeth Knight, ii., 5
    Elizabeth S., ii., 16
    (De Peyster), Estelle, i., 112
    Eugene Augustus, i., 83
    Family, ii., 3, 17
    Gilbert, ii., 6, 7, 13
    Henry, ii., 11
    Henry, ii., 12
    Henry B., ii., 16
    Henry W., ii., 12
    Herman, ii., 12
    James, ii., 7
    James, ii., 11
    James, ii., 17
    James (Colonel), ii., 16
    (Van Horne), Johanna, ii., 6
    John, ii., 7
    John, ii , 11
    John, ii., 11
    John, ii., 17
    John (of Oak Hill), ii., 12
    John (Colonel), ii., 5
    John (Rev.), ii., 3, 4
    John G., ii., 112
    John Henry (Rev.), ii., 13
    John P., ii., 16
    John Swift, ii., 12
    John William (Admiral), ii., 16
    Johnston, ii., 12
    Johnston II., ii , 12
    (Delafield), Julia, i , 82
    Katherine Van Brugh, ii., 5
    Louis, ii., 12
    Margaret, i., 139
    Margaret, ii., 11

Livingston, (Vetch), Margaret, ii., 6
    Margaretta Schuyler, ii., 7
    Maria K., ii , 11
    (Decare) Mary, ii , 11
    (De Peyster., Mary, i , 113
    (Penn Allen), Mary, ii., 12
    (Thong), Mary, ii., 7
    (Delafield), Mary C., i., 83
    Maturin (Judge), i., 82
    Maturin, ii., 17
    Maturin II , ii , 17
    Peter, ii., 7
    Peter R., ii., 11
    Peter R., ii., 12
    Peter Van Brugh, ii., 7–9
    Philip, ii , 5–7
    Philip, ii , 7, 8
    Richard (Lieutenant-Colonel), ii., 16
    Robert, i., 118; ii., 4–5
    Robert, ii., 7
    Robert, ii , 17
    Robert (of Clermont), ii., 6, 7, 10, 11, 13
    Robert (Nephew), ii., 6, 7, 17
    Robert Cambridge, ii., 11, 12
    Robert Cambridge II., ii , 12
    Robert Cambridge III., ii., 12
    Robert Cambridge IV., ii., 12
    Robert R. (Chancellor), ii , 13, 14
    Robert R. (Judge), ii., 10, 11, 13
    Sylvia, ii., 12
    Walter, ii., 11
    Walter [1740], ii., 12
    William (Governor), ii., 7, 9, 11, 12
Lloyd (Delafield), Anne S , i , 85
Longfellow, Frederick H., i., 85
    Julia Delafield, i., 85
Low, Isaac, i., 69
Lubbertse, Cornelia De Peyster, i , 102
Lynch, Thomas, i., 118

M

McAdam, Anne Charlotte De Lancey, i., 97
— John L., i., 97
    William I., 69
McEvers, Charles, i , 69
McGee (Barclay), Fanny, i , 20
Madison, James, i., 49, 50
Mann (Fish), Emily N., i., 141
Markoe (Cruger), Ann, i., 72
Marshall (Barclay), Margaret, i., 20
Maur-Rhys, ii., 22
Maxwell (Cruger), Sarah J., i., 73
Mead (Duer), Elizabeth, i., 132
— Orlando, i., 132
Milledoler (Beekman), Abian Steele, i., 32

Milledoler, Philip (Rev. Dr.), i., 31
Montgomery, Hannah S., i., 69
Moran, Daniel E., i., 84
— (Delafield), Elizabeth B., i., 84
Morris, A. P., ii., 34
    Anna M., ii., 35
    Anna R. Russell, ii., 36
    Annie C., i., 35
    (De Peyster), Augusta M., i., 112
    Eleanor R., ii., 36
    Elizabeth S. Fish, i., 139
    Emily Lorillard, ii, 36
    Family, ii., 21
    Fordham, ii., 36
    Francis (Commodore), ii., 36
    Gerard Walton, ii., 35
    Gouverneur, ii., 29
    Gouverneur II , ii., 33
    Gouverneur III., ii., 35
    Gouverneur IV., ii., 35
    Helen Van Cortlandt, ii., 34
    Henry, ii., 35
    Henry Lewis, ii., 36
    Isabella Graham, ii., 26
    Jacob (General), ii., 33
    James (Captain), ii., 34
    John (Captain), ii., 22
    Katrintje Staats, ii., 29
    Lewis (Chief Justice), ii., 24
    Lewis (Colonel), ii., 22
    Lewis (Colonel), ii., 34
    Lewis III., ii., 28
    Lewis IV., ii., 29
    Lewis Gouverneur, ii., 34
    Lewis Spencer, ii., 36
    Martha J. Cary, ii., 35
    Mary Cox, ii., 34
    Mary Walton, ii., 32
    Randolph, ii., 35
    Richard, ii., 29
    Richard (Captain), ii , 21
    Richard (Judge), ii., 32
    Richard Lewis (Dr.), i., 139
    Richard Valentine II., ii , 35
    Richard Valentine (Commodore), ii., 34
    Robert (of Fordham), ii., 34
    Robert Hunter (Governor), ii., 28
    Robert Hunter II., ii., 34, 35
    Sarah Pole, ii., 23
    Sarah Gouverneur, ii., 29
    Sarah Ludlow, ii., 32
    Staats Long, ii., 29
    William, ii , 22
Morse (Delafield), Elizabeth B., i., 85
    Sidney, i., 85
Munro, Frances De Lancey, i., 97
    Peter Jay, i., 97

Munson (Delafield), Mary P., i., 82
— Judge, i., 82

Neely, Henry A., i. 83
    Henry A. (Rev), i , 83
    (Delafield), Mary F., i., 83
Neilson, John (Dr.), i., 139
— Margaret A. Fish, i., 139
New York Society Library, i., 18
Nicolls, Richard (Governor), i., 56, 57, 67
North, Maria Duane, i., 123
    William (General), i., 123
Northcote, Edith Fish, i., 141
    Oliver, i , 141

O

Oakley, Matilda C. C., i., 72
    Thomas J. (Chief Justice), i., 72
Octave (De Peyster), Mary, i., 107
Ogilvie, J. (Rev.), i., 16
Oldfield (Barclay), Lillie, i., 20
Osgood, Alfred (Rev.), ii., 45
    Alfred T.,ii., 46
    Caroline T. Lawrence, ii., 46
    Catharine R. Montgomery, ii., 47
    Clara Runyon, ii., 46
    Daniel (Rev.), ii., 42
    David (Rev.), ii., 46
    David L., ii., 46
    Family, ii., 41
    Frances, ii., 46
    Harriet K., ii., 46
    Harriet K. Ladd, ii., 46
    Henry (Dr.), ii., 42
    Herbert L. (Professor), ii., 47
    Howard (Rev.), ii , 46
    Howard Lawrence, ii., 47
    Isaac (Colonel), ii , 42
    John (Colonel), ii., 42
    John (Captain), the founder, ii., 41
    Joseph (Dr.), ii., 43
    Julia, ii., 45
    Kendall (Dr.), ii., 42
    Maria Bowne Franklin, ii., 45
    Maria Caile, ii., 46
    Martha Brandon, ii., 45
    (Genet), Martha B. II., ii., 45
    Mary M., ii., 46
    Paulia C. Pelt, ii., 46
    Peter (Captain), ii., 42, 43
    Samuel (Captain), ii., 42
    Samuel (Colonel), ii., 43, 44
    Samuel (Rev.), ii., 45
    Samuel Stillman, ii., 46

Index

Osgood (Field), Susan M., ii., 45
    Thaddeus (Rev), ii., 42
    Walter Franklin, ii., 45
Osterburg (Cornell), Mary C., i., 62

P

Paine (Delafield), Eliza, i., 83
Paterson (Van Rensselaer), Cornelia, ii., 219
    William (Governor), ii., 219
Paul (Astor), Mary D., i., 8
Pell, Adelia Duane, i., 123
— George W., i., 123
— James D., i., 123
— John A , i., 123
— Richard M., i., 123
— Robert L., i., 123
Perry O. H. (Commodore), i., 41
Peters, Hugh (Rev.), i., 146
Phillips, Margaret Wendell, ii , 243
    Wendell, ii., 243
    William, ii., 243
Pool (Duer), Sophia L., i., 132
Potter, Abigail Stevens, ii., 55
    Alice Key, ii., 55
    Alonzo (Bishop), ii., 53
    Anna, ii., 55
    Anna Knight, ii., 53
    Charles Henry, ii., 55
    Clarkson N., ii., 54
    David T., ii., 55
    Edward Tuckerman, ii., 55
    Eliphalet N., ii., 55
    Eliza Rogers, ii., 55
    Esther Sheldon, ii., 53
    Family, ii., 51
    Frank Hunter, ii., 55
    Frances Seton, ii., 55
    Frances Tileston, ii., 55
    Harriet D. Jones, ii., 55
    Helen Fuller, ii., 55
    Henry Codman (Bishop), ii., 55
    Horatio (Bishop), ii., 53
    Horatio, Jr., ii., 55
    Howard, ii., 55
    James Neilson, ii., 55
    Jane Burlingame, ii., 51
    John, ii., 53
    John, ii., 53
    John, ii., 53
    Joseph, ii., 53
    Julia Blatchford, ii., 53
    (Delafield), Louisa, i., 83
    Margaret Pollock, ii., 55
    (Thompson), Maria, ii., 55
    Mary J., ii., 55
    Mary Jane, ii., 55

Potter, Mary J. Tomlinson, ii., 55
    Mary L Brown, ii., 55
    Paraclete, i., 83
    (Delafield), Paraclete, i., 83
    Phœbe, ii., 55
    Phœbe Arnold Greene, ii., 51
    Robert, the founder, ii., 51
    Robert B. (General), ii., 55
    Robert Minturn, ii., 55
    Ruth Fisher, ii., 53
    Sarah M. Nott, ii., 53
    Sarah Porter, ii , 55
    Thomas, ii., 53
    Virginia Mitchell, ii., 55
    William A., ii., 55
    William Bleecker (Professor), ii., 55
Prime (Delafield), Emily, i., 83
    Frederick, i., 83

R

Ramsay (Cruger), Martha, i., 72
Rapalje, Agnes Bergen, ii., 67
    Aletje Cornell, ii., 65
    Anna Denys, ii., 64
    Annetje, ii., 64
    Augustus, ii., 70
    Catalina Trico, ii., 64
    Catalyntje, ii , 64
    Cornelius, ii., 65
    Cornelius, ii , 66
    Daniel, ii., 64
    Daniel, ii., 65
    Daniel, ii., 66
    Daniel, ii., 67
    Daniel (Major), ii., 67
    Daniel (Rev.), ii., 67
    Derrick, ii., 66
    Elizabeth, ii , 64
    Elizabeth Remsen, ii., 66
    Elizabeth Van Mater, ii., 70
    Ellen Hardenbrook, ii., 68
    Ellen Maria, ii., 69
    Family, ii , 63
    Folkert, ii , 66
    George, ii., 66
    George, ii , 66
    George, ii., 68
    George, ii., 69
    George, Jr , ii , 66
    George A., ii., 69
    George B., ii., 68
    George Bernard, ii., 69
    Gilbert V. M., ii., 70
    Hilletje Van Vechten, ii., 65
    Jacob, ii , 64
    Jacob, ii., 65
    Jacob, ii , 69

Index

Rapalje, Jan, the founder, ii., 63
   Jan, Jr., ii., 64
   Jannetje, ii., 64
   Jeronimus, ii , 64
   Jeronimus, ii., 65
   Jeronimus, ii., 66
   Jeronimus, ii , 66
   Joanna Antonides, ii., 65
   John, ii., 67
   Judith, ii., 64
   Marritje, ii., 64
   Matilda Polhemus, ii., 66
   Michael, ii., 67
   Phœbe, ii., 66
   Rem, ii., 66
   Rem, ii., 68
   Samuel, ii., 67
   Sarah, ii., 66
   (Bergen) (Bogaert), Sarah, ii 64
   Sarah Brinckerhoff, ii., 65
   Sarah E., ii., 69
   Sarah E. Staples, 69
   Sarah Klock, ii , 65
   Sarah Van Vechten, ii., 65
   Susan E. Provost, ii , 68
   Tunis, ii., 65
   Tunis, ii , 66
   Tunis, ii., 66
   Williamson, ii., 67
Rathbone (Cruger), Susan M. W , i., 73
Reade, Joseph, i., 107
   (De Peyster), Sarah, i., 107
Remsen, Abraham, ii., 75
   Abraham, ii., 76
   Aert, ii., 76
   (Dorlandt), Anna, ii., 75
   (Adriense), Catalina, ii., 75
   Charles (Dr), ii , 79
   Christopher, ii., 75
   Daniel, ii., 75
   Elizabeth de Peyster, ii., 78
   Family, ii , 73
   (Hegeman), Femmetje, ii., 75
   Garrett, ii., 76
   Georgiana D., ii , 78
   Hendrick, ii., 77
   Hendrick, ii , 77
   Henry, ii., 77
   Henry, ii., 78
   Henry, ii., 79
   (Schenck), Heyltie, ii., 76
   (Vanderbilt), Hildegong, ii., 75
   Ira (Dr), ii , 79
   Isaac, ii., 75
   Isaac, Jr., ii., 75
   Jacob, ii., 75
   Jacob D., ii., 79

Remsen, Jan, ii., 75
   Jane Suydam, ii., 78
   (Van Nostrand), Jannetje, ii., 75
   Jannetje Rapalje, ii., 74
   Jeremias, ii., 75
   Jeromus, ii., 75
   Jeromus (Captain), ii., 76
   John, ii., 75
   Joris, ii., 75
   Lilian Livingston, ii , 79
   Luke, ii., 76
   Mary Delprat, ii., 78
   (Howard), Phœbe, ii., 76
   Phœnix, ii., 79
   Rem, ii., 75
   Rem, ii., 76
   Rem II , ii., 75
   Rem III , ii , 75
   Rem Jansen, the founder, ii , 74
   Robert G., ii., 78
   Robert G. (Dr.), ii., 79
   (Adriense), Sarah, ii , 75
   William, ii., 78
   William, ii., 79
Renwick (Henry), Agnes, ii., 86
   Anna L. Aspenwall, ii , 88
   Annie Cooke, ii., 90
   Claire Rhinelander, ii., 91
   Edward B., ii., 91
   Edward S., ii , 88
   (Brown), Eliza C., ii., 91
   Eliza S. Crosby, ii., 90
   (Wittingham), Elizabeth, ii , 91
   Elizabeth A. Brevoort, ii , 90
   Ellen J. Wise, ii., 91
   (Hurry), Emily A., ii , 91
   Emily D. Hicks, ii., 91
   Evelyn Smith, ii , 91
   Family, ii., 83
   Frederick W., ii., 90
   Frederick W. II., ii., 91
   Gertrude Sears, ii., 91
   Harold S., ii., 91
   Harriet McDonell, ii , 91
   (Schaff), Helen S., ii., 91
   Henry, ii., 90
   Henry B., ii , 86
   (Smedburg), Isabella, ii., 86
   James, ii , 87
   James (Professor), ii , 84
   James, the founder, ii., 84
   James, the martyr, ii., 83
   James A., ii., 90
   (Wilkes), Jane, ii , 86
   (Callender), Jane J , ii , 90
   Jane Jeffrey, ii., 84
   Julia Kortright, ii., 90

Index 263

Renwick, (Munroe), Laura, ii , 90
    Margaret A. Brevoort, ii., 86
    (Brown), Mary C., ii., 91
    (Strong), Mary C., ii , 91
    Mary H. Rhinelander, ii , 86
    (Swan), Mary R., ii., 90
    (Sedgwick), Meta B., ii., 91
    Philip B., ii., 91
    Robert J., ii., 86
—   Robert J. II., ii., 90
—   S. Stanhope, ii., 91
—   Viola Blodget, ii., 90
—   William, ii., 84
    William C., ii , 91
    William R., ii , 90
    William W., ii., 91
Rhinebeck (from Beekman), i., 27
Riker (Duane), Grietje, i., 118
Rives, Francis R., i., 120
Roberts (Cruger), Elizabeth, i., 73
    John, i., 81
    (Delafield), Mary, i , 81
Robinson, Beverly, i., 131
    (Duer), Catherine, i., 131
    Frances Duer, i., 130
    Hamilton E. Duer, i., 130
    Morris, i., 131
Rochester, Margaret M. De Lancey, i. 98
    Thomas F. (Dr.), i., 98
Rogers, Susan L. Fish, i , 141
    William E., i., 141
Romaine (Cruger), Mary, i., 73
Roosevelt, Albert C., ii., 102
    Albert J , ii., 101
    Alice Lee, ii., 101
    Anne L. Jackson, ii., 102
    Annetje Bogaert, ii., 97
    Charles H., ii., 102
    Claas, the founder, ii., 95
    Clinton, ii., 101
    Cornelius V. S., ii., 98
    Cornelius V. S. II., ii., 99
    Edith Carow, ii., 101
    Elbert, ii., 101
    Family, ii., 95
    Helborne, ii., 102
    Henry E., ii., 102
    Hillotje Jans, ii., 96
    Hyltje Syverts, ii., 96
    Isaac, ii., 97
    Jacobus, ii., 97
    Jacobus II., ii., 97
    James, ii., 97
    James I., ii., 97
    James II , ii., 98
    James A., ii., 99
    James H., ii., 101

Roosevelt, Jane M. Young, ii., 101
    Jannetje Thomas, ii., 95
    Johannes, ii., 96
    John (Captain), ii., 97
    Lydia M. Latrobe, ii , 98
    Margaret Barnhill, ii., 98
    Martha Bullock, ii., 100
    Mary Van Schaick, ii., 98
    Nicholas, ii., 96
    Nicholas, ii , 97
    Nicholas (Lieutenant), ii., 98
    Peter T., ii., 101
    Robert B., ii , 99
    Samuel M., ii., 98
    (Schuyler), Sarah, ii., 97
    Silas W., ii , 99
    Theodore, ii., 99
    Theodore (President), ii., 100
    Washington, ii., 101
Rusher (Cruger), Frances E., i., 75
Rutgers (Lispenard), Alice, ii., 108
    Anthony, ii , 107
    Anthony, ii., 108
    Anthony (Captain), ii., 109
    Anthony II , ii., 108, 19
    Anthony III., ii., 108
    Catarina de Hooges, ii., 107
    Catharina Meyer, ii., 108
    (Bedloe), Catharine, ii., 109
    (LeRoy), Catharine, ii , 109
    (Van Horne), Catharine, ii., 108
    Catharine de Peyster, ii., 108
    Cornelia Benson, ii., 107
    (LeRoy), Cornelia, ii., 109
    Elizabeth Beekman, ii., 109
    Elizabeth Williams, ii., 108
    (Lispenard), Elsie, ii., 108
    (Marshall), Elsie, ii., 108
    (Schuyler), Elsie, ii., 107
    (Provoost), Eva, ii., 108
    Family, ii., 105
    Gerard, ii., 112
    Gertrude Gouverneur, ii., 108
    Harman, ii., 106
    Harman (Lieutenant), ii., 109
    Harman III., ii., 108
    Harman IV., ii., 109
    Harman H , ii., 107
    Hendrick, ii., 108
    Hendrickje Vandewater, ii., 107
    Henry (Colonel), ii , 109
    (Bleecker), Margaret, ii., 106
    Margaret Bayard, ii., 112
    (Barclay), Mary, ii., 19
    Peter, ii., 108
    Robert, ii., 109
    Robert II., ii., 112

Index

Rutgers, Rutgers Jacobsen, the founder, ii., 105
— Tryntje J. Van Breesteede, ii., 106

S

Sackett, Hannah De Lancey, i., 95
    Joseph (Rev.), i., 95
Sanders (Beekman), Catherine, i., 31
Sands, Charles, i., 85
— (Delafield), Lettice L., i., 85
Schermerhorn, Abraham, ii., 121
    Adeline E. Coster, ii , 122
    Aeltje, ii., 119
    Ann Elliott Huger Laight, ii., 122
    Arnout, ii., 119
    Arnout, ii., 120
    Beyer, ii., 118
    Bruce, ii., 123
    Burr (Dr.), ii., 123
    Catharina, ii., 119
    Catharine, ii., 120
    Cornelia, ii., 118
    Cornelius (Judge), ii., 123
    Daniel C., ii., 123
    Edmond H., ii., 122
    Elizabeth, ii., 121
    (Brevoort), Elizabeth, i., 42
    Elizabeth Bussing, ii., 121
    (Auchmuty), Ellen, ii., 122
    Esther, ii., 120
    Family, ii., 117
    Frederick Augustus, ii., 122
    George, ii., 121
    Helena, ii., 118
    Henry A., ii., 122
    Henry Augustus, ii., 123
    Hester ii., 120
    Jacob, the founder, ii., 117
    Jacob, Jr., ii., 118
    James, ii., 121
    James J., ii., 122
    Jannetje, ii., 118
    Jannetje, ii., 136
    Jannetje Segers, ii., 118
    Johannes, ii., 119
    John, ii., 120
    John, ii., 121
    Lucas, ii., 118
    Mary, ii., 120
    Marytje Beekman, ii., 119
    Nachtilt, ii., 118
    Neeltje, ii., 118
    Peter, ii., 120
    Peter, ii , 121
    Peter, the younger, ii., 121
    Peter Henry, ii., 122
    Sarah, ii , 120

Schermerhorn, Sarah Cannon, ii., 119
    Sarah Jones, ii., 122
— Symon, ii., 118
    Symon, ii., 119
    Symon, ii., 120
    Willementje, ii., 119
    Willempie Viele, ii , 118
    William B., ii., 123
    William C., ii., 122
Schieffelin (Barclay), Sarah S., i., 20
Schuchardt (Delafield), Elizabeth, i., 84
Schuchardt Frederick, i., 84
Schuyler (Church), Angelica, ii., 132
— Anna de Peyster , i., 106
    Anthony (Rev.). ii., 135
    Arendt, ii., 127, 128
    Arent, i., 106; ii., 135
    Brandt, ii., 127
    (De Peyster), Catharine, i., 106
    (Malcolm) (Cochran), Catherine, ii, 132
    Catherine Van Rensselaer, ii., 130
    (Morton), Cornelia, ii , 132
    Cornelia Van Cortlandt, ii., 130
    Elizabeth Ten Broeck, ii., 132
    Elizabeth Van Rensselaer, ii., 132
    Eugene, ii., 137
    Family, ii., 127
    (Hamilton), Elizabeth, i., 132
    George Lee, ii., 133
    George W., ii., 136
    Georgina, ii., 134
    Grace Hunter, ii., 133
    John, ii., 127
    John, ii., 133
    John B., ii., 132
    John Bradstreet, ii., 132
    Louis Sandford (Rev.), ii., 135
    Louisa Lee, ii., 134
    Margaret S., ii. 129
    (Van Rensselaer), Margarita, ii., 132
    Margherita Van Schlichtenhorst, ii., 127
    Mary A. Sawyer, ii., 133
    Montgomery, ii., 136
    Montgomery (Rev.), ii , 135
    Montgomery, Jr., ii., 136
    Myndert, i., 106
    Philip, ii., 132
    Philip (Captain), ii., 136
    Philip (Colonel), ii., 129
    Philip (General), i., 138; ii., 129
    Philip (Major), ii., 134
    Philip, the founder, ii., 127
    Philip J., ii., 132
    Philip Jeremiah, ii., 133
    Pieter (Colonel), i., 106
    Pieter (Colonel), ii., 129
    Pieter (Mayor), ii., 127

Index

Schuyler, Rensselaer, ii., 132
Scott, John W. (General), i , 138
   Sir Walter, i., 39, 40
Sharp, Richard, i., 69
Shepherd (Cruger), Caroline M., i., 74
Shipman, Edgar, i., 84
   Harriet C. Delafield, i., 84
Simpson, Sampson, i., 69
Sloane (Barclay), Priscilla D., i., 20
Smith, Atkinson, ii., 146
   (Cruger), Caroline, i., 71
   Catherine Duer, i., 132
   Charles Bainbridge, ii., 147
   Charles Vincent, i., 132
   Christiana, ii., 142
   Elizabeth Hartley, ii., 142
   Elizabeth Lynsen, ii., 146
   Elizabeth Scott Williams, ii., 144
   Eugene Keteltas, ii., 147
   Family, ii., 139
   Frances Peartree, ii., 142
   James, ii., 142
   James (Dr.), ii., 146
   Jennet Livingstone, ii., 145
   John, ii., 142
   John, ii., 144
   John Taylor, ii., 147
   John Witherspoon, i., 130
   Joshua Hett, ii., 146
   Keteltas, ii., 147
   Mary Hett, ii., 144
   Mary Taylor, ii., 147
   Mehetabel Hooker, ii., 144
   Samuel, ii., 142
   Sarah H. Duer, i., 130
   Susan Webber, ii., 146
   Susanna Odell, ii., 142
   Thomas, ii., 142
   Thomas, ii., 144
   Thomas, ii., 146
   Thomas, Jr., ii., 147
   William, ii., 141, 142
   William, ii., 146
   William II., ii , 142
   William (Chief-Justice), ii., 144
   William (Judge), ii., 142
   William Peartree, ii., 144
   Willimina Stodart, ii., 147
Steuben, Baron, i., 123
Storrow (Cruger), Julie G., i., 75
Sturgis, Charles, i , 84
   Cornelia Delafield, i., 84
   George, i., 84
   Mary Delafield, i., 84
Stuyvesant, A. Van Horne, ii , 157
   — Amelia Schuchardt, ii., 157
   — Anna, ii., 156

Stuyvesant, (Bayard), Anna, ii., 153
   Balthazar, ii., 155
   (Onderdonk), Caroline A., ii., 157
   Caroline Hoppock, ii., 157
   (Mortimer), Catherine A., ii., 157
   Catherine Ackerley, ii , 157
   — Catherine A. Cheesebrough, ii., 157
   — Catherine L. Reade, ii., 156
   — (Neill), Catherine S., ii., 157
   — (Ten Broeck), Cornelia, ii., 156
   Cornelia U. Bergen, ii., 158
   (Fish), Elizabeth, i., 139; ii., 156
   Elizabeth Slechtenhorst, ii., 156
   Elizabeth T. Kendall, ii., 157
   F. Schuchardt, ii., 158
   Family, ii., 151
   Fanny J Gibson, ii., 157
   Gerald, ii., 157
   Gerard, ii., 158
   Gerardus or Gerard, ii , 156
   (Rogers), Gertrude, ii., 157
   Harriet L. Seward, ii., 157
   (Dudley-Olmsted-Mayo), Helen C. ii., 157
   (Sandford), Helen M., ii., 157
   Helen Rutherford, ii., 156
   Henry, ii , 157
   Jane A Browning, ii., 157
   John R , ii., 157
   John R., ii., 157
   Joseph Reade, ii., 157
   (Winthrop), Judith, ii., 156
   Judith Bayard, ii., 153
   Judith Bayard II., ii., 156
   (Winterhoff), Julia H., ii., 157
   Julia Martin, ii , 156
   Margaret A. Mildeberger, ii., 157
   (Van Rensselaer), Margaret L., ii., 157
   (Wainwright), Margaret L., ii., 157
   Margaret Livingston, ii , 156
   Marie Beekman, ii., 156
   Mary A. Yates, ii., 157
   Mildred N. Floyd, ii., 158
   Nicholas W., i., 28; ii., 155, 156
   Nicholas W. II., ii., 156
   Nicholas W. III., ii., 157
   Peter, i , 139
   Peter, ii., 156
   Peter, ii., 156
   Peter, ii., 156
   Peter G., ii., 156
   Petrus (Governor), i., 26, 102; ii., 151, 152
   Robert, ii., 157
   Robert R., ii., 157
   Robert Reade, ii., 157
   (Pillot), Rosalie, ii., 157

Stuyvesant, Rutherford, ii., 158
    Susan Barclay, ii., 156
    Susan R. Van Horne, ii., 157
    Van Horne, ii., 158
    Van Rensselaer, ii., 157
Summers, Andrew, i., 83
    (Delafield), Helen, i., 83
Suydam, Henry, i., 132
— (Duer), Louise, i., 132
Swamp, Beekman, i., 27
Swift, Dean, i., 40

T

Tallmadge, Benjamin, i., 81
    (Delafield), Harriet W., i., 81
Tappen (Livingston), Caty, ii., 166
    Charles Barclay (Colonel), ii., 168
— Christoffel, ii., 165
— Christopher, ii., 166
— Christopher, Jr., ii., 167
— (Clinton), Cornelia, ii., 167
    Cornelia Kiersted, ii., 167
    Cornelia Vas, ii., 166
    Family, ii , 163
    Frederick D., ii , 169
    Henry Philip (Rev.), ii., 168
    John, ii., 168
    Jurian, the founder, ii., 164
    Jurian (II.), ii., 165
    Peter (Dr.), ii., 166
    Sarah A. B. Littell, ii., 170
    Sarah Schepmoes, ii., 165
    Tunis, ii., 165
Throckmorton, Captain, i., 56
Thurman, John, i., 69
Todd, Adam, i., 5
Todd (Astor), Sarah, i., 5
Toler (De Peyster), Julianna, i., 113
Travers (Duer), Ellen, i., 132
    William, i., 132

Van Baal (De Peyster), Mary, i., 105
Van Boogh (Beekman), Catherine, i., 28
Van Buren, Abraham, ii., 177
    Abraham (Colonel), ii., 179
    (Duer), Ann, i., 132
    Anna Hoes, ii., 177
    Angelica Singleton, ii , 177
    Ariaantje B. Meindersen, ii., 176
    Ariaantje G. Vanderberg, ii., 176
    Barent, ii., 176
    Barent, ii., 177
    Benjamin, ii., 176
    Catalyntje Martense, ii., 174

Van Buren, Catalyntje V. B. Schermerhorn, ii., 176
    Catalyntje Witbeck, ii., 177
    Catharine Quackenbosch, ii., 177
    (Van Deusen), Cornelia, ii , 176
    Cornelia Salisbury, ii., 176
    Cornelius, the founder, ii , 174
    Cornelius, ii., 176
    Cornelius, ii., 177
    Elizabeth Vanderpoel, ii., 179
    Family, ii., 173
    Frank Roe, ii., 180
    Hannah Hoes, ii., 179
    Hendrick, ii., 176
    Howard, ii., 180
    Johannes, or John, ii., 176
    John, i., 132
    John (" Prince "), ii , 179
    John Dash, ii., 179
    John Dash, Jr., ii., 179, 180
    Lawrence, ii , 179
    Maes, ii., 175
    Margrietje Van Vlechten, ii., 176
    Maria G. Van Alen, ii., 177
    Maria Litner, ii., 177
    Maria Vanderberg, ii., 176
    Maria Winne, ii , 177
    Maritje Quackenbosch, ii., 176
    (Vosburgh), Marritje, ii., 176
    Marritje Briesch, ii., 176
    Marritje Hun, ii , 176
    Marritje Vanderpoel, ii., 176
    Marten, ii., 174
    Martin, ii., 176
    Martin, ii., 176
    Martin (President), ii., 177
    Petrus, ii., 176
    Peter, ii., 177
    Robert, ii., 180
    Singleton, ii., 180
    Tanneke Adams, ii., 176
    Thenotje Vanderberg, ii., 176
    Tobias, ii., 176
    Tobias, ii., 176
    Tobias, ii , 177
    Tobias, ii., 177
Van Cortlandt, Ann Stevenson, ii., 191
    (De Lancey), Anne, i., 91 ; ii , 187
    Anne S. Van Schaack, ii., 188
    Annetje Loockermanns, ii., 186
    Augustus, ii., 190
    Catharine Beck, ii., 191
    (Mathews), Catharine T. R., ii., 191, 192
    Catherine Clinton, ii., 191
    Catherine de Peyster, ii., 188

Index

Van Cortlandt, Catherine Ogden, ii., 188
   (Schuyler), Cornelia, ii., 187
   Elizabeth Cuyler, ii., 190
   (Phillipse), Eva, ii., 187
   Family, ii., 185
   Frances Jay, ii., 188
   Frederick, ii., 186
   Frederick, ii., 188
   Gertrude, i., 29
   (Beekman), Gertrude, ii., 187
   (Ver Planck), Gertrude, ii., 188
   Gertrude Schuyler, ii., 187
   Helen Barclay, ii., 190
   Jacobus, i., 9; ii., 187
   James (Colonel), ii., 190
   James S. (Captain), ii., 191, 192
   Joanna Livingston, ii., 189
   Johannes, ii., 187
   Johannes, ii., 188
   (Bayard), Margaret, ii., 187
   (De Peyster), Margaret, i., 106
   (Van Rensselaer), Maria, ii., 187
   Mary W. Ricketts, ii., 188
   Oloff, the founder, ii., 186
   Philip, ii., 188
   Philip (Colonel), ii., 188
   Philip (General), ii., 189
   Pierre, ii., 191
   Pierre (Colonel), ii., 191
   Pierre (General), ii., 190
   Pierre (Lieutenant-Governor), ii., 188, 189
   Romeyn B., ii., 191
   Stephanus, i., 91, 92 ; ii., 186
   Stephen (Colonel), ii., 188
   Steven, ii., 186
   William R., ii., 188
Van Cott, Alexander H., ii., 201
   Caroline Case, ii., 200
   Claes, the founder, ii., 197
   Cornelius, ii., 198
   Cornelius, ii., 198
   Cornelius, ii., 199
   Cornelius (Postmaster), ii., 200
   Cornelius, Jr., ii., 198
   David, ii., 198
   David H., ii., 201
   Family, ii., 197
   Fanny Thompson, ii., 201
   Gabriel, ii., 199
   Gabriel, ii., 202
   Gabriel, Jr., ii., 199
   Joshua M., ii., 199
   Joshua M. (Dr.), ii., 200
   Lincoln, ii., 202
   May Richardson, ii., 202
   Nellie Praa, ii., 198

Van Cott, Richard, ii., 199
   Richard, ii., 202
   Thomas, ii., 199
   Thomas, ii., 200
   Wickfield, ii., 202
Vanderbeeck, or Vanderbeek (for Remsen), ii., 73, 74
   Rem Jansen, ii., 74
Vanderbilt, Alfred G., ii., 210
   Alice Gwynne, ii., 210
   Alva Smith, ii., 210
   (Parker) (Lafitte), Catherine, ii., 209
   Consuelo (Duchess), ii., 210
   Cornelius, ii., 206
   Cornelius, ii., 210
   Cornelius, ii., 210
   Cornelius (Commodore), ii., 205
   Edith S. Dresser, ii., 210
   (Osgood), Eliza, ii., 209
   (Webb), Eliza Osgood, ii., 210
   Elsie French, ii., 210
   (Sloane), Emily, ii., 209
   (Thorn), Emily, ii., 209
   (Allen), Ethelinda, ii., 209
   Family, ii., 205
   (Twombly), Florence Adele, ii., 210
   Frances Crawford, ii., 209
   Frederick W., ii., 210
   George, ii., 210
   (Whitney), Gertrude, ii., 210
   Gladys, ii., 210
   Grace Wilson, ii., 210
   Harold., ii., 211
   Jan, the founder, ii., 205
   Jeremiah, ii., 206
   John, ii., 206
   (Shepard), Margaret Louisa, ii., 210
   (La Bau), Maria A., 209
   Maria L. Kissam, ii., 210
   (Clark) (Niven), Marie L., ii., 209
   (Cross), Phebe, ii., 209
   Reginald, ii., 210
   Sophia Johnson, ii., 209
   (Torrance), Sophia, ii., 209
   Virginia Fair, ii., 211
   William H., ii., 209
   William K., ii., 210
   William K. (II.), ii., 211
Van Fez, Anthony Jansen, ii., 229
Van Rensselaer, Catherine Livingstone, ii., 218
   Cornelia Paterson, ii., 219
   Cortlandt, ii., 223
   Cortlandt (Rev.), ii., 223
   Cortlandt (Rev.), ii., 223
   (Cruger), Euphemia W., i., 73
   Family, ii., 213
   Gratz, ii., 223

268 Index

Van Rensselaer, Harriet E. Bayard, ii., 220
 Hendrick, ii., 218
 Henry, i., 84
 Henry (General), ii., 221
 Howard (Dr.), ii., 220
 James (Major), ii., 223
 James T., ii., 213
 Jan Baptiste, ii., 217
 Jeremiah, ii., 222
 Jeremias, ii., 217, 223
 Jeremias (5th Patroon), ii., 218
 (Delafield), Katherine, i., 84
 Kiliaen, the founder, ii., 215
 Kiliaen (of Albany), ii., 218
 Kiliaen (Captain), ii., 221
 Kiliaen (Colonel), ii., 222
 Kiliaen K., ii., 222
 Margarita Schuyler, ii., 219
 Maria Van Cortlandt, ii., 218
 Mary B. Tallmadge, ii., 223
 Maunsell (Rev.), ii., 222
 Philip, ii., 223
 Philip L., ii., 223
 Solomon, ii., 222
 Solomon (Colonel), ii., 219
 Stephen, ii., 218
 Stephen (8th Patroon), ii., 219
 Stephen (9th Patroon), ii., 220
 Stephen (Colonel), ii., 223
 Stephen (Rev.), ii., 221
 Steven (6th Patroon), ii., 218
 William, ii., 221
 William, ii., 223
 William B., ii., 220
 William P., ii., 223
Van Salee, Anthony Jansen, ii., 229
Van Schaick (Barclay), Cornelia, i., 16
 Elizabeth, i., 70
 (Roosevelt), Mary, ii., 98
 Peter, i., 70
Van Sichlen (for Van Siclen), ii., 227
Van Sickelen (for Van Siclen), ii., 227
Van Sickle (for Van Siclen), ii., 227
Van Sicklen (for Van Siclen), ii., 227
 — George, ii., 230
Van Siclen, Abraham, ii., 233
 Abraham (Lieutenant), ii., 233
 Andries, ii., 233
 Anthony, ii., 228
 Arthur, ii., 255
 Bennett (Judge), ii., 255
 Cornelius, ii., 233
 Cornelius (of Gravesend), ii., 232
 De Witt Clinton, ii., 234
 Eva Jansen, ii., 228
 Family, ii., 227
 George W., ii., 235

Van Siclen, George Washington, ii., 235
 Grace C. Hogarth, ii., 255
 Gysbert, ii., 233
 Ferdinand, ii., 232
 Ferdinand, ii., 233
 Ferdinandus, the founder, ii., 228
 Ferdinandus, Jr., ii., 231
 Henry, ii., 234
 Jacobus, ii., 233
 James (Captain), ii., 233
 James C., ii., 235
 Jan of Raritan, ii., 233
 Johannes, ii., 231
 Johannes, ii., 233
 Johannes (of New Lots), ii., 233
 John Sydney, ii., 234
 John T., ii., 235
 Joseph (Captain), ii., 233
 Lyman, ii., 234
 Mary Van Nuyse, ii., 232, 233
 Matthew, ii., 235
 Moses E. (Lieutenant), ii., 234
 Peter, ii., 233.
 Peter, ii., 233
 Reinier, ii., 231
 Reinier, ii., 233
 Reinier, ii , 233
 Reinier (of Flatbush), ii., 232
 Richard, ii., 234
 Sarah Gregory, ii., 235
Van Siechelen (for Van Siclen), ii., 227
Varick, Richard (Colonel), i., 122, 123
Voltaire, i., 15

W

Waldorf, Hotel, i., 8
 Town of, i., 3
Waldorf-Astoria, i., 9
Wallace (Delafield), Edith, i., 83
 Matthew G. (Rev.), i., 83
Walton, Jacob, i., 72
 Mary De Lancey, i., 95
 William, i., 69, 95
Warren, Peter, (Sir), i., 92
 Susan De Lancey, i., 92
Washington, George, i., 47, 48, 71, 72
Watts, Ann De Lancey, i., 92
 John, i., 92
 John, i., 97
 Jane De Lancey, i., 97
 (De Peyster), Mary J., i., 97
Webster, Sarah Fish, i., 141
 Sidney, i., 141
Wendell, Abraham, ii., 241
 — Abraham, ii., 242
 — Abraham, ii., 244

Wendell, Adelbert C., ii., 246
    Anna Glen, ii., 243
    Anna Melvin, ii., 246
    Ariaantje Visscher, ii., 241
    Barrett (Professor), ii., 245
    Benjamin R., ii., 246
    Benjamin R., Jr., ii., 246
    Burr, ii., 246
    Cathalina Hun, ii., 246
    Cathalina Van Benthuysen, ii., 245
    Catharina Van Vechten, ii., 244
    Cornelius, ii., 246
    Dorothy Sherburne, ii., 245
    Edith Greenough, ii., 245
    (Quincy), Elizabeth, ii., 242
    Elizabeth Quincy, ii., 242
    Elizabeth Sanders, ii., 242
    Elizabeth Staats, ii., 241
    Elizabeth Wendell, ii., 244
    (Staats), Elsie, ii., 242
    Ephraim, ii., 243
    Evert, the founder, ii., 239
    Evert, Jr., ii., 242
    Family, ii., 239
    Frances Roberts, ii., 246
    Garrett, ii., 245
    Gertrude Lansing, ii., 245
    Harman (Dr.), ii., 246
    Harmanus, ii., 243
—   Harmanus (Sheriff), ii., 245
—   Harmanus C., ii., 246
—   Hendrick, or Henry, ii., 244
—   Hermanus, ii., 243
    Jacob, ii., 243
    Jacob H. (Captain), ii., 245
    Jeronimus, ii., 241
    John, ii., 241
    John, ii., 242
    John, ii., 242
    John, ii., 245
    John (of Boston), ii., 242
    John Harmanus (Captain), ii., 244
    John Lansing, ii., 245
    Katrina de Kay, ii., 242

Wendell, (Phillips), Margaret, ii., 243
    Maria Lansing, ii., 244
    Maria Visscher, ii., 242
    Maritie Meyer, ii., 241
    Maritje Vosburgh, ii., 241
    (Oothout), Marritje, ii., 242
    Mary Ren Van Nes, ii., 241
    Peter (Dr.), ii., 245
    Philip, ii., 241
    (Holmes), Sarah, ii., 243
    Sarah Kip, ii., 246
    Sarah Oliver, ii., 243
    Susanna de Trieux, ii., 241
    Thomas, ii., 241
    William, ii., 246
    William F., ii., 246
    William H., ii., 246
Westcott (Duer), Maria, i., 131
Whetten (Captain), i., 39
    (Brevoort), Sarah, i., 39
Wilkes, Charles (Admiral), ii., 86
    Jane Renwick, ii., 86
Willemson, Derike, i., 146
    (Gardner), Mary, i., 146
William Street, i., 27
Williamson (Cruger), Louise E. A., i., 73
Willing (Astor), Ava, i., 9
Willis (Cruger), Laura A., i., 74
Wilson, Eleanor J. Duer, i., 131
—   George T., i., 131
Winthrop, John, i., 146
Woodbury, Cornelia Delafield, i., 85
    Theodore, i., 85
Wright (Barclay), Clara, i., 20
    Edward, i., 84
    Katherine F. Delafield, i., 84
Wyeth (Delafield), Charlotte H., i., 85
    Leonard, i., 85

Z

Zeng (DeLancey), Josephine M. de, i., 98
    William S. de, i., 98